D0876172

Families and Kinship in Contemporary Europe

Palgrave Macmillan Studies in Family and Intimate Life
Series Standing Order ISBN 978-0-230-51748-6 hardback
⠀⠀⠀⠀⠀⠀⠀⠀⠀⠀⠀⠀⠀⠀**978-0-230-24924-0 paperback**
⠀⠀⠀⠀⠀⠀⠀⠀⠀⠀⠀⠀⠀⠀*(outside North America only)*

You can receive future titles in this series as they are published by placing a standing order. Please contact your bookseller or, in case of difficulty, write to us at the address below with your name and address, the title of the series and the ISBN quoted above.

Customer Services Department, Macmillan Distribution Ltd, Houndmills, Basingstoke, Hampshire RG21 6XS, England

---

Families and Kinship in Contemporary Europe

Rules and Practices of Relatedness

Edited by

Riitta Jallinoja
University of Helsinki, Finland

and

Eric D. Widmer
University of Geneva, Switzerland

© Riitta Jallinoja and Eric D. Widmer 2011

All rights reserved. No reproduction, copy or transmission of this publication may be made without written permission.

No portion of this publication may be reproduced, copied or transmitted save with written permission or in accordance with the provisions of the Copyright, Designs and Patents Act 1988, or under the terms of any licence permitting limited copying issued by the Copyright Licensing Agency, Saffron House, 6–10 Kirby Street, London EC1N 8TS.

Any person who does any unauthorized act in relation to this publication may be liable to criminal prosecution and civil claims for damages.

The authors have asserted their rights to be identified as the authors of this work in accordance with the Copyright, Designs and Patents Act 1988.

First published 2011 by
PALGRAVE MACMILLAN

Palgrave Macmillan in the UK is an imprint of Macmillan Publishers Limited, registered in England, company number 785998, of Houndmills, Basingstoke, Hampshire RG21 6XS.

Palgrave Macmillan in the US is a division of St Martin's Press LLC, 175 Fifth Avenue, New York, NY 10010.

Palgrave Macmillan is the global academic imprint of the above companies and has companies and representatives throughout the world.

Palgrave® and Macmillan® are registered trademarks in the United States, the United Kingdom, Europe and other countries.

ISBN 978–0–230–28428–9   hardback

This book is printed on paper suitable for recycling and made from fully managed and sustained forest sources. Logging, pulping and manufacturing processes are expected to conform to the environmental regulations of the country of origin.

A catalogue record for this book is available from the British Library.

A catalog record for this book is available from the Library of Congress.

10 9 8 7 6 5 4 3 2 1
20 19 18 17 16 15 14 13 12 11

Printed and bound in The United States of America

Contents

List of Figures

List of Tables

Series Editors' Preface

The remit of the *Palgrave Macmillan Studies in Family and Intimate Life* series is to publish major texts, monographs and edited collections focusing broadly on the sociological exploration of intimate relationships and family organization. As editors we think such a series is timely. Expectations, commitments and practices have changed significantly in intimate relationship and family life in recent decades. This is very apparent in patterns of family formation and dissolution, demonstrated by trends in cohabitation, marriage and divorce. Changes in household living patterns over the last twenty years have also been marked, with more people living alone, adult children living longer in the parental home, and more 'non-family' households being formed. Furthermore, there have been important shifts in the ways people construct intimate relationships. There are few comfortable certainties about the best ways of being a family man or woman, with once conventional gender roles no longer being widely accepted. The normative connection between sexual relationships and marriage or marriage-like relationships is also less powerful than it once was. Not only is greater sexual experimentation accepted, but it is now accepted at an earlier age. Moreover heterosexuality is no longer the only mode of sexual relationship given legitimacy. In Britain as elsewhere, gay male and lesbian partnerships are now socially and legally endorsed to a degree hardly imaginable in the mid-twentieth century. Increases in lone-parent families, the rapid growth of different types of stepfamily, the de-stigmatization of births outside marriage, and the rise in couples 'living-apart-together' (LATs) all provide further examples of the ways that 'being a couple', 'being a parent' and 'being a family' have diversified in recent years.

The fact that change in family life and intimate relationships has been so pervasive has resulted in renewed research interest from sociologists and other scholars. Increasing amounts of public funding have been directed to family research in recent years, in terms of both individual projects and the creation of family research centers of different hues. This research activity has been accompanied by the publication of some very important and influential books exploring different aspects of shifting family experience, in Britain and elsewhere. The *Palgrave Macmillan Studies in Family and Intimate Life* series hopes to add to this list of influential research-based texts, thereby contributing to existing knowledge and informing current debates. Our main audience consists of academics and advanced students, though we intend that the books in the series will be accessible to a more general readership who wish to understand better the changing nature of contemporary family life and personal relationships.

We see the remit of the series as wide. The concept of 'family and intimate life' will be interpreted in a broad fashion. While the focus of the series will clearly be sociological, we take family and intimacy as being inclusive rather than exclusive. The series will cover a range of topics concerned with family practices and experiences, including, for example, partnership; marriage; parenting; domestic arrangements; kinship; demographic change; intergenerational ties; life course transitions; step-families; gay and lesbian relationships; lone-parent households; and also non-familial intimate relationships such as friendships. We also wish to foster comparative research, as well as research on under-studied populations. The series will include different forms of books. Most will be theoretical or empirical monographs on particular substantive topics, though some may also have a strong methodological focus. In addition, we see edited collections as also falling within the series' remit, as well as translations of significant publications in other languages. Finally we intend that the series has an international appeal, in terms of both topics covered and authorship. Our goal is for the series to provide a forum for family sociologists conducting research in various societies, and not solely in Britain.

Graham Allan, Lynn Jamieson and David Morgan

Notes on Contributors

Dr Elisabeth Beck-Gernsheim was Professor of Sociology at Hamburg University and the University of Erlangen-Nuremberg, Germany. Currently she is a visiting professor at NTNU/Trondheim (Norway). Her main areas of research are migration and ethnicity, reproductive technology, family and gender and individualization.

Dr Laura Bernardi is Professor of Demography and Sociology of Life Course, Director of the Laboratory for Life Course Studies and Deputy Director of the National Centre for Competence in Research 'LIVES' at Lausanne University, Switzerland. Since 2010 she is Book Editor of the *European Journal of Population*. Her publications are mainly in the area of family and fertility studies and involve longitudinal, multilevel and social network analyses in a multidisciplinary perspective.

Dr Roberta Bonini is a lecturer in social policy and quantitative methodology at the Catholic University of Milan, Italy and a coordinator of 'Family Social Policy' at Lombard Regional Institute for Research. Her research interests include family solidarity, intergenerational relationships and family social policy.

Ivan De Carlo is a Ph.D. student and lecturer at the Department of Sociology, Geneva University, Switzerland. His doctoral dissertation analyzes interpersonal and social trust development in a configurational perspective.

Dr Anna-Maija Castrén is Docent and a Research Fellow at the Department of Social Research (sociology), Helsinki University, Finland. Her research themes include social networks, intimate relationships, family transition, post-divorce family configurations and weddings.

Dr Antònia Gomila has previously worked as a researcher in several European universities and institutes and as a lecturer at the private university CESAG in Majorca, Spain. Currently she is working at the Department of Philosophy, University of the Balearic Islands. Her current research is about the role of the family in the school and in the education of children.

Roland Hauri is currently working on a doctoral thesis on families' Christmas celebrations. He is a research and teaching assistant at the

Institute for Practical Theology, Bern University, Switzerland. His research interests include family and child studies, social inequality and mixed methods.

Dr Andreas Hirseland is a senior researcher at the Department 'Joblessness and Social Inclusion', Institute for Employment Research (IAB), the German Federal Employment Agency (BA), in Nuremberg, Germany. His scientific interests are research design and methods, especially qualitative methods, longitudinal studies on the dynamics of poverty and the labour market, the reform of job replacement, social inclusion and state subsidized employment, and the transformation of the welfare state.

Dr Riitta Högbacka is a lecturer and postdoctoral scholar at the Department of Social Research (sociology), Helsinki University, Finland and a visiting scholar at California University, Berkeley, US. Her research interests include transnational adoption, globalization and rural gender studies.

Dr Riitta Jallinoja is Professor Emerita at the Department of Social Research (sociology), Helsinki University, Finland. Her research interests have covered a wide range of topics, for example, women's movement, modernization, individualization, family transitions, familism, family configurations, marriage and kinship. Her current research is about the dynastic family, its ideal-typical appearance in royal dynasties and family enterprises and the emergence of the 'bare' family.

Dr Sylvia Keim is a research scientist at Rostock University, Germany. Her research interests focus on social networks, family sociology and qualitative research methods. Her publications include 'Fertility-Relevant Social Networks: Composition, Structure, and Meaning of Personal Relationships for Fertility Intentions' (with A. Klärner and L. Bernardi; *Current Sociology*, 57(6) 2009).

Dr Florence Maillochon is a sociologist at the National Centre for Scientific Research (CNRS; Centre Maurice Halbwachs; ERIS) in Paris, France. She studies different topics from a relational perspective (using social network concepts), such as youth sexuality and risk behaviours as well as French wedding ceremonies. She also works in gender studies with the production of statistics on violence against women.

Dr Sara Mazzucchelli is a sociologist and a research fellow at the Athenaeum Centre for Family Research and Studies, Catholic University of Milan, Italy. She has developed her research on company welfare;

family, gender and work; and social and cultural transformations of the family, focusing in particular on conjugal and parental trajectories and interactions. She is a member of the organizational and scientific committee of the Family & Work Award (promoted by Lombardy Region, ALTIS – Postgraduate School Business & Society, ASAG-Postgraduate School of Psychology). She is also author and co-author of several articles in national and international journals.

Dr Anna Oppo has been Professor of Sociology at Gagliari University, Italy, but is now retired. Her long-term research interests include history of family, family and kinship relations, and women's changing roles in family and society. She is the author of various books and articles on the Sardinian family history, kinship structures and cooperation as well as conflicts among kin members.

Dr Giovanna Rossi is Full Professor of Family Sociology at Catholic University of Milan, Italy. She is also regular researcher at the Department of Sociology and Secretary of the Athenaeum Centre for Family Research and Studies. She has carried out extensive and documented research focusing on family topics: social and cultural transformations of the family, changing generational values, pro-social exchanges, relationships between family and work, socialization, family-based communities and family migration, planning policies regarding family, elderly and minors, and best practices of service networking models with a special focus on family associations. She is also author and co-author of many books and over 130 scientific contributions on national and international journals.

Dr Caroline Ruiner is a research associate at the Faculty of Philosophy and Social Sciences, Augsburg University, Germany. Her doctoral dissertation was about the formation of couple making. Her scientific interests are family sociology including marriage, qualitative methods, especially panel analysis and sociology of knowledge.

Dr Werner Schneider is Professor of Sociology at Augsburg University, Germany. His scientific interests are family sociology including marriage, youth and childhood, body, health and illness, sociology of death and dying, sociology of knowledge and poststructuralist discourse theory, and qualitative methods.

Dr Carol Smart is Professor of Sociology and Co-Director of the Morgan Centre for the Study of Relationships and Personal Life at Manchester University, UK. Prior to this she was Professor of Sociology at Leeds

University. She is author of several books, the most recent being *Personal Life* published in 2007 by Polity. For more information visit http://www. manchester.ac.uk/morgancentre/people/smart/index.html.

Dr Dana Sýkorová is Docent/Professor of Sociology at the Faculty of Social Studies, Ostrava University and the Philosophical Faculty of Palacký University in Olomouc, Czech Republic. Her research and publication activities focus mainly on the issues of family sociology (kinship, family help and aid) and gerontology (personal autonomy and social integration of the seniors). She has participated in a number of research projects funded by the Czech Science Foundation.

Dr Eric D. Widmer is Professor at the Department of Sociology, Geneva University, Switzerland, with an appointment at the Centre for Life Course and Lifestyle Studies (Pavie). His long-term interests include intimate ties, family and other interpersonal relations, life course research, social norms and social networks. Along with others, he has been developing research on families in a configurational perspective, using the Family Network Method (FNM). Eric D. Widmer is the author of various books and articles.

Dr Ulrike Zartler is an assistant at the Institute of Sociology, Vienna University, Austria. Her interests in research and teaching cover different aspects of family research, with a focus on family transition processes and research on children and childhood.

Part I
Outlining Relatedness

1
Introduction

Riitta Jallinoja and Eric D. Widmer

Over the last two or three decades, individualism has provided a grand frame of reference for family sociologists in their interpretations of the transformation of families and family life. Carol Smart (2007b: 17) characterizes individualism as the 'big idea' that became hugely popular and that seemed to offer an explanation for everything. In the 1980s and 1990s, in a world that witnessed the triumph of individualization it was natural that numerous studies on family transition examined certain phenomena in this light. Subjects like the increase in divorce, blended families, cohabitation, 'living-apart-together', 'parenting-across-households', same-sex and single-parent families were all regarded as new family arrangements whose logic was interpreted similar to that of individualism. In the 1990s, three names were unparalleled for their theorizing about these phenomena in accord with individualization theory: Anthony Giddens (1991, 1992), Ulrich Beck and Elisabeth Beck-Gernsheim (1999, 2002; Beck-Gernsheim, 2002). They were the protagonists at the centre of the scene, where changes in family and intimate lives were categorized and theorized as the thousands of references to them indeed prove. This approach also attempted to liberate society from traditions and other normative constraints that the 'monolithic' family, or the notion of the nuclear family had previously set. In this context, criticism was unanimously directed at Talcott Parsons, who seems to bear the main responsibility for modelling families normatively on the nuclear family format (e.g. Jamieson, 2005: 191–4; Smart, 2007b).

However, since 2000 in particular more and more voices are sceptical of individualization as an interpretative instrument. These critical assessments target Giddens, Beck and Beck-Gernsheim, leading to (or at least it should lead to) bewilderment. Why on earth are the same scholars, who until recently were considered the harbingers of a new and fresh approach and prized with utmost favours, now critiqued?

In this respect, the lots of Giddens, Beck and Beck-Gernsheim are comparable with the one of Parsons, who was applauded in the 1940s, 1950s and still in the 1960s, but whose status as a leading family sociologist (and also as a leading sociologist) collapsed at the turn of the 1970s (Chambers, 2001; Gerhardt, 2002).

The necessity for the change in perspective is justified, first, by empirical studies which continually bear witness to the persistence of the family form and marriage – institutions that some time ago were thought to represent the fading past. Looking back to history provides another type of argumentation; findings derived from long-term historical studies show that divorce, blended families, cohabitation, living-apart-together and single-parent families have existed for ages, although often under different names and for reasons distintct from those that account for the current states of families. These studies indicate that transition has not proceeded linearly in one direction, but has materialized in waves (Laslett et al., 1980).

It is also good to remember that the family and marriage were targets of criticism long before Giddens, Beck and Beck-Gernsheim published their books about the effects of individualization. Theories of family decline have been expounded ever since family sociology began. Durkheim for instance raised serious concerns about the ability of families to maintain significant functions in modernity and envisioned a society in which occupational and professional groups would replace families as a principal group of moral solidarity. During the 1920s and 1930s a large number of empirical investigations in the US assumed that families were going through a historical stage of massive disorganization (Popenoe, 1988). In the 1960s and 1970s, some radical intellectuals and scholars even called for the death of the family (Cooper, 1971), not so much in the name of individualism but with the intention to substitute the family for a better community, that is, communes. Thus, the aim was not to celebrate the birth of the totally independent and isolated individual but to give birth to communality that, as the advocates of the revolution remarked, would generate authentic relationships grounded on voluntary participation, which was considered impossible in the family. Giddens, Beck and Beck-Gernsheim did not refer to these radical endeavours when they postulated the individualistic family transition, to say nothing of the free-love movement that attracted bohemian artist circles in the US and elsewhere in the mid-nineteenth century (Stoehr, 1979). In this light the latest individualistic formulation of the variety of different family patterns looks like a moderate version of the comprehensive change introduced by the radicals; in this moderate version, families do not disappear, but undergo a transformation which makes family a target of choice, which in turn multiplies family patterns.

When challenging individualism as an omnipotent sociological tool kit, family sociologists found, or more correctly, rediscovered relationality, or the embeddedness of the individual in family and kin relationships. At a very general level, the approach means shifting the focus away from individuals to relationships and to socially significant ensembles that are constituted by these relationships. This approach has stimulated empirical research on, for instance, inter- and intra-generational relationships. A number of terms are used to characterize the essence of this new approach, the most frequent of which include relationality, relatedness, embeddedness, togetherness, belongingness, entourage, and configuration. To see families as configurations extending beyond the nuclear family brings relatives and friends back to family sociology and the focus on informal rules underpinning the actual organization of families (Widmer and Jallinoja, 2008). Interest in relationality, social networks, social capital, communities, and communality has been on the increase in sociology, but the dispute over individualism still lays the foundation for assessing different approaches to relatedness. For example, the work of Etzioni (1996) who was one of the forerunners of the revival of community studies and whose famous description of the communitarian order attracted wide attention, is not satisfactory for those contemporary family sociologists who situate relatedness at the centre of their research. Perhaps Etzioni relies too much on idealized familism when characterizing the recent fate of the family and delineating its desirable future (Morris, 1996: 229; Jamieson, 2005: 914). For the same reason Brigitte and Peter Berger (1984), the strong proponents of the nuclear family have been largely absent from the recent family sociological literature. Just as with the neoconservatives (Steinfels, 1980), they are left on the margins of the renewed family sociological discussion.

In our proposal here for a new perspective on family sociology, we are confronted with a difficult task. Individualism appears to be waning as a frame of reference and relationality is set to conquer the empty space that the dislodged individualism is leaving behind. Both of these strands have a long history, which weakens their plausibility to alone represent the specific nature of the contemporary time on their own. One solution can be, as many authors before us have suggested, that we do not regard individuality and relatedness as alternative orientations, which by turns not only dominate family sociological debates but also organize family practices, but we should instead take the coexistence of individuality and belongingness at face value (Adam, 1996). In reality, they have co-existed since the nineteenth century. Our task is to investigate their mutual relation – how they are interwoven with each other. Even while we question the normative model of the nuclear family as proposed by the functionalist sociologists of the 1950s, we believe that efforts to trace the models of family organization, discern their underlying structures and informal rules, and ascertain their contribution to the larger society should be back on the agenda of family sociology.

This volume aims to find a pathway to a better understanding of the ways in which contemporary individuals continuously make and remake their families within various structural and cultural constraints. The first step to be taken is to investigate *processes* through which families come into existence – in different constellations and through different transactions, keeping in mind some families are also terminated. The word 'relatedness' captures this idea well and this is why it is included in the title of the volume. The aim is to take under scrutiny such processes that shed light on the essentials of the making of relatedness in late modernity, as constituted through families and kinship above all. In the following we portray this as it is displayed in more detail in this volume, through different themes and empirical data from different European countries.

The first part of the book is reserved for the introduction to the notion of *relatedness*. After the introduction written by Jallinoja and Widmer, Smart delineates the relational approach and develops five concepts that indicate an unconventional approach to the making of families. Relationality is the elementary concept, with memory, biography, embeddedness, and imaginary giving it substance. However, these do not take shape merely as individual endeavours, but in relatedness to significant others. The collage of instruments suggested by Smart is also meant to be an invitation to complement relationality with other concepts which have hitherto been examined as essentially individual activities but which should also be examined as socially constituted. This demonstrates that families are made and remade in different constellations, some in nuclear or otherwise closed forms, some in much more extended ensembles.

In Part II we concentrate on *family assemblages* or family gatherings. Their significance is in the symbolic presentation of one's family, which entails solemnizing one's family and putting it on display, privately and publicly. In get togethers family members and kinfolk mark the boundaries of their family configurations beyond the nuclear family. The sequence of family gatherings through a lifetime is like an extended narrative, which expresses and reaffirms relationships within the family and between families, following life stories from cradle to grave, and charting and celebrating major turning points in the family's history (Jones, 2007: 8). In this volume, we examine four different forms of family assemblages. W*eddings and Christmas festivities* are typical family celebrations and very common across Europe. They are particular in that they have maintained their ritualistic character, following the old rituals as they were designed in the nineteenth century with surprising accuracy (Gillis, 1997: 88–107). They have remained a highly stylized cultural performance involving several family members that is repeated, has a formal structure, and involves symbolic behaviour (Pleck, 2000: 10). Yet we must remember that families often personalize them, adding idiosyncratic elements. Castrén and Maillochon elaborate, on the one hand, how bilaterality and equality direct the ways guest lists are drawn up for weddings and, on the other hand, how personal aspirations and constraints give rise to variation in this respect. Hauri looks at the Christmas celebration from the same perspective, showing that two to three days are needed to celebrate Christmas accordingly, that is, according to the principles of bilaterality and equality. These two traditions of family assembling also show that the range of family configurations varies; weddings tend to gather a wide range of relatives together, while at Christmas festivities the scope is much more limited.

The two other family gatherings examined do not occur face-to-face, but are embodied in symbolically significant customs that in our cultures have come to indicate belongingness (Rochberg-Halton, 1986: 169; Bourdieu, 1990: 9). These are customs surrounding *family photos* and *obituaries* or death announcements in newspapers. Gomila examines the photos people put on display. Here people are making families through pictures; this is feasible, because pictures include a reference to the relationship, embody kinship ties, and are valued as tangible evidence of friendship and family bonds. Family photos, when grouped on tables or bookshelves are much like domestic altars. Jallinoja's analysis of obituaries or death announcements in newspapers draws similar findings. Obituaries are mediate relationships whereby the mourning survivors, by being present in the obituary signal their belongingness to each other. In the obituaries, the ranking of the relatives on the lists of mourners is of vital importance. Obituaries and family photos carry us into an invisible world of 'pieces of paper' that when made visible uncover a whole range of family life hitherto more or less unnoticed in family sociology.

In Parts III and IV, we move on to delineate the *making and re-making of families* on a more daily basis, in everyday practices, but even here the focus is on practices which can be seen as encapsulated episodes of family making. Life circles are at the centre, but at certain times the chain of events is condensed into a distinctive episode with its own formation logic. In this sense, episodes resemble family assemblages, albeit of long duration and less ritualistic.

Part III focuses on the *transition to conjugal living and parenthood* from a configurational perspective. The three chapters stress the important collective implications of this transition. Bernardi and Oppo's chapter examines how young adults experience LATAP (living apart together at the parents' home), that is, making the journey from their parents' home to their own. In some European countries, particularly in Italy, this living arrangement is a typical transition to couplehood. While some scholars underline the influence of rising individualization on couple formation, leading to the increasing diversity and individually tailored definition of couple relationships, the configurational perspective, followed by Bernardi and Oppo, highlights the young couple's sensitivity to the adjustment in interdependencies throughout the couple-formation process. On the one hand, the couple's choices are linked to the commitments and compromises with relevant others in the families of origin (mainly parents, but also siblings). On the other, the coupling process tends to modify values, norms and previous practices of the group of relatives so that both the children's individual choices and the maintenance of family cohesion and affection can be sustained.

Keim considers in her chapter how the transition to parenthood is interrelated with the attitudes and behaviours of one's network members. The personal relationships and social networks in which individuals are embedded shape their expectations and views on family formation. The composition of social networks either contributes to the continuity of fertility-related attitudes and behaviour over time, or fosters the emergence of 'new' forms of family formation. In many cases, this means the retraditionalization of attitudes and behaviour and a change in network structure towards the inclusion of more traditional bonds. This is linked to the need for social support, especially in childcare, in a context which only inadequately provides childcare facilities. Overall, the chapter stresses the collective dimension of becoming or not becoming a parent. Instead of resulting from purely personal decisions with merely personal consequences, the process of becoming a parent can better be understood when interdependencies with a fairly large number of friends and family members are taken into account.

Högbacka's chapter on adoption reveals how adoptive parents struggle to have a child of 'their own', which would complete their nuclear family. Understanding the family in this way leaves no space for biological parents, and arouses an intense fear of them whenever they make an appearance (even symbolically). In other cases, however, parents choose an open adoption, where ties with biological parents are maintained. This *de facto* leads to a more configurational perspective of their families; by acknowledging the special tie between their adopted children and the biological parents of those adopted children they open up the boundaries of their nuclear family unit. To a certain extent, families that chose open adoption face concerns similar to post-divorce families, where children are shared between several households. In transnational adoption, these questions are more critical, due to the hierarchy that prevails between the South and the North and to differences that exist in family cultures of these two regions; with southern regions favouring open family systems, and northern areas featuring more exclusive family configurations.

In Part IV the focus is on the remaking of families, with four examples of the mechanisms of family formation later in life. Ruiner examines how *money mediates the couple relationship*, also serving as a good example of research on materials and objects that have a social meaning beyond their immediate function. Money is 'relationship money', differentiated as 'my money' – 'your money' – 'our money'. In this kind of situation, 'synchronization' is a key concept, playing a decisive role in handling changes and establishing and maintaining stability and continuity. Sýkorová's chapter is about *making families due to old age*, which in fact means the remaking of families due to the necessity of senior care, usually involving the adult children of elderly parents. The basic concept here is 'ambivalence', emerging as a mixture of contradictory feelings, with both expectations of and tendencies towards closeness and distance. Ambivalence then creates a particular type of foundation for the reorganization of family ensembles, consisting in this case mainly of the members of the family of origin who once lived together but have since lived apart. In the reorganization of these family relationships, each party seeks a balance between autonomy and mutual dependency.

The next two chapters draw attention to situations where family members who used to live together now live scattered apart. Whatever the reason behind the separation, dissolved families require re-making in new constellations. Zartler outlines her study on *reassembling families after divorce*. Examined from the perspectives of the mother, father, and children, this study provides valuable information about the different ways family members experience their relationships vis-à-vis each other and with newcomers to their family circles. The biological aspect still appears to be a very clear boundary. In addition, family-wise dyadic relationships, mother-child, father-child, and co-parental relationships clearly bear witness to differences between the parties of the dyads in regard to how the relationship in question is assessed. Beck-Gernsheim illuminates another type of scattered family, the rapidly growing variety of *transnational families*. More and more often family members are disseminated across the world due to a new division of labour, whereby mothers travel far away from their homes to look after other mothers' children, while their own children stay behind with their grandmothers, sisters, and aunts as their caregivers. This gives rise to a global hierarchy of care, which may lead to more destabilization in poor countries.

In Part V relatedness as *social capital* provides us with an important complementary perspective meant to specify the very character of belongingness. When looking at family relationships as social capital, the interest lies in the quality of relationships. The chapter by Rossi, Bonini, and Mazzucchelli discusses the fundamentals of family social capital in the theoretical perspective. It raises the importance of four elements: *network*, namely the structural dimensions of social capital, such as the density of ties; *trust* as the expectation of a social actor that others will carry out beneficial or harmless actions made under the conditions of uncertainty; *reciprocity* as knowing that giving something one will get something in return, not only at an instrumental level but also at a symbolic and relational level; and *cooperation* as a way of interacting together that can also establish itself also without external control mechanisms. The various dimensions should be taken into account when dealing with the contribution of families to social integration and personal well-being. Rather than being the containers of individuals, led by their personal preferences without concern for consequences, families remain a highly interconnected group in late modernity. This perspective is taken over by De Carlo and Widmer, who focus on the interrelations between various elements of social capital such as its structural dimensions, reciprocity, and trust. It shows that social capital is not an attribute of all family relationships but that it has to be produced and maintained through active relationships which are not fully granted by family status, such as being a father or a mother. Overall, this part of the book stresses the interest of working with the concept of social capital in family research.

For practical reasons, the findings in most of the chapters are based on empirical data stemming from one European country. But the nation-based data are not meant to limit our analysis to the presentation of country-wise family formation processes; instead we assume that the findings are also valid across Europe, wherever the type of dynamics found in country-specific research appears. More important than this, though, is that we must seek the fundamentals of the family-making processes; in other words, we have to strive to detect what is universal in the variations arising from the different relational contexts. To do this we have to go beyond individual inclinations towards more structural analysis, based on *rules* that have much say in the making of families. The question of rules is not examined in a separate section here, but the exploration of these rules is a thread running through all the chapters.

Rules have not been a topical theme in recent family sociological research. This is because individualism as a frame of reference reluctantly examines rules unless they are scrutinized critically, as constraints of free choice. The term 'rule' should not be seen as equivalent with the term 'norm'; that is to say, rules are neither clearly pronounced obligations nor are they externally imposed on individuals to force them to act in a desired way. Rather we should attempt to perceive rules as informal, as a kind of tacit knowledge, an unspoken understanding of how relatedness through families and kinship is made. Rules can also be regarded as the habitualization of practices (Berger and Luckmann, 1981), which is a dialectic process. Rules come into existence in the repetitive makings of relatedness and rules structure the makings of relatedness. In this process, rules change and new rules may emerge. In addition, no rule is absolute, as there is always some freedom of choice (Lévi-Strauss, 1969) not to mention the intentional breaking of rules. Because of its obscure nature, the term 'rule' is not meant to be set in stone. We could just as well use alternative terms like 'principle', 'structure', and 'order', in a manner of Lévi-Strauss (1969) himself.

The aim of this book is to discover rules that organize and structure the workings of family- and kinship-making processes in late modernity. These rules are abstract in the sense that they are applied in different assembling and relatedness-making contexts. We did not predefine the rules that we would like to elaborate on; rather they were derived from the different data sets. Some of the rules we delineate in this book are familiar from classical sociology and anthropology, while others are taken from individualization theory. For example, the rules of genealogical proximity, bilaterality, monogamy, and equality are from the former. They are most influential in family assemblages. The organization principles rooted in individualization are focused on negotiations between family members and relatives. Negotiations are needed, due to ambivalence between individual interests, aspirations, and expectations on the one hand, and obligations set by families on the other.

In negotiations controversial views are synchronized, but even here the rules of reciprocity and genealogy, for instance, leave their mark. The last chapter, *Afterthoughts*, examines in detail the workings of the rules and how they are interwoven with more individualistic orientations. In this context we also set up a bridge between not only generalizations and practices that tend to vary but also between social bonds and individualization – aiming at an informed theoretical discussion on relatedness in an individualized late modern world.

At the end of the last chapter we also examine some obvious limitations this collection of articles entails. We are well aware that they do not capture the full diversity of family forms that currently exist in the European context. In particular, same-sex relationships and the issues of ethnicity, class, and religion and their impact on family-formation processes are not extensively dealt with. This was not the result of an explicit disregard for such realities; rather it stems from the current tendency of doing family research in Europe which, for the most part, continuously focuses sociological research on families with heterosexual partners and their biological children. It is also true that in most studies grounded in a small number of in-depth interviews it is not possible to include a wide range of diversities. As a consequence, researchers have to limit the scope of their scientific interests. We hope that the addition displayed at the end of the afterthoughts supplements the analysis we have made in this book.

2
Relationality and Socio-Cultural Theories of Family Life

Carol Smart

In this chapter I propose to take some of the ideas I initially developed in *Personal Life* (Smart, 2007b) a little further. The purpose of that book was to start a process of reconceptualization of the sociology of relationships by putting a reflexive (social) self (Burkitt, 2008) into the centre of this approach as opposed to the isolated individual of theories of individualization. This means that here I first revisit the conceptual tools I worked with but then try to expand them while also taking account of my own dictum about trying to write relationships differently. This means that this chapter does not follow strictly the conventions of sociological writing (Gordon, 2008) and the reader will come across a number of 'digressions' en route.

Conceptual foundations

One of the first conceptual foundations of the new approach to a sociology of family life was created by the work of David Morgan (1996). He instigated a move away from seeing family as an institution towards mapping family practices and understanding families as constituted by what they do. This refreshed the ways sociology could think about family life and provided a terminology which has allowed us to speak differently. The second shift is to be found in the work of Janet Finch and Jennifer Mason (1993, 2000a) which has expanded the narrow ways in which sociologists have thought about how we relate to our 'relatives' and whom we include in our spheres of intimacy. It was Finch and Mason who insisted that we think 'relationally' when we focus on families and kin. Third, there is the new anthropology of kinship (Carsten, 2004), which rejected traditional structuralist thinking on kinship and allowed for a much more fluid conceptualization to emerge. Fourth, there is the semi-autobiographical work of authors such Carolyn Steedman (1986, 1992) and Annette Kuhn (1995), which points to the significance of memory, place and history to an understanding of the workings of family life (both in the present and the past). Fifth, the work of John Gillis (1997, 2004) in the area of social history has contributed to an understanding of the ways in which families inhabit both personal and cultural imaginaries and has explored how these two imaginaries intersect. His focus on cultural memory and practices/ rituals that support these memories has brought sociology closer to recognizing the importance of everyday activities as well as the realm of the imagined. Finally, the significance of space/place and the recognition of the material culture of family living have also been restored to sociological thinking. This has emerged from both autobiography and visual methods (particularly the emphasis on family albums and the meaning of home), as well as from the anthropology of everyday life (Chapman and Hockey, 1999; Miller, 1998).

Multi-dimensional personal life

Combined with a desire to find a more textured way of conceptualizing and representing family life and relationships has been the struggle to find ways of capturing the multi-dimensionality of relationships and personal life. Multi-dimensionality requires sociology to speak of (or write of) many issues, layers, places, eras and meanings all at the same time. This is not possible of course, but if the purpose of capturing these many dimensions is sufficiently serious then non-conventional methods and alternative codes for writing and representing need to be embraced. Les Back (2007), for example, calls for 'artful description' which will capture the texture of lives. He argues,

> Conceptual and theoretical work should not climb to a level where the voices of the people concern[ed] [*sic*] become inaudible. Rather, theoretical ideas and concepts hover above the ethnographic ground in order to provide a vocabulary for its explication. This is a kind of description that is committed and dialogic but not just a matter of 'letting the research subjects speak'.
>
> (Back, 2007: 21)

Back is here inviting sociologists to connect much more with what is significant in everyday life and to use ethnography as a kind of check against tendencies towards overly theorized accounts. But equally he is not satisfied with some contemporary practices which leave respondents to speak for themselves as if the sociologist needs to do no work in making sense of everyday life. So there are no easy remedies for Back and hence his insistence that sociologists adopt a more varied and engaged form of writing. Thus, for example, in his own attempt to capture and account for the rich lives of his respondents, Back uses photographs. These include photographs of significant places, events and 'real' people, often his own family members. Part of his argument is that photographs can convey more than words can. But his argument is also that using photographs is not enough since they too are loaded with many potential meanings, not all of which are easily decoded. So it is also important to consider how we construct and write the text, how we integrate the spoken word, and how we use data (including photographs) to be evocative, descriptive and deep at the same time.

Following a related set of concerns A. Gordon (2008) has argued that sociologists are really positioned as modern storytellers – but she argues that they have not reflected upon this hugely responsible task and have been limited, and perhaps careless, about the stories they construct because they underestimate the power of the story and its potential reach. She argues,

> Sociology, in particular, has an extraordinary mandate as far as academic disciplines go: to conjure up social life. [...] As a mode of apprehension and reformation, conjuring merges the analytical, the procedural, the imaginative, and the effervescent. But we have more to learn about how to conjure in an evocative and compelling way.
>
> (Gordon, 2008: 22)

Gordon's notion of 'conjuring up social life' conveys the way in which the sociologist is not an outside observer who documents what he or she has found, but someone who tells stories which others take to be real and true. Thus sociological accounts of families and relationships have a responsibility not to represent the lives of others as one-dimensional and impoverished. In her book Gordon focuses on haunting as being precisely the kind of monumentally important phenomenon that sociology fails to notice. The hauntings she refers to are the aftershocks of such traumatic events as slavery or fascist dictatorships which leave marks on successive generations and which are carried – to use evocative terminology – in the soul, but which also become manifest in actions, beliefs and ways of being. She argues that without some kind of understanding of these ripples and hauntings,

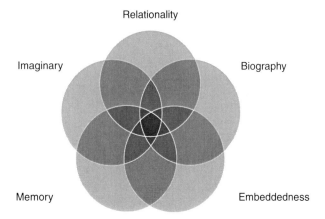

Figure 2.1   The toolbox of concepts

sociologists cannot begin to understand the lives of the people they seek to encompass in their research.

These dual concerns about sociology's ability to capture and reflect multi-dimensional lives, along with my specific concerns about impoverished stories about family life and personal lives, has led me to two conclusions. The first is to the construction of what I have called a toolbox of concepts. The aim of this toolbox is to produce a collage and, as Back would say, this collage should not render real lives/voices 'inaudible' nor so artful that they are incomprehensible. Rather it should enable the sociologist to be more attentive to a wider range of dimensions of lived life. The second conclusion is that sociology needs to embrace more actively different ways of writing and representing sociological knowledge and insight. In this chapter I focus more on the first point than the second but, as noted above, I shall incorporate certain writing practices in the text as a means of demonstrating the second point rather than articulating it in a more abstract way. Put more simply, I shall try to 'do' it rather than 'write about' it. But first I shall reflect upon the tools in the box in turn.

Relationality

The concept of relationality has its roots in feminist philosophical discussions of the self, which in turn have their roots in much longer traditions of philosophy. Although the specific term 'relationality' may not have been used, feminists in the 1990s developed a concept of the self which was a relational one, that is to say the self was deemed to develop inter-subjectively and through social interaction (Griffiths, 1995; Meyers, 1997; Held, 1993). It was a concept opposed to the fully autonomous individual of Hobbesian and other post-Enlightenment thought. Hence in this conceptualization the self is always to be found in a web of relationships and constituted by such interconnections. This philosophical stance, which always sees the individual in context and as untenable if conceptualized as solitary and self generating, found its way into sociology, particularly into symbolic interactionism and later into feminism. This emphasis on interaction, not as something that isolated individuals may or may not 'choose' to engage in, but as a precondition for the construction of the self, has been taken up into analyses of family and kin relationships. Thus threads of this perspective can be found in the following argument by Finch and Mason:

> First, we think that kinship operates at, or is to found at, the level of negotiated relationships more than structures or systems. [...] Essentially, this is why we wish to jettison both the idea of kinship as a structure and the concept of individualism in favour of one of *relationism*. Second, we want to suggest that kinship is constituted in *relational practices*, with the privilege that this concept gives to actors' reasoning, actions and experiences.
>
> (Finch and Mason, 2000a: 164)

Finch and Mason come to this point of view through their empirical study of kinship obligations where they found that people made decisions (about wills, or about moving, or about caring) in relation to others and not simply in terms of their own specific or separate needs and desires. Importantly this term relationality also captures a way of thinking that ordinary people have as a consequence of being a part of a web of connectedness where their concept of self (and self value) is tied into how they behave towards significant others. For example Mason (2004), in exploring the ways in which people explain decisions to move home, found that their relationships with others was very significant in their reasoning. Thus the term relationality conjures up the image of people existing within intentional, thoughtful networks which they actively sustain, maintain or allow to atrophy. Indeed, the combination of relationality with the term 'practices' (Morgan, 1996) also emphasizes the active nature of relating and reduces the idea that relationships are simply given (and hence unchanging) through one's position in a family genealogy.

Relationality, as deployed by Finch and Mason, is a mode of thinking and reflecting which influences decisions, actions and choices, and which also forms the context for the unfolding of everyday life. It is enmeshed with all the other concepts I shall describe here, which is why it is hard to speak of relationality without invoking the connectedness of the self with others; equally the past (which is captured in memories) is part of how we relate to people in the present. I shall deal with memory next:

Memory

As Misztal (2003) points out, memory is far from just being the ability to recall past events. Individual memory is formed and shaped by others around us and through the process of language development, since to have memories requires speech. It is speaking about events (with others) which fixes them in memory and also gives a shape to experiences that can then be shared over and over again. Thus individual memory is profoundly social because it relies on communication to become a memory and on context to be meaningful. The significance of this attention to memory for the understanding of family and relationships is considerable. Our earliest memories are formed in the context of families – with parents or caring adults and with siblings. Regardless of whether these are good or bad memories they carry a particular significance because of their primary status and because they are formed in the company of people who are so important to a child. This can often give rise to nostalgia, which, when associated with life histories, genealogies and family photograph albums, is particularly strong and alluring. The emotional reaction people often have to recalling these memories can create a sentimental aura around the past of 'the family'. So, often memories of this sort appear to be embellished, bringing into focus a perpetual summer and dimming the routine drudgery of everyday life. In this sense these personal memories of families past play tricks on us yet, sociologically speaking, this is important because it explains why the family of the past occupies such a special place in our internal emotional calibrations of personal significance. There is therefore a circular processes in which families occupy a special place in the 'laying down' of strong or important memories, but in turn the feelings generated by remembering one's childhood in a family create anew the sense that these are special memories and thus feed into the experience that families are particularly special places. Thus ironically the more work we do in Western cultures on family memories and

Figure 2.2 Digression 1: A memory of mine
One of my family photographs from around 1951–2 taken in Regent's Park Zoo, London
This is a photograph of my brother at an age of around five years. It is of a type which was typical in England in the 1950s of highly stylized poses to capture 'special' moments of childhood. It is, however, hard to imagine an event less typical of everyday life and so it is a figment of imagination on many levels. However, for me it nonetheless works its magic and takes me straight back to the 1950s, that particular zoo which I loved (being unaware of the politics of curating live animals), and it also reminds me of the relative rarity of such outings in those days. I remember that this outing was with my mother and her best friend (just caught in the snap). My father was not there and this then reminds me that he would hardly ever be there – but this was not unusual for fathers in the 1950s of course. But the poignancy of this photograph also lies in the fact that I know what was to become of the key figure, my brother. So I do not read this photograph simply as a sociologist (understanding fatherhood in the 1950s, see Brannen et al. 2004), nor only as a visual critic who takes the genre of idealized, innocent childhood to task, but also as an emotionally connected person who recalls that at the age of three she loved her older brother a great deal, but who much later fell out with him and was not able to reconnect properly with him before his untimely death. Such is the power of the photograph to evoke memories and to condense threads of a life into one frozen image.

tracing lines of heritage, the more we contribute to the iconic status of families in the cultural imaginary.

It is important of course to acknowledge the chameleon nature of memory. Bloklan (2005) argues that memory has magical qualities in that it changes shape and colour depending on who is recalling events or processes, when they are doing so, and arguably why they are doing so. She stresses that memory is linked to the present and this is particularly important for understanding families. It seems that there are particular moments when we remember our childhoods or our family history. These may be done collectively at times of cultural celebration (for example, Christmas or weddings) or they may be more individual acts, such as when a parent dies, when children are born, or simply with ageing. Memories can change to suit an audience or to fit a newly crafted identity better. Memory therefore works in unstable ways notwithstanding that it almost always appears to have the status of the most authentic and most signifying act of identity creation.

Biography

Michael Rustin (2000) has argued that the discipline of sociology still cannot quite grasp the sociological significance of the individual life story. Yet a few lives – purposively selected – can capture a complex moving picture of social change and connections with networks of kin, economic trends, and often migration and other large scale events or processes such as wars. These stories can be located in an understanding of local and dominant economic systems as well as being situated in time. But perhaps more significantly they can offer the experience of living through certain times; they can deal with the meanings that individuals attribute to events and relationships and they can explain, to a degree, motivations, desires and aspirations. These methodologies provide what have become known as 'thick descriptions' (Geertz, 1973; Mason, 2002) because they create both deep and dense understandings of processes and interactions. As Rustin argues, as long as these descriptions relate to a sociological perspective which is always interested in social contexts then what emerges has a broader significance than the life of one or two individuals.

The biographical turn (as it has become known) has particular salience for understanding family relationships. Most important is the ability to grasp movement through time (for example, one decade to the next) but also movement through the life course (for example, from being 20 to being 30 years of age).

Figure 2.3   Digression 2: A short bio-pic of my father
*Clockwise from top left: 1) my father as a boy on a beach probably in 1925 with his
sister and cigarette smoking father (who died when my father was 12). 2) My father as
a young man, note the style of the trousers. 3) My father in the army during WWII in
the Middle East or maybe Italy where he was captured, some time between 1940 and
1945. 4) My father on his wedding day in West London, September 1940, on the eve
of being called up.*

    *If I had the space in this chapter I could use this life to tell the story of a segment
of working class life in London from 1925 to 1945. It would entail accounts of being
orphaned and having to leave school at 12 (in 1928/9), of being brought up by older
siblings and trying to find work during the great depression of the 1930s, of hardship,
survival, heavy drinking and entrepreneurship. The story would show shifting political
affiliations – from Labour to Conservative, perplexing but typical perhaps of the post-
war disaffection of the small businessman. It could cover too some aspects of the kind
of haunting spoken of by Gordon. Those ripples through later post-war life of the ghosts
of comrades killed and mistreatment fear and near starvation in prisoner of war camps.
I could then compare the lifestyles and life chances of the next generation born into the
comforts of Welfare State and National Health Service in the post-war decade. It might
then be possible also to account for the huge divide that opened up between these generations born into such different worlds – yet so intimately connected.*

Biography can also capture the different experiences of different members of families or kin groups rather than treating them as a homogeneous whole with one world view and one shared set of experiences. Of course there are disadvantages too. Biography relies on memory and as I discuss above memory is unstable and fluid. But biographical methods deploy what might be seen as little anchors for memory which give shape to stories. These may be photographs, objects, accounts written in previous times, documentary evidence and so on. Thus, at least where studies of family life are concerned, materiality becomes an important feature of the biographical method. Not only do material objects elicit memories and stories, but they 'speak' themselves of particular decades, or of specific tastes, or even of impoverishment or affluence. Anthropologists such as D. Miller (1998, 2001), and T. Chapman and J. Hockey (1999) have emphasized the importance of homes, as well as objects and forms within homes and the (changing) meanings of a home. But they also point to the ways in which the social organization of the home gives insights into social relationships. In this way 'things' are entirely relational; they may be kept as a memento of a parent or relative, or they may be reminiscent of previous homes, or they may signify an ongoing relationship. Thus Hecht argues that furniture, décor and ornaments

> are more than mere 'things', they are a collection of appropriated materials, invested with meaning and memory, a material testament of who we are, where we have been, and perhaps even where we are heading.
>
> (Hecht, 2001: 123)

It is of course the way that things are invested with meaning that matters most to the sociological imagination.

Embeddedness

> I have tried to think of memories which might not involve people and connections. I have found it impossible. I find connections with other people colour and frame every important building block in my remembered, imagined, conscious self.
>
> (Griffiths, 1995: 20)

This quotation from Morwenna Griffiths links this concept of embeddedness through the bridging notions of memory and connections to the concept of relationality with which I began this discussion. Griffiths (1995) discusses the development of a concept of the self and suggests the impossibility of thinking about remembering herself (growing up as a child) without also acknowledging the 'self' in its connections with other people. She conjures up the idea of the web as a metaphor for explaining how the self is made up of lots of strong but flexible strands and how those strands are connected to surrounding circumstances. She creates visions of intricate entanglements which are between different selves and those surrounding circumstances. The web also hints at the difficulty of disentangling and becoming completely autonomous. These evocative ideas can also be appropriately applied to understanding how each generation is linked with and connected to the generations that have gone before. The idea can also be suggestive of connections which can be gossamer light most of the time, but remain strong at times, which can be virtually invisible and yet exert a painful tug from time to time. I suggest that this can be the way in which important personal relationships work over time. Typically one thinks of genetic kin in this regard, where relationships can ebb and flow and yet be reactivated at times of need. But this is also often the case for strong friendships which only need refreshing with the occasional contact and yet retain a foundational place in the emotions.

Taking this idea of connections in a slightly different direction, Bengtson et al. (2002) deploy the concept of 'linked lives' as a way of describing chains of relationships across generations. With his colleagues he carried out a longitudinal study of families across several generations creating rich data on the ways in which different generations grow up (in different eras) and also how they relate to one another across time and epochs. They argue that individual life trajectories are meaningful in the context of the other lives with which they are linked. So the lives of 'individuals' should not be seen in isolation from the other lives which run in parallel, cross or interfere with those of the main protagonists in the study. But more than this they argue that it is important to theorize how each personal life is also embedded in a web of relationships which includes people who have gone before. Previous generations leave their mark on present generations. Elements of the past are carried forward and help to form the 'new' person who is in practice taking forward a (small) part of the past.

This conceptualization of families across time captures an element of family life that can offer ontological security and a sense of continuity. Indeed once we start to look for these linkages (which may be quite metaphorical, imaginary or even concrete) it is possible to see how even

Figure 2.4 Digression 3: Photos from a graduation ceremony[1]
Photographs reproduced with kind permission from Ed Swinden, 2008, and with the agreement of the students and parents at the ceremony
I can see striking similarities in both of these photos between mother and daughter and these similarities are suggestive of invisible links – if not exactly bonds. The bonds that may or may not exist are dependent upon the meanings the actors give to these similarities and, of course, it is quite possible that the people themselves do not see the same or any similarities. Looking like one's mother when one is 21 years old may not seem attractive, although everyone must surely be familiar now with the experience of becoming middle aged and looking in the mirror only to see one's mother or father looking back. This is an important moment of recognition; it is a kind of haunting too. I can see echoes of the generation before in the younger women. Moreover, getting these young people and their parents to talk of resemblances produced great merriment and much teasing. There were cries of delight and horror and parents absolutely relished speaking of resemblances. It was, in this context – a proud moment of course – a way of expressing love and affection. At other times these same resemblances may seem less charming.

something as chimerical as family resemblances can become a form of bonding and a way of embedding each generation in some way in the generation(s) that went before.

Of course these links and feelings of embeddedness – especially within a genetic family – can be experienced as psychologically and emotionally suffocating. These signs can remind one of how hard it is to be free of one's family and kin. Where lives have become interwoven and embedded it becomes impossible for relationships simply to end. We now appreciate that family relationships do not necessarily end with death and that people have symbolic means, and even practices, which sustain elements of love and closeness or even hate and bitterness. We also know that even those who have fled problematic families engage in imaginary conversations or carry emotions about their families in perpetuity. These relationships can therefore be described as very 'sticky'; it is hard to shake free from them at an emotional level and their existence can continue to influence our practices and not just our thoughts. *More hauntings!*

Embeddedness is therefore neither a good nor bad quality in family relationships. But as a concept it seeks to reflect the tenacity of these bonds and links, while also grasping the extent to which family members and close kin actually feel a part of one. Family relationships seem to be unique in possessing these haunting powers and I shall say more about this below. But here I wish to stress the materiality of these feelings and associations and hence the importance of always putting the person in the context of their past, their webs of relationships, their possessions and their sense of location.

Imaginary

This concept is used to express the ways in which relationships exist in one's imagination and thoughts. But these relationships are not simply located in one's imagination; they have a rich life there. Thus we might imagine that our relationships could be better or stronger or more supportive; we might try to deal with disappointments or arguments; we might compare our relationships with those gone before or with those we imagine that other people have. Our relationships are in part sustained by the workings of our imaginations and significant others may present themselves there in chimerical forms rather than as 'true' likenesses. Families may be full of secrets and lies that are unknown to many, giving the 'illusion' of respectability or closeness when neither is entirely 'true'. Hence the shock a child might receive on discovering they were adopted; or the kind of distress that can be felt on the discovery of illegitimate sibling or prior marriages (Smart, 2009). The following passages from Margaret Forster's *Hidden Lives* (1996) (a semi-fictionalized biography) captures this kind of shock, but it is necessary first to give the segment some context.

There are 3 daughters who, on the day in question in 1936, have buried their beloved mother (a widow) and they have gone back to her house for the funeral reception. There is a knock at the door and one sister opens it to a stranger, another woman, who says she has come to find out whether she had been left anything in the Will because she too is a daughter of the deceased.

Shock could not adequately describe the sense of outrage in the parlour. It was a trick. What else could it be but a disgusting attempt to extort money? Jean's and Nan's faces were flushed with fury, Lillian's pale with distress.

(Forster, 1996: 10)

Later the sisters find their mother's Will.

> 'I knew it was a lie,' [Lillian] said triumphantly and passed the will over to her sister. It was unequivocal. [...] No mention whatsoever of any fourth daughter. No need for panic. No need to revise the revered character and conduct of the good, the wise, the kind, the gentle, the generous, the honest, the almost saintly Margaret Ann, their beloved mother.
>
> (Forster, 1996: 11)

What is interesting in the story that follows, however, is the way in which evidence grows of the existence of a fourth daughter and yet this is suppressed in the family. Moreover no attempt is made to find out who the woman at the door was; she was simply erased. The daughters were determined not to change their vision of their mother regardless of potentially looming evidence.

Forster's story goes on to account for why her grandmother had disguised her past and the illegitimate child she had borne before she married; she also explains why her mother and aunts could not have absorbed the truth because they could not have understood the awful economic and social constraints facing the Margaret Ann. Had they accepted the truth of this event they would have felt they had to abandon their love and affection for their mother and they would have also felt betrayed in some way. Little wonder therefore that they could not do this. But the granddaughter (Forster herself) was born in different times and she could piece together the full story with equanimity and without judgement. This personal memoir is therefore a social history because Forster situates her forebears in their place and time and paints for the reader the rich context of the lives of working class women. But the book is also a demonstration of the workings the imaginary. Her grandmother created a family to fit with the cultural and normative expectations of respectable working class family life in the 1930s and 1940s. The family was both real and a work of fiction. Moreover it was a fiction that her daughters strove hard to maintain.

Gillis deals with precisely this issue. He argues,

> Symbolic universes vary from culture to culture, and over time as well as space. What sets the modern era apart is its dependence on the smallest of all possible symbolic universes – the communities of feeling and fantasy we call our family worlds, worlds of our own making that, as such, are subject to all the foibles and finitudes of human existence.
>
> (Gillis, 1997: 61–2)

Gillis also refers to two realms of family life: the families we live 'with' and those we live 'by'. The latter inhabit our imaginations but they also impinge on our daily existence. Families we live 'by' are therefore not simply imaginings because we actively try to create this imagined family in the here and now. Thus Gillis refers to such activities as going on family holidays, collecting family videos and having family get-togethers as ways in which we shape the flawed family into a more perfect shape. This is what Margaret Forster's grandmother, mother and aunts were doing in her memoir. So the realms of 'by' and 'with' are not separate with one set in substance and one in imagination, rather they overlap in everyday practices as we conduct our family lives. But it is important to recognize that the 'idealized' family we live by is a social, historical and cultural phenomenon. As Gillis implies above, this symbolic universe is widely culturally shared and its components are not arbitrary or unique, rather they would be readily recognized by almost anyone who shares that specific culture at a given time. Of course in the case of Forster's story her mother and aunts shared the cultural vision of what a good family and a good mother was with their own mother's generation. However, by the time of Forster's generation the power of that symbolic universe had waned and she could 'break the spell' so to speak by searching out and speaking of the secret. So this realm of the imaginary should not be understood as a personal quirk or longing of an individual family, it is formed by and influenced by dominant ideals at any given time. Moreover this work of imagination is also a family practice and thus, as Gillis argues, through this means we actively engage in sustaining the cultural imaginary of family life. It is an iterative process.

All of the conceptual tools I have described (relationality, memory, biography, embeddedness or connectedness, and the imaginary) are immanent within each other and also overlap. It is hard, although not impossible, to write of one without calling upon another. So they are connected to one another and it is not my intention that they should be inevitably separated out in some kind of instrumental way. Nor have I argued that all must be followed as if, taken together, they provide some kind of template. Rather the point is that these concepts open up other ways of seeing (Berger, 1972) and can bring into the field of personal life and relationships an additional depth of meaning. They provide a way of 'telling stories' differently and, as I have argued, following Gordon, sociology has a responsibility for the stories it tells. Of course other concepts might work as well as these and A. Gordon's notion of 'hauntings' is one such theme which sets the sociological imagination off in new directions. Equally Les Back's idea of sociology as an 'art of listening' pushes the sociologist into a different position regarding his or her research. It requires a new kind of thoughtfulness for the task. But the concepts I have used suggest a slightly different direction. My purpose has been to restore the person and the personal into the sociological enterprise and to work outwards from this point to account for engagements and meaningful interactions while maintaining personal meanings as a kind of barometer for interpretation. Clearly, not all of sociology should adopt this approach nor would I wish to suggest this. However, in the field of family and personal relationships there is a need to strive to invest accounts of family life with everyday meaningfulness and the challenge to how we listen and how we 'artfully' describe and evoke remains omnipresent.

Part II
Assembling Families

3
Making Family at a Wedding: Bilateral Kinship and Equality

Florence Maillochon and Anna-Maija Castrén

In this chapter we study weddings as family gatherings, as get-togethers of people who are important in the lives of young couples. A wedding is no longer a rite of passage in the sense of being the first step into adulthood and getting married is no longer correlated to leaving the parental home, living in a couple relationship or even having children. Many people live independently, disconnected from their parents' everyday life, and have a family of their own prior to marriage or even totally outside marriage. However, a wedding can still be considered as a rite of passage for the young couple; it reconfigures the social bond between the partners and, for many couples, a wedding offers a means to obtain social recognition of their relationship from their parents (Maillochon, 2008).

A wedding marks a crossroads in a life history: with marriage a new social unit starts to evolve (a couple as 'us' and as a family[1]) and two formerly separate personal networks become intertwined to produce a shared marital network (Rands, 1988). In addition to the couple, a larger group of people become involved, notably the parents and other members of the immediate family, along with the couple's friends. For this very special day kin, friends, neighbours, and colleagues gather together. To paraphrase Berger and Kellner (1988) on marriage, a wedding is the 'building of a small world'. Our intention is to follow this building process by looking at the wedding guests – who have not been systematically analyzed in the research literature – and the rules influencing their selection.

Just as marriage has changed from a social institution controlled by kin groups and collective interests into companionship (Burgess and Locke, 1945) entered into through individual choice, so have weddings turned increasingly into an expression of the personality and preferences of the couple rather than those of their parents (Pleck, 2000; Leeds-Hurwitz, 2002; Boden, 2003). The strengthening of individualism during the twentieth century in Western societies emphasized the individual's point of view. It also led to the democratization of personal relationships (Giddens, 1991; Beck and Beck-Gernsheim, 1995). The idea of marriage as a companionship (Burgess and Locke, 1945) and as a couple relationship (Giddens, 1991) more than as a social institution implies equality between partners. Both are as responsible for the future and well-being of the relationship and, in a heterosexual relationship, neither the male nor the female perspective should dominate. Men and women alike are considered accountable for the happiness or unhappiness of the relationship. This aspect of partners as equals is also acknowledged in the organization of weddings and, despite the everyday remarks about weddings as the woman's fairytale day (referring mainly to visual appearance), the essential decisions are made by the couple as 'us', that is, in mutual understanding about 'our' wedding.[2]

Individual choices are embedded in social constraints. One of the social and structural prerequisites affecting marriage and the family-to-be is the system of bilateral or cognatic kinship in Western societies, which means that both the mother's and father's relatives of both genders are considered as relatives. In contrast to patrilineal and matrilineal systems of descent, the bilateral method of kin reckoning leads to a large group of relatives where the kin group cannot be unanimously delineated, since ego's relatives will always have relatives to whom ego is unrelated (Eriksen, 2001: 98). The kin group membership is thus open to negotiation. What follows in the context of weddings is not only that kin from both the bride's and the groom's sides are expected to be present but also that the couple needs to decide on the categories of relatives and the actual people they invite to their wedding.

Reconciling the individualistic principles that emphasize the importance of personal preferences and the equality of partners with the structural constraint of a bilateral kinship system is a challenge; it creates practical problems when organizing a wedding and deciding which relatives to exclude and which ones to invite and thus include in the newly forming kin group of the family-to-be. Couples are faced with a difficult question: where do their family and relevant kin begin and where do they end?

In the selection of guests brides and grooms confront one of the main dilemmas in the contemporary study of kinship and family in the Western world, namely the process of family deinstitutionalization (Shorter, 1975; Beck and Beck-Gernsheim, 1995). This implies that relations between relatives are more elective and more of a personal choice, and no longer a principle of social organization. Kinship can be seen as a network of interpersonal relationships, a 'kindred' as Freeman (1961) and Mitchell (1963) argued. In this respect, bilateral or cognatic kinship in Western societies is a challenge, and according to Déchaux (2002: 230), in contemporary societies it is difficult to know what constitutes family membership when descent is cognatic and the individual is at the centre of family ties.

Much of the recent analysis proposes that the progress of individualism in contemporary societies opens up either a quite pessimistic perspective (Castel, 1995) or an optimistic one leading to self-development (De Singly, 1996, 2000). Our aim is to reconsider the question of social relations and bonding without taking a stand in the debate but by describing the rules affecting the everyday practices of the family. In this we follow F. Weber (2005), who, on the basis of an empirical study, has outlined different ways of belonging to a family: 'maisonnée' (family members gathered together in everyday life), 'parentèle' (family defined by elective choices) and 'lignée' (family defined through origin and descent: who do people descend from). In a similar manner our aim is to depict the practices of guest selection that mould the composition of the family in-group in contemporary weddings.

Data and methods

In this study, weddings are analyzed in terms of a relational (Smart, 2007b) and configurational (Elias, 1978; Gribaudi, 1998) perspective on social phenomena. This means that instead of focusing solely on a specific dyad, the couple relationship, we consider the larger network of relationships in which the particular dyad is embedded (Widmer et al., 2008). We develop a relational approach that conflates sociological analysis grounded on personal interview data – where people talk about their relations – with a systematic investigation of those relations. This methodological approach thus combines two theoretical perspectives on social phenomena – social constructivism and social realism – that are conventionally kept apart.

The data come from two European societies, France and Finland. They make a good pair of countries to study, since they share significant similarities in their demographic trends relating to couple formation and marriage.[3] Despite the two locations and the cultural differences, our goal is not to perform cross-national comparison. Instead the material has been treated as one data corpus. The main purpose of the article is to describe the micro-level dynamics related to the relational aspects of weddings and, in this respect, the points of convergence are more salient than the differences.

The study is restricted to heterosexual couples with mainstream cultural and ethnic backgrounds in France and Finland. Couples are in the same stage of the life cycle, nearing age 30, which is the mean age at first marriage in the two countries.[4] They live in urban localities (metropolitan Paris and Helsinki) and are marrying for the first time. All have lived together prior to the wedding (from six months to six years) and none of the couples have children.

The sample comprises 12 French and 12 Finnish couples,[5] whose wedding guests are analysed. The couples represent different socioeconomic groups although most of the respondents have a college or a higher education and only one French woman has no education after high school. The respondents were found[6] through self-recruitment by various channels: Internet discussion groups, religious functions, wedding boutiques, commercial exhibitions and snowballing.

The study is based on two kinds of data collected from couples: comprehensive interviews carried out with bride and groom, and exhaustive information about the guests. The couple interviews focused on the wedding but other issues were also discussed, like the history of the couple's relationship and their reasons for getting married. The couples' hesitations regarding the guest list, as well as their obligations, were discussed in detail. The interviews took place at the couple's home or at the university, and they lasted from 1.5 to 4 hours.

After the interviews, the couples filled in detailed questionnaires about themselves, including personal and family background and the guests invited to the wedding. All the guests were described in a systematic way in the questionnaires: personal information (name, age, place of birth and residence, occupation, marital status) as well as relational information (who invited this person, who met this person first, when and in what context, what is his/her relationship to the bride/groom, how often has this person been met face-to-face or otherwise).

The interviews were analysed thematically by type and content of answers. The guest lists were analysed from several angles, the most central being each guest's relationship to the couple. The possible disparities between the representation given by the couples in the interviews about guest selection, and the factual outcome revealed by exhaustive examination of the guest lists offers insight into the ways in which values of individualism are reconciled with the structural constraint of bilateral kinship.

The way the family in-group is defined for the weddings is not the straightforward end result of applying the principles derived from indivualism or bilateral kinship as if they were fixed rules. Instead, the practices observed in the selection of wedding guests are more diverse. Our intention is to examine in detail the invited family members, to see which relatives are invited and to identify the practices determining the selection of relatives at weddings.

The constraint of bilateral kinship and the relatives to be invited

The research literature on contemporary weddings provides us with only a very general description of wedding guests: extended family and friends (Currie, 1993). Not many details about which relatives or which friends are given. In France, the historically oriented studies of Martine Segalen (1980, 1981) show that weddings in rural France were both a familial celebration as well as a local festive event. The bride's family organized the festivities for a large circle of villagers that included family members, extended kin and neighbours. In rural Finland, likewise, the wedding festivities involved various categories of people (Heikinmäki, 1981).

Nowadays couples want to choose the guests by themselves on the grounds of personal preferences even though their parents may still contribute largely to the expenses (Castrén and Maillochon, 2009). Deciding who shall be invited reinforces the separateness of the couple from their parents (Maillochon, 2002). Even though decision-making powers for the wedding arrangements have passed from the parents to the couple, the couple is not freed from structural and familial constraints. Bilateral kinship as a structure defines certain groups of people as potential guests, and the bride's and groom's family members and relatives must all be considered at this point.

Bilaterality of kinship is not discussed in the interviews. It is so axiomatic that it needs no reflection. As the couples' mothers' relatives are as much kin as their fathers' relatives, so are the brides' relatives as much kin in respect to the couple as the grooms' relatives. Both families are considered as important and neither should be favoured. Fairness is required and family members occupying equivalent structural positions must be treated in the same way.

However, the guest lists show that this is not what happens; the norms are never applied in a consistent manner because there is no consensus on what categories of relatives should be invited. A closer look at the data reveals that invited relatives can be divided into three groups on the basis of the kin categories included in each group. The groups are organized according to the genealogical closeness of the categories.

The *first* group comprises people who are most self-evidently invited and always present at weddings. The categories are: parents of the bride and groom and step-parents, if there are any; siblings of the bride and groom, their spouses and children, and step-siblings, if there are any; and lastly, the grandparents, even when they are unlikely to attend due to old age or illness. Exclusion of any member of the bride's or groom's family of origin is possible only for a particular and a grave reason.

The *second* group includes siblings of the bride and groom's parents and cousins with their families. Among all couples in this dataset there are at least a few parents' siblings on the guest list and very often they are all invited even though the couple does not consider all of them as especially close.

The *third* group of invited relatives includes individual kin from unforeseeable categories such as parents' cousins, bride's or groom's second cousins, great-aunts and in one case the sister of the bride's aunt's husband.

Couples who invite a large kin network and conform to formal bilaterality in the sense that all relatives occupying an equivalent position in the genealogical structure are treated similarly, are quite seldom observed in this dataset. This is the case, however, with the Finnish couple Sara and Jouni, who invite all the cousins but none of the more distant kin. They explicitly state in the interview that it is the cousins 'where the fun ends' and this boundary can be observed in their guest list.

In many other cases, however, the practices are more varied, even concerning the first group, which is often the most self-evident. For example, in some families where the parents are divorced, bilaterality is not observed. Two French grooms, Brice and Paul, did not want to invite their divorced fathers, with whom they were no longer in contact. Likewise, other family quarrels can disrupt the self-evidence of the first group. For example, Florent will not invite his sister, who is no longer in contact with their mother. He is also trapped in a cruel dilemma as to whether he should invite his grandmother, whom he loves very much but with whom his mother has broken off all ties.

The selection of wedding guests becomes less straightforward as the genealogical distance grows. There is much more negotiation in respect to the second group even though some couples invite all the people belonging to these categories. Invitation strategies make the choice of some more evident than of others. Some cousins, aunts or uncles are clearly preferred because of emotional closeness. This is the case for Kirsi and Timo, a Finnish couple, who invited only those aunts and uncles they liked. The third group is even more complicated. Even though the couples talk about where they have set the boundary regarding guest selection, it is clear that they have been influenced by their parents (Castrén and Maillochon, 2009).

In the majority of cases, couples have agreed on a shared 'strategy' with regard to inviting certain kin categories, such as cousins. It is therefore very interesting to see that one Finnish couple, Suvi and Jaakko, has totally diverging strategies for deciding which relatives to invite and which not. The boundary for Suvi is between her own cousins, who are invited with their children, and her mother's cousin, who is not invited even though Suvi had discussed it with her mother. Jaakko on the other hand has a completely different attitude towards his relatives. He does not want to invite people with whom he feels distant and whom he meets very rarely; he invites only one cousin on his father's side and he has to disappoint his mother about another cousin whom Jaakko is not eager to invite. Nevertheless, and quite surprisingly, the guest list includes one of Jaakko's father's cousins and two second cousins. The couples' parents are clearly influential, but the personal attitudes of the bride and groom towards family members and kin more generally affect the guest selection. The importance given to these relations may differ between the spouses-to-be, and these differences can be considered as a legitimate explanation for the imbalance between the two families.

Inviting is not an innocent act. It makes the family into a substantive reality by defining its borders: who is in, who is out (Maillochon, 2009a). Inviting testifies to the strength of the ties, since all couples emphasize that they want to invite only people with whom they are 'close' and, as we have seen, also people belonging to a certain kin category. Some of the aunts, uncles and cousins are invited even if they are not that important emotionally because they 'belong' to the extended family or because they cannot be left out. They may be emotionally very close and important for one of the couple's parents, for example. With the selection of their kin guests, the bride and groom make decisions on what kind of family or kin group they wish to have. Within formal constraints, they still have some latitude for choices through which to express their personal preferences and value orientations. In that sense it is not a question of more family or less family, or more personal choice in exchange for less institutional control, as was observed by Déchaux (2002, 2003) when studying transmission in contemporary families. For Déchaux individualism is not incompatible with maintaining descent that organizes the transmission of kinship, but it must be viewed more from a dialectical than a binary perspective. It then becomes possible to conceive the paradox that 'the self is linked to descent: it is by inheriting, or refusing to inherit, that one becomes oneself' (Déchaux, 2002: 232). Inheriting not only places individuals within a structure but also enables them to become themselves. Inheriting means accepting descent: it is not only a fate but also a personal – though limited – choice. When preparing their wedding party, couples want to become themselves and set themselves free from familial constraints, yet they still want or need some kin to be invited. When choosing their kin guests and delimiting who is in and who is out, couples define the borders of kinship and act upon their choice (Maillochon, 2009a). They not only reveal the shape of the family, but also give it substantive reality.

Equality in the relationship understood as fairness between two families

As mentioned, bilaterality is a structural feature of Western kinship whereby family members from both sides are understood as kin. This point is not discussed in the interviews. What is discussed, however, is fairness between the two family groups and between the spouses-to-be. For the couples interviewed, it is thus more a question of equality than structural balance, and equality and fairness can be seen as important contemporary norms complementing bilaterality.

According to the bilateral mode of kin reckoning, families of the bride and groom should be treated in an equal manner. In the ideal situation, the couple could invite the same kind of kin guests, with approximately the same number of people from each side. This is rarely possible, however, since the size and the structure of their families only very seldom match. Also the manner in which the bride and groom perceive family bonds and value their importance is rarely identical.

A question arises: how should bilaterality and equality be balanced? And what would actually be fair for everybody: the intention to invite the same type of relatives or to invite the same number of guests?

A Finnish couple, Kirsi and Timo, for example, talked explicitly about the balance between her and his side. They said that they have had to bargain with each other (if you can invite that person I can have this one). Meanwhile, some other Finnish couples with a quite large difference between the numbers of guests (like Suvi and Jaakko, who had very different attitude towards kin, and Sara and Jouni, who applied a formal interpretation of categorical balance) discuss the subject only briefly or not at all. For example, Sara and Jouni just mention the size of Jouni's extended family as an explanation for the imbalance.

In the French data the number of kin guests is discussed in interviews especially when there are considerable differences between the two sides. Couples feel compelled to explain why one side is more numerous than the other as if they were suspected of unfairness regarding one or the other family. The size of the family is offered as an explanation and the couples base their arguments on the structural differences between families. For Fabienne and Florent's wedding the final list of invited kin – direct ascendants of the couple, uncles, aunts and cousins – comprised a total of 53 people from her side and 10 from his. This is because neither his mother nor his father has any sisters or brothers. Similarly, see Table 3.1 for Véronique and Brice, and Guilaine and Paul. However, sometimes the structural differences between the two sides are only a part of the story, and other criteria are also used in selecting the guests. This is clear in the two last-mentioned cases, where the grooms decided not to invite their divorced fathers. And as a consequence of the parents' divorce, the paternal relatives seem to have lost importance since none of the aunts, uncles, or cousins from Brice's or Paul's fathers' sides are present at their weddings.

Agreeing upon equal numbers of guests on each side calls for considerable bargaining and is rarely the result of strict bilaterality; on the contrary. For example, Diane and Pierre do not observe the bilateral norm which would disadvantage the bride who has lost both of her parents. Instead, they decided to invite a similar number of relatives from both sides as a matter of fairness: Diane invited the parents of her sister's husband to replace her family of origin. Marie and Christophe decided to invite a similar number of relatives in order to be 'equal' and also to reduce the influence of Christophe's quite dominating family, which he characterized as a huge and powerful 'matrilocal tribe'. The case of the Finnish couple Liina and Pekka is also illuminating. Pekka's extended family is substantially larger than Liina's, and since they mutually decided to have only a small wedding party for family members (and later a bigger party for friends), they had to restrict the number of his aunts and uncles in the guest list. Dramatic cutbacks were not needed on Liina's side, so with this strategy they managed to end up with balanced numbers of kin guests from both sides at the party held in Liina's home town. Formal bilaterality is thus not observed consistently and in these cases, inviting equal numbers of family guests on either side is

Table 3.1 Breakdown of guests for each wedding

	Kin & parents' friends		Couple's friends & acquaintances			All together		Total of guests
	Bride's side	Groom's side	Bride's side	Groom's side	Mutual	Bride's side	Groom's side	
Finnish couples								
Arja & Joonatan	27	22	9	4	8	36	26	70
Kirsi & Timo	15	14	13	16	6	28	30	64
Marja & Aleksi	23	16	19	15	4	42	31	77
Suvi & Jaakko	43	13	10	11	1	53	24	78
Sara & Jouni	23	47	8	11	0	31	58	89
Minna & Toni	26	43	20	23	9	46	66	121
Venla & Arttu	15	28	6	8	1	21	36	58
Aila & Ville	26	25	36	28	0	62	53	115
Hanna & Tuomas	22	35	24	26	6	46	61	113
Liina & Pekka	9	10	23	31	0	32	41	73
Helena & Mikko	4	16	7	16	0	11	16	27
Kirsti & Oskari	28	10	12	1	0	40	11	51
French couples								
Carole & Simon	13	16	21	30	3	34	46	83
Marjorie & Cédric	7	12	2	14	3	9	26	38
Noelle & Thomas	29	25	16	13	2	35	38	85
Nina & Yann	44	35	44	15	12	88	50	150
Sandra & Sylvain	36	37	10	16	4	46	53	103
Sabine & Charles	40	29	2	8	6	42	37	85
Claire & Thomas	25	14	22	16	2	47	30	79
Marie & Christophe	15	20	16	10	3	31	30	64
Diane & Pierre	21	19	6	17	2	25	38	65
Véronique & Brice	25	8	10	17	2	35	25	62
Fabienne & Florent	53	10	7	10	0	61	20	81
Guilaine & Paul	48	6	18	10	1	66	16	83
Mean value	26	21	15	15	3	40	36	80

considered as the best way to obtain a fair balance between bride and groom: not a formal equivalence but an effective one.

Emphasis on the bride's family

In this dataset of 24 weddings, bride's family and kin represents the largest group of people with a mean of 26 persons (compared to the groom's side with a mean of 21 persons). Despite the variation, it is the kin guests from the bride's side that form the largest category of wedding guests, especially in French weddings. The bride's relatives and her parents' family friends are more numerous than those of the groom in 14 cases (out of 24).

The size differences of the bride's and groom's extended families offer only a partial explanation for the imbalance in wedding guests, and it is important to note that there are no structural reasons why the brides' families in this dataset should be systematically larger than the grooms'. A more detailed look at the cases shows that the female side of the family plays a dominant role at the beginning of the family career.

In France, weddings were traditionally arranged at the home town of the bride (Segalen, 1980, 1981). Also in many parts of Finland, the tradition was to arrange the wedding festivities, or at least a part of them, in the bride's home village (Heikinmäki, 1981). Since many young couples nowadays live together and separately from their parents prior to marriage, this tradition has waned. Similarly, the bride's family is no longer considered as being solely responsible for the wedding expenses and in most cases the costs are shared. However, in some cases the bride's home town is chosen as the wedding venue, especially if the bride's parents still live nearby. This is the case for three Finnish couples and eight French couples. In all these cases the brides have lived away from their parents for some years either in metropolitan Helsinki or in Paris. In the interviews the choice of wedding venue was discussed as a neutral matter related to practical issues (such as availability of more attractive and more reasonably priced premises and services) and not as something that factually gives precedence to the bride's family.

Even though the 'matrilocality' of the wedding is no longer predetermined and the interviewed brides and grooms report having chosen jointly the type of wedding that 'reflects who they are' (referring to both partners) and that expresses their personalities and preferences, the wedding preparations still remain a women's affair. Brides are much more involved in the arrangements than their grooms, along with the women from the bride's side of family (mother and sisters particularly)

(Maillochon, 2009b; Sniezek, 2005). This 'managerial' position (Boden, 2003) grants them power to negotiate the solution reached for the dilemma between the constraints of bilateral kinship and balanced proportions of guests, for example.

The preference given to the bride's family is illustrated in the mechanism of bargaining when the extended families are of very different sizes. The cases of Diane and Pierre, Marie and Christophe, and Liina and Pekka have already been presented. In the first case, the bride's side was favoured through inviting the in-laws of the bride's sister, and in the second and third, the bride's side is favoured in the sense that the groom's group of relatives is clearly smaller than it would have been had the bilateral norm been observed formally. What is highly interesting, however, is that when the groom's extended family is smaller than the bride's, no adjustments are made to balance the numbers. We have already mentioned the cases of two French grooms, Paul and Brice, whose weddings were not attended by their fathers due to the parents' divorce. In these cases there was no substitution or compensation, and the groom's side remained considerably smaller than the bride's (8 for Brice vs 25 for Véronique; 6 for Paul vs 48 for Guilaine). In the French data, a clear substitution happened only when there was a deficit on the bride's side.

The imbalance in the numbers of guests, in the choice of wedding venue or in the resolution of the problem generated by the bilateral kinship on the one hand and the expectation of fairness and equality of partners on the other, indicates the dominance of the wife's significant people over those of the husband in the social life of the new family. It has been observed, for example, that despite the principle of bilaterality, there is an emphasis on the matrilineal side in many Western societies (Jonas and Le Pape, 2008) especially in relation to care (Weber et al., 2003).

However, it seems that the imbalance between the two sides is more often structurally grounded in the Finnish cases than it is in the French ones. In the Finnish dataset there is either a clear difference in the size of extended family or in the personal attitude and commitment towards kin. The proportions of kin guests differ because the bilateral mode of kin reckoning is observed formally even when there are considerable differences in the family sizes. In the case of Sara and Jouni, for example, the reasons for the imbalance are clearly structural; the groom's extended family is much bigger than the bride's and the couple agreed to invite guests on the basis of kin category (aunts, uncles and cousins). Jouni has six aunts and uncles and 13 cousins while Sara has only three aunts and uncles and six cousins. Likewise, in the cases of Venla and Arttu, and Kirsti and Oskari the differences derive from an unequal number of aunts and uncles in the first place. The other legitimate explanation seems to lie in the importance personally attached to family members and relatives by the bride and groom. In the case of Suvi and Jaakko, the bride-to-be was reported as being very 'keen on relatives' and so it was clear that she was more eager to invite her family members and kin than he was. The constraints of bilateral kinship are much less binding in the French dataset, where more emphasis is given to the equal sizes of guest groups, at least when this does not disadvantage the woman.

Discussion: from the structural constraint of bilateral kinship to formal equality in the couple

An American historian, Pleck (2000: 1), begins her book on rituals with an apposite sentence: 'At certain times of year or moments in life it is important "to have a family" and difficult to be without one'. A wedding is definitely such a moment. Families of both the bride and groom are indispensable on the occasion, due to the system of bilateral kinship in Western societies. A wedding initiates the formation of a new kin group, and it is the first occasion when all the people connected by the new union come together. Some of the guests may meet next time at the Christening of the couple's first child or at some other family ritual, some maybe never. Nevertheless they are now all connected and part of the young couple's kin group.

The practice of guest selection is not unanimously dictated by bilateral kinship or the cognatic family. In the context of individualistic societies, people distance themselves from social norms, especially those considered traditional and delimiting, and become eager to decide for themselves. This prevalent tendency also encourages young couples to view bilaterality in terms of equality between guests on the bride's side and those on the groom's side, rather than in terms of female and male lineages. Equality in the number of guests invited by the woman and the man apparently preserves the idea of equivalence attached to bilateral kinship although it may lead to large differences in the structure of the new kin group. Equivalence and equity are important determinants in choosing the kin guests for the wedding, but in the era of individualism they seem to derive from the principle of gender (partner) equality rather than from the structural equilibrium in kinship. Nevertheless, the equality of partners is not self-evident in this data and relatives and family friends on the bride's side are favoured in many cases. And quite often the disparity can be explained by social differences in the bride's and groom's social status or family background (Maillochon, 2002).

The family in contemporary societies is shaped not only by social and structural norms but also by individual preferences. This transformation should not, however, be interpreted as implying the disappearance of norms and the consecration of individualism. The empirical analysis of the family groups gathered to celebrate the birth of a new family unit presented here invites us to think in new ways about the dilemma of structural versus individual construction of family and, beyond that, of social reality. The question needs to be raised in a more dialectical than binary perspective: individual choices are made under various structural constraints, and they not only reveal the reality of the family, but also contribute to shaping it.

4
Christmas Celebration, an Annual Family Gathering

Roland Hauri

After the examination of wedding practices in the previous chapter, in this chapter another assembling event is analyzed: Christmas celebration. Families – in particular families with minor children – attach great importance to this event, and the planning and performing often take up considerable time and attention. Nevertheless, Christmas celebration is a topic that is rarely addressed in family research. Mostly, this family event is mentioned in studies investigating family rituals.

The term family ritual refers to collective family activities such as shared meals, weekend excursions, or family gatherings. Through their special meaning and their repetitive nature, family rituals serve to stabilize the family and contribute to the shared identity of its members (Wolin and Bennett, 1984). Bennett, Wolin and McAvity (1988: 215) assume that 'rituals are condensed versions of family life as a whole. Their performance clarifies roles, delineates boundaries, and defines rules'. Thus Wolin, Bennett and Jacobs (1988: 232) emphasize that 'rituals provide a particularly rich and accessible window into the family's private world'.

Wolin and Bennett (1984) distinguish between three different types of family rituals: family celebrations, family traditions and patterned family interaction. Christmas feasts are considered as family celebrations. According to these authors, family celebrations 'assert the larger group identification for the nuclear family' (Wolin and Bennett, 1984: 404).

At first glance, the family's Christmas celebration seems to be rather a religious event than a family event. The notion is widespread that the celebration of Jesus' birth stands in the foreground of this occasion. Therefore, scholars like Wolin and Bennett (1984) or Fiese and Kline (1993) consider it as a religious celebration. However, as a result of a historical examination of the festival's origins, Miller (1993: 11) concludes that 'all interpretations of Christmas acknowledge the central image of the family in its celebrations'. Tracing the origins back to the fourth century, his investigation reveals a 'direct correspondence in time between the birth of the festival and a major shift in the norms and practices of family life, which led to the foundation of the idealization of the nuclear family that has continued in Western Europe ever since' (Miller, 1993: 14).

According to Weber-Kellermann (1988), the family's Christmas celebration as we know it today has developed in the first half of the nineteenth century. She highlights the link between the evolution of the Christmas feast and the foundation of the bourgeois family. In this era, the bourgeoisie began to emphasize the privacy of the family. At the same time, Christmas celebration moved from public space to the domestic area. These historical findings indicate that the family's Christmas feast is not solely a religious event, but also a family event.

Research on contemporary Christmas celebrations also acknowledges that family issues stand in the foreground of these occasions. What happens during the celebration seems less important for the participants than who is present at the celebration. In a study on Christmas feasts, Audehm and Zirfas (2001) show that the absence of a family member is a much bigger disaster than, for instance, a burning Christmas tree. The authors conclude that at Christmas, the family expresses its intactness by the physical presence of all family members. By performing this assemblage, the family marks those who belong to the family.

The conjoint performance of family gatherings results in collective experiences among the participating family members. According to Mannheim (1982), such experiences are constitutional to small groups – so-called communities of experience. With reference to Mannheim (ibid.), any family can therefore be considered as a 'conjunctive experiential space', established by shared experiences and actions.

A configurational perspective on families takes similar considerations into account. In family research, the concept of family configurations has recently developed in order to overcome the limitations of family understandings that emphasize the cohabitation of the family members (Widmer and Jallinoja, 2008). Central to the configurational perspective is the focus on actualized relationships rather than institutional criteria such as living in a common household. Family configurations are circumscribed as 'sets of directly or indirectly interdependent persons sharing feelings of family belonging and connectedness' (Widmer et al., 2008: 3). Instead of a specific place of living, the sense of belonging to a family is significant. This sense of belonging emerges by sharing a focus such as common activities: 'Configurations come into being and evolve because individuals share some activities or have a strong common concern for something or someone' (Widmer et al., 2008: 4). Therefore, family activities play a crucial part to the constitution of families.

With regard to a family's Christmas celebrations, Wulf (2006: 399) highlights: 'Regardless of the differences in perception of Christmas [...], the practical occurrence of this Christmas ritual has a binding effect on all the participants'. The regular repetition – the annual performance of the gathering – contributes significantly to this binding effect. Furthermore, through enactment and re-enactment year after year, participating family members incorporate schemes of perceptions, appreciation and action. According to Bourdieu (1977), these schemes are part of the habitus of a person. Therefore, the habitus is developed when participating in family events like Christmas celebrations. Since the habitus is a generative principle, 'a disposition that generates meaningful practices' (Bourdieu, 1977: 170), the schemes acquired in family events will shape social practice – particularly family life – in the future. Consequently, it is assumed that the way families celebrate Christmas has an impact on other parts of family life.

Referring to family celebrations, Wolin and Bennett (1984: 404) point out that 'spouses must negotiate some degree of agreement regarding the format their celebrations will follow, generally drawing heavily upon their experience in their family of origin'. In the context of families' Christmas celebrations, particularly the decision as to who will be participating has to be negotiated. This negotiation is affected by the bilaterality of kinship in Western societies. In contrast to patrilineal and matrilineal systems of descent, bilateral kinship reckons both father's and mother's relatives of both genders as relatives (Goody, 1983). In order to include the kin from both sides, many families celebrate Christmas more than once, whereas each celebration has its own constellation of participants.

The main interest of this study lies on who is participating at Christmas celebrations of families with children. It is argued that families celebrate with significant family members, whether they live in the same household or not. Relevant to the participants is primarily a common feeling of connectedness. Therefore, in accordance with a configurational perspective on families, the group of individuals participating at a Christmas celebration is regarded as a family configuration that can vary extensively from family to family. Mainly based on a survey of more than 1300 families in Switzerland, diverse types of family configurations are identified.

In this chapter, first the underlying data is described. Then attention is drawn to the participants of the Christmas gathering. Based on the individuals attending the gathering considered as the most important, a typology of family configurations is constructed. Thereafter, the configurations are compared to each other with respect to other dimensions of the family assemblages. It will be apparent that the configuration affects the shaping of this assembling event. Finally, the chapter closes with some conclusions.

Data

This study includes quantitative as well as qualitative data sources: a survey on the one hand, and several case studies on the other hand. The main focus is put on the survey of families with children aged six or nine conducted in German-speaking Switzerland in autumn 2005. The selected probability sample containing 3243 families was stratified according to large regions of Switzerland and to commune size. The questionnaire – sent to the children's home address – was completed either by the child's mother or the child's father. The parents decided themselves which one of them was going to participate. The response rate was 41 per cent therefore data analysis is based on 1344 questionnaires.

The sample shows the following characteristics: 85 per cent of the respondents are mothers, 15 per cent fathers. 92 per cent of the parents live in two-parents-households and 8 per cent in one-parent-households. On average 2.4 children live in a household. The children's age ranges from a few months to 26 years. 15 per cent of the families contain at least one non-Swiss parent, and in 19 per cent of the families at least one parent has a university degree. Compared with the Swiss Household Panel, a representative household survey in Switzerland, families with three or more children are over-represented, whereas households with non-Swiss parents and one-parent-households are under-represented.

The questionnaire contained items related to different aspects of the family assemblages at Christmas. Since many families celebrate Christmas more than once, the main focus is on the celebration rated as the most important by the parents. Four aspects of this main celebration stood in the foreground: the participating individuals, the celebration's components, the atmosphere and the meaning ascribed to the celebration. Who was present at the gathering was recorded by an open-ended question. However, the respondents had to clarify whether the named persons were relatives from mother's or father's side, or whether they were non-relatives. In order to gain information about the celebration's components, respondents were presented a list of 13 possible objects and activities, for instance Christmas tree or singing Christmas carols. They were asked to indicate for each component if it occurred and how important it was. The importance was reported on a three-point scale with the values 'very important', 'less important' and 'not important', but analysis was conducted on the basis of a dichotomous scale distinguishing between 'very important' and other values. The atmosphere at the main celebration was measured by a list of 11 adjectives, for example festive, cosy or conflictual. Responses were made on a four-point scale ranging from 'agree' to 'disagree'. In order to structure the multiple facets of the atmosphere, a factor analysis based on the adjectives' ratings was conducted, revealing four independent factors labelled as sociability, quietness, contemplativeness and formality. The celebration's meaning was detected by presenting 11 statements beginning with 'It was important', for example 'It was important that the children had fun", or 'It was important that the family could be together'. The respondents' agreement was measured on the same four-point scale as for the atmosphere.

As mentioned earlier, most of the survey data refer to the Christmas celebrations rated as the most important by the parents. In order to consider the complexity of the different celebrations over Christmas, the study also includes additional case studies based on interview data of 12 families with a child aged nine or ten. In each family, the child, parents and grandparents were interviewed on how the family celebrates Christmas.

Family configurations at Christmas celebrations

First, attention is drawn upon the participants of the family assemblage at Christmas. Referring to the concept of family configuration, different types of family configurations will be distinguished. The typology will be based on the individuals attending the Christmas gathering that is considered as the most important by the parents. But before constructing the typology of family configurations, I will present some descriptive data concerning the participants.

Who is present at a particular assemblage depends on the participants at other gatherings over Christmas. Therefore, it is necessary to detect how many celebrations take place before analyzing who is participating at the main event. Data show, as assumed, that most families celebrate Christmas more than once: in 27 per cent of the families, only one gathering takes place, whereas 43 per cent celebrate twice and 25 celebrate three times. In 88 per cent of the families grandparents are attendant at at least one Christmas gathering. 44 per cent of the families celebrate with grandparents as well as without grandparents.

Approximately one third of the families celebrate their main event as a nuclear family. Those family constellations are labelled as nuclear family when the six- or nine-year-old child celebrates exclusively with parents and siblings, or with stepparents and stepsiblings, irrespectively if these family members live in the same household or not. In one-half per cent of these families, parents or siblings living outside the household are attendant, for instance parents living separately or adult siblings with their own household.

Out of the other two-thirds of the families that expand the nuclear family at Christmas, 89 per cent celebrate with relatives, 5 per cent with non-relatives, and 6 per cent with both relatives and non-relatives. Of the celebrations with relatives, 56 per cent are with relatives of the mother's side, 27 per cent with relatives of the father's side and 17 per cent with relatives of both sides. For both mothers and for fathers, the celebration with their own relatives is more important than the celebration with relatives of the other side.

The relatives most often attending the main Christmas celebration are grandparents. In 60 per cent of the families at least one grandparent is present. In 4 per cent even great-grandparents participate.

So far, little empirical research has constructed whole typologies of family configurations. In recent years, there are the studies of Widmer (2006) and Widmer and Sapin (2008) that identify different types of family configurations, both applying an empirical inductive procedure by means of cluster analysis. The typologies they present are quite similar to each other. Widmer and Sapin (ibid.) for instance distinguish between five family types: nuclear, family of orientation, kinship, post-divorce and friendship. But in contrast to the study on Christmas celebrations presented here, the identification of the various family configurations is not directly based on actual family life. Instead, in both studies the respondents were simply asked to list all individuals they consider as significant family members. Furthermore, the data of the two studies derive from rather specific populations: on the one hand from young adults, on the other hand from individuals undergoing psychotherapy.

In comparison with the method Widmer (2006) as well as Widmer and Sapin (2008) are applying, in this study the family configuration will be constructed conceptually deductively, and not empirically inductively. The classification includes the distinctions between relatives and

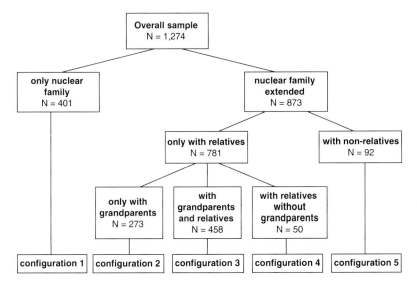

Figure 4.1 Typology of family configurations at the main Christmas celebration

non-relatives, and the subdivision of relatives into direct lineage and other kin. Figure 4.1 gives an overview on the construction of the typology based on 1274 families.

First, the families celebrating as a nuclear family were separated from those celebrating with additional people. Then, based on the distinction between relatives and non-relatives, the latter families were divided into families celebrating solely with relatives and families celebrating with non-relatives, some of them additionally with relatives. Finally, the families with relatives were split into three groups referring to the distinction between direct lineage and other kin.

In Figure 4.1, these five types of family configurations will be described. In order to illustrate that the main Christmas celebration is often complemented by other coexisting celebrations, each description begins with a short case study showing the diverse celebrations over Christmas. Out of 12 case studies, the most typical cases are selected. Then, based on the survey data, the composition of the family configuration at the main celebration will be presented in detail.

Nuclear family

Family A is composed of the mother, the father and two daughters six and eight years of age. Both grandparents of the mother's side are still alive; on the father's side the grandfather has already died. The mother has two younger twin sisters, the father an older and a younger sister.

Family A celebrates Christmas three times. The main event takes place at the home of family A in the evening of 24 December. It is celebrated as a nuclear family, with mother, father and both children attending. The two other feasts, rated as less important by the parents, take place 25 and 26 December. At one celebration, family A meets the relatives from the father's side, the grandmother and the two aunts with their families. At the other celebration, family A meets the relatives from the mother's side, both grandparents and the two aunts with their families. Both celebrations take place at the home of the respective grandparents.

Family A belongs to the family configuration type that celebrates the main Christmas event as a nuclear family. This configuration type contains 31 per cent of the sample. As explained earlier, the term nuclear family is used for those family constellations when the six- or nine-year-old child celebrates exclusively with parents and siblings, or with stepparents and stepsiblings, irrespectively if these family members live in the same household or not. In one-half per cent of these families, parents or siblings living outside the household are attendant, for instance parents living separately or adult siblings with their own household. In this group, the proportion of one-parent-households is only 4 per cent, which is clearly below average. But it is remarkable that more than three quarters of these one-parent-households celebrate not only with one parent: in some cases the parents living separately join the celebration, and in another case the single parent's partner living in a different household is present. Therefore, celebrating as a nuclear family means in 99 per cent of the cases that two adults are celebrating with children. Three quarters of these families have at least one other celebration besides the main celebration. In comparison to the other types, there are a high proportion of families that celebrate three or even more times (41 per cent). In most of the cases, grandparents are present at at least one of the additional celebrations. Although the main event is performed as nuclear family and without grandparents, 73 per cent of the families still celebrate with grandparents over Christmas.

This type corresponds to the family configuration of Widmer and Sapin (2008), which is labelled as 'nuclear'. Most important to the families of this type is the inner family circle. The families refer to the traditional family image: the significant family is the nuclear family, composed of a mother, a father and children, generally living in the same household. Even the few one-parent households in this type seem to correspond with the traditional image, since most of them are complemented by a second parent at Christmas. Although the families focus on the nuclear family, grandparents and other kin are still of certain importance. The relationships to the relatives, preferably to the relatives of both parents' sides, are often substantially maintained. In many families, this leads to three or more family gatherings over Christmas.

Nuclear family with grandparents (and great-grandparents)

Family E consists of the father, the mother, and three sons aged four, six and nine. The grandfather of the father's side has already died, the grandmother of the father's side and both grandparents of the mother's side are still alive. The father has two older sisters, the mother one older brother.

Family E celebrates Christmas twice, whereas the most important celebration takes place at the home of family E in the evening of 24 December. All living grandparents are invited: the father's mother as well as the mother's parents. On 27 December the family celebrates Christmas a second time. The second celebration, which takes place at the home of the grandmother of the father's side, is rated as less important than the first celebration. Besides the grandmother, both sisters of the father with their families are present.

Family E belongs to the family configuration type that expands the nuclear family along the direct lineage at the main Christmas celebration. This configuration type contains 21 per cent of the sample. Grandparents – or step-grandparents – and sometimes great-grandparents of the six- or nine-year-old child join the nuclear family. In 49 per cent of the families grandparents of the mother's side are present, in 33 per cent grandparents from the father's side. In 5 per cent it is not clarified from which side the grandparents come. 13 per cent of the families celebrate the main Christmas event with grandparents from both sides. In 4 per cent of the families even great-grandparents are participating besides the grandparents. Many families of this type celebrate Christmas twice (47 per cent). In comparison to other types, three or more celebrations are relatively rare (22 per cent).

This type is consistent with the family configuration of Widmer and Sapin (2008) that is called the 'family of orientation'. Families of this type significantly include members of the direct lineage in their family life. With the attendance of grandparents and sometimes great-grandparents, these families reach across households. This configuration type attaches great importance to the relationships between children, parents and grandparents. In contrast to the previous type, not only two generations are involved in family life, but three or even four. Christmas is generally celebrated with the grandparents of both sides, but most often separately as indicated by the relatively high frequencies of two gatherings over Christmas.

Nuclear family with grandparents and other relatives

Family F is composed of the two parents and their three daughters, who are aged six, nine and thirteen. Both grandparents of the father's side as well as both of the mother's side are still alive. The father has three younger triplet brothers of whom one has already died, and a younger sister. The mother has a younger brother and a younger sister.

Family F celebrates Christmas three times. The most important feast takes place at the home of the grandparents of the mother's side, in the afternoon and evening of 24 December. Besides the grandparents, both siblings of the mother with their partners participate. One of the two other less important celebrations is performed as nuclear family event on 23 December. Only the father, the mother and the three daughters are present. The other celebration is on 25 December when all three remaining siblings of the father and their families meet at the home of the father's parents.

Family F belongs to the family configuration type that expands the nuclear family not only by grandparents and great-grandparents, but also by other relatives. This configuration type contains 36 per cent of the sample. In 38 per cent of the cases the additional relatives are aunts and uncles of the child aged six or nine, in 51 per cent of the cases they are aunts and uncles as well as cousins. Only 10 per cent of these families celebrate the main Christmas feast with more distant kin.

The relatives derive more often from the mother's side than in the previous configuration type, namely in 58 per cent of the families. Reaching 17 per cent, the proportion of families celebrating with relatives of both sides is also higher.

Great-grandparents are attending the main Christmas event in 9 per cent of the families. Therefore, the percentage of celebrations with great-grandparents is significantly higher than in the previous type. As opposed to the previous types, in this type the attendance of children in addition to those of the nuclear family is possible. In 58 per cent of the families, relatives who belong to the same generation as the child aged six or nine are present. Like the previous type, families tend to celebrate Christmas twice (50 per cent). Relatively seldom, the event with grandparents and other relatives is the sole event over Christmas (24 per cent).

This type corresponds to the 'kinship' configuration of Widmer and Sapin (2008). Families of this configuration type consider the extended family as the significant family. Relevant is the whole family network, and not just single ties to certain kin. More frequently than in the previous type, relatives of both parents' sides are conjointly involved in Christmas gatherings. For adults as well as for children, it is possible to maintain family relationships to exponents of the same generation across the household boundaries. At the same time, the gatherings of three or four generations provide the opportunity to establish relationships across generations.

Nuclear family with relatives but without grandparents

Family J consists of the father, the mother, and two sons aged nine and sixteen. None of the grandparents are alive. The father has two older sisters, a twin brother and a younger step-sister. The mother has a brother and a sister, both older than her.

Family J celebrates Christmas only once. The celebration takes place at the home of Family J, in the evening of 24 December. Besides both parents and the two children, there are relatives of both sides attending: from the mother's side, the sister and the brother respectively the children's aunt and uncle participate, as well as the brother's wife and her mother. From the father's side, the step-sister is present. Although there are no grandparents, the grandparents' generation is still represented by the uncle's mother-in-law.

Family J belongs to the family configuration type that celebrates the most important Christmas event with relatives, but without grandparents and great-grandparents. This configuration type contains 4 per cent of the sample and corresponds to the previous type, with the difference that relatives of the direct lineage are missing. In 8 per cent of these families the grandparents' generation is still represented by a single aunt or uncle of the parents, but in the remaining 92 per cent this generation is completely absent.

In 22 per cent of the families, the nuclear family is extended by aunts and uncles of the child aged six or nine, in 56 per cent by aunts and uncles as well as cousins. More distant kin appear in 18 per cent of the families. This percentage is almost twice as big as in the previous type. In 68 per cent, the relatives stem from the mother's side of the family, in 32 per cent from the father's side. In this type, not a single family celebrates with relatives from both sides.

Among all types, this type has the largest proportion of families celebrating Christmas twice (58 per cent), and the smallest proportion celebrating just once (18 per cent).

There is no configuration in the study of Widmer and Sapin (2008) that corresponds to this type. The families of this configuration type significantly include relatives in their family life, but the members of the direct lineage are absent. In most of the cases the nuclear family is therefore expanded only by exponents of the same two generations as the nuclear family.

Despite the absence of grandparents at the main gathering, it is assumed that grandparents are often present at coexisting assemblies, because in this type, one single event over Christmas is relatively rare.

Nuclear family with non-relatives (and relatives)

None of the case studies fall into this type of family configuration, which is characterized by the attendance of non-relatives at the most important Christmas celebration. This configuration type contains 7 per cent of the sample. In addition to the non-relatives, in more than half of the families of this type also relatives take part in the main event (54 per cent).

According to the responding parents, in three quarters of the families the non-relatives are friends and colleagues, sometimes participating with their partners, children, or other relatives. One tenth of the families report that non-related godparents of the children are present, another tenth mention neighbours. However, it is impossible to distinguish clearly between these groups of non-related persons. For instance, godparents can also be named as friends. Besides the non-related adults, in 30 per cent of the families there are also non-related children participating at the main Christmas event.

In 41 per cent of these families grandparents are present; in 14 per cent they are the only relatives attending the celebration. If relatives are present, relatively often they stem from both sides, from the mother's as well as from the father's side (31 per cent). In this group, the proportion of families celebrating Christmas just once is the highest of all types (38 per cent).

This type corresponds to the 'friendship' configuration of Widmer and Sapin (2008). With reference to Weston (1991) they also speak of 'chosen families''. The families of this configuration type are characterized by the inclusion of non-related individuals. Family life is not restricted to relatives. But the presence of non-relatives does not mean that kin ties are unimportant. Often, relatives are attendant in addition to the non-relatives, quite frequently even relatives of both parents' sides. Besides the main assemblage, in quite a few families, there are no other gatherings over Christmas.

Differences between configurations with regard to other aspects of the assemblage

After constructing a typology of family configurations, the question arises whether the diverse configuration types differ with regard to other aspects than simply the participants. In other words: is a particular configuration associated with a specific format of assembling? In order to answer this question, I consider the following three aspects: the celebration's components, the atmosphere and the meaning which is ascribed to the celebration.

A descriptive analysis of the celebration's components shows the following results. In nearly every family, the most important celebration contains a meal (98 per cent), a Christmas tree (97 per cent) and the exchange of presents (96 per cent). Less frequent but still quite common are the Christmas decoration (84 per cent), the singing of Christmas carols (75 per cent) and the Nativity Set (68 per cent). Other components occur even more rarely. For instance, 53 per cent of the families report listening to music and the Nativity Story from the Bible is read or told only in 29 per cent of the families. If they occur the Christmas tree, the Nativity set and the Nativity story from the Bible are most often rated as very important.

A comparison of the five family configurations shows substantial differences in some components (see Table 4.1). The nuclear family type seems to attach less importance to the festive meal than other types do. It is the only type with several families that celebrate Christmas without a meal. And if a meal is part of the gathering, it is rated in only 59 per cent of the cases as very important. In comparison with the other types, this type most frequently sings Christmas carols and reads or tells the Nativity story from the Bible. Furthermore, the exchange of presents is most often rated as very important. The family type celebrating with grandparents shows similar values as the overall sample. However, the percentage of families that consider the meal as very important is below average. In contrast, the type gathering with grandparents and other relatives attaches great significance to the festive meal, which is most often considered as very important. In addition, this type has the highest percentage of families singing Christmas Carols during the gathering. The type with relatives but without grandparents relatively often celebrates Christmas without traditional components like Christmas carols or the Nativity story from the Bible. The type including non-relatives in the assemblies has the highest percentage of families celebrating Christmas without Christmas carols. Furthermore, presents are clearly less important than in other types.

Table 4.1 Components of the main celebration depending on family configuration (percentages)

		only NF	with GP	with GP and RL	with RL without GP	with NR	Overall sample
Meal							
Occurrence	$\chi^2 = 29.06^{***}$	96	99	100	100	99	98
Importance	$\chi^2 = 15.42^{**}$	58	61	74	64	69	65
Presents							
Occurrence	$\chi^2 = 2.04$	95	97	95	95	98	96
Importance	$\chi^2 = 15.42^{**}$	53	43	42	49	34	45
Christmas carols							
Occurrence	$\chi^2 = 16.87^{**}$	78	71	78	68	62	75
Importance	$\chi^2 = 2.48$	73	73	68	73	68	71
Nativity story from the Bible							
Occurrence	$\chi^2 = 15.45^{**}$	36	29	26	16	26	29
Importance	$\chi^2 = 1.61$	81	78	77	75	71	78

Note: N = 1266; percentages on 'importance' refers to those families where the corresponding component actually occurred; NF = nuclear family; GP = grandparents; RL = relatives; NR = non-relatives; ** = p < .01; *** = p < .001.

Table 4.2 Atmosphere at the main celebration depending on family configuration (mean)

		only NF	with GP	with GP and RL	with RL without GP	with NR	Overall sample
Sociability	F = 5.46***	3.42	3.48	3.56	3.52	3.46	3.49
Contemplativeness	F = 6.05***	3.06	3.00	2.91	2.81	2.76	2.96
Quietness	F = 14.20***	3.01	2.94	2.72	2.69	2.74	2.86
Formality	F = 1.24	1.37	1.42	1.42	1.53	1.37	1.40

Note: N between 1233 and 1234; NF = nuclear family; GP = grandparents; RL = relatives; NR = non-relatives; item values: 1 = disagree, 2 = disagree somewhat, 3 = agree somewhat, 4 = agree; F = one-factorial analysis of variance; *** = p < .001.

Regarding the atmosphere at the Christmas gathering, descriptive analysis of the four detected factors show that sociability has the highest score, followed by contemplativeness and quietness. A comparison of the five family configurations reveals significant differences in the factors sociability, contemplativeness and quietness (see Table 4.2).

It is striking that families celebrating their main event as a nuclear family have the highest contemplativeness and quietness scores, but the lowest sociability score. With the addition of grandparents the assemblages obtain a more sociable, but less contemplative atmosphere. Families with gatherings including the extended family show the highest sociability score of all family types. But the ratings for contemplativeness and quietness are below average. Assemblages with relatives but without grandparents have relatively low contemplativeness and quietness scores, but the sociability score is above average. When non-relatives are present, the assemblages have the lowest contemplativeness score.

When parents are asked what was important at their previous Christmas celebration, they most often mention issues related to the children and to the family as a whole. Out of the 11 listed statements, the statements 'It was important that the children had fun", and 'It was important that the family could be together' are most strongly agreed with.

A comparison of the family configurations shows significant differences in a few statements (see Table 4.3). Families assembling as a nuclear family most strongly affirm the statements 'It was important that the family could be together' and 'It was important to remember Jesus' birth'. But the agreement with the statement 'It was important

Table 4.3 Meaning of the main celebration depending on family configuration (mean)

It was important		only NF	with GP	with GP and RL	with RL without GP	with NR	Overall sample
that the family could be together.	F = 10.65***	2.95	2.89	2.92	2.78	2.70	2.90
to preserve a family tradition.	F = 4.18**	2.08	2.14	2.32	2.16	2.01	2.18
to remember Jesus' birth.	F = 6.97***	2.27	2.10	1.93	1.88	1.99	2.08

Note: N between 1246 and 1258; NF = nuclear family; GP = grandparents; RL = relatives; NR = non-relatives; item values: 1 = disagree, 2 = disagree somewhat, 3 = agree somewhat, 4 = agree; F = one-factorial analysis of variance; ** = p < .01; *** = p < .001.

to preserve a family tradition' is below average. With the addition of grandparents and other relatives, remembering Jesus' birth becomes less important, but the relevance of preserving a family tradition increases. Interestingly, families celebrating with relatives but without grandparents show relatively low agreement with the statement 'It was important that the family could be together' although they gather exclusively with relatives. Less surprisingly, the lowest agreement with the statements 'It was important that the family could be together' and 'It was important to preserve a family tradition' is reported in families where non-relatives attend the assemblage.

Conclusion

Provided that Christmas celebrations are regarded as family rituals, we can assume that these gatherings 'provide a particularly rich and accessible window into the family's private world' (Wolin et al., 1988: 232). Family assemblages at Christmas particularly show which individuals are part of the family world. Based on a configurational perspective, the present study reveals that families vary significantly with regard to the participants of the family gatherings at Christmas. The composition of the assembling families differs in several respects. On the one hand, the diversity refers to different possibilities in shaping intergenerational relationships within the family. For instance, grandparents seem to be of different relevance when families gather at Christmas. On the other hand, differences are detected with regard to the inclusion of non-relatives in family life.

The diversity appears on two levels: the first level refers to differences in the format of the main Christmas celebration, the second level to the combination of different coexisting celebrations over Christmas.

At the main Christmas gathering, five different types of family configurations appear. These types largely correspond to the family configurations described in the studies of Widmer (2006) and Widmer and Sapin (2008). This correspondence is remarkable because the typologies of the aforementioned studies are constructed on the grounds of respondents' listing of significant family members, and in the present study the typology is directly based on actual family praxis. Furthermore, additional analysis shows that the family configurations do not vary only with regard to the participants. Other aspects, such as the celebration's components or the atmosphere, are closely related to the configurations. Therefore, the results suggest that families shape their gatherings depending on the participating individuals.

In addition to the main Christmas celebration, in many families there are supplemental gatherings. The coexistence of several assemblies can be seen as a result of the bilaterality of kinship. Since relatives from father's and mother's sides are reckoned as relatives, families try to gather with relatives from both sides over Christmas. As the analysis shows, there are different strategies how to include both sides: in some families, assemblies with relatives from father's as well as mother's side take place. But often there is only one side of the relatives present, which means that other gatherings are needed.

By performing family assemblages, families mark who belongs to the family. But the gatherings are influenced by several constraints. For instance, if some relatives dislike each other, conjoint gatherings are impossible. Or family members may live too far away to participate. Consequently, sometimes individuals are missing although they are considered as family members. However, it is argued that the actual performance is of great importance, since the attendants incorporate schemes of perceptions, appreciations and actions on the grounds of concrete practice. These schemes will shape social practice – particularly family life – in the future.

In order to detect the main assemblage over Christmas, parents were asked which gathering is considered as the most important. Therefore, in this study, the parents' perspective is taken into account. But in regard to family perceptions, the parents' perspective can differ significantly from other generations' perspectives such as those of the children (see Zartler, this volume).

This study is mainly based on a cross-sectional survey. Unfortunately, this approach leads to a static picture of family configurations in the context of families' Christmas celebrations. But family configurations are dynamic family phenomena. Therefore, in order to investigate corresponding processes and developments over time, further research is needed.

5
Family Photographs: Putting Families on Display

Antònia Gomila

The analysis of the family biography through pictures is less than new in family studies. Bourdieu has led a better understanding of it, and other studies about the family have used photography both as a method of analysis and as a theoretical framework in which to understand the family as a social construction (Kuhn, 1995; Miller, 1998; Chalfen, 1987). Nevertheless, in the present context, in which visual experiences and images are omnipresent in everyday life, the symbolic content and its capacity of representation turn photographs into one of the most valuable parts of the material culture of the family, and therefore, an object of analysis for the study of family relations and the idea of the family.

Family photographs function as visual rhetoric. They are 'presented for the purpose of communication, symbolic and involve human intervention' (Foss, 2004) and, as such, elicit both emotional and rhetorical responses, resulting from the attribution of meaning to them. It is in this sense that we affirm that the depiction of family photographs – like obituaries, weddings, birthdays, Christmas festivities – are a form of family assemblages. Family photographs are the visual representations of bonds, personal relations, interactions and shared emotions that express a social and individual conception of family configurations. But also, they involve a process of assemblage, as the meaning of the family photography has to be understood in a dynamic process of family display (Finch, 2007: 66) that embraces the production, the classification, the storage (albums, boxes and so on), the exhibition (in walls, in screens, in mobile phones, in handbags), the exchange and the narratives around and about them.

The concepts of imagination, memory, relationality, embeddedness and biography that allow the exploration and visualisation of the way families construct themselves (Smart, 2007b: 37), find in family photography not only a form of graphical expression of an idea, but a tool through which this process takes place. Taking pictures, organising, arranging and exchanging them, as well as the steps involved in the decision making of all these processes, are ways of practising the family and a way of constructing both a public and a private depiction of it from a representation of its own. It could be interpreted as a space in which official and practical kinship – the double dimension of the family as Bourdieu (1977: 35) states – are linked. It is also the analysis of the family display of photographs that allows us to go along with the transformations of the family experiences and the way they are thought of in the process of construction and definition of themselves.

Therefore the understanding of the process of presentation, re-presentation and construction of the family throughout the visual images suggests a multidimensional approach. All the domestic images displayed in a house, whether they are pictures of the individual family members or group pictures, both personalise the dwelling and, at the same time, make the family a collective. In this sense, the depiction of family images provides the double dimension of the concept of family configurations as stated by Widmer and Jallinoja (2008: 2), which blends both dimensions of the concept 'family': the *particular* and the *general*, or, to put it in Bourdieu's terms: the *official* and the *practical*. That is, a clear representation of the collective–public/individual–private dichotomy. As Jallinoja explains, following Bourdieu (1977), the presentation of the family through family portraits is a self-representation of the family, which is at the same time particular (as they refer to a particular family) and general, since all of them manifest belongingness through family bonds. Therefore, the internal dimension of the family pictures deals with identity and personal life that goes beyond the domestic sphere of relationships and roles. The pictures remind the family members who they are and what is their place in the group, allowing them to identify themselves as such. Photographs are then not only an element that reproduces the image of cohesion and embeddedness that the family wants to give of itself as a group (Bourdieu, 1979), but also an element that contributes to the reinforcement of this cohesion (Belleau, 1996: 68) through the construction of the personal identity of a member of this group. At the same time, they have a public dimension in the sense that the exhibition of family pictures articulates a real and a virtual (an ideal/official) version of the family. They tell not only who is part of the family – and when, where and how they are – but also what are the rules that structure and organise the projection of the family to the outside world; a projection that cannot be dissociated from the social system of values nor from an 'idealised' model that corresponds with the meaning of 'the family' in the social imaginary.

Furthermore, the social organisation and the rules involved in the domestic display of family images refers to a cultural form of social relations inside the family in a particular society and, therefore, a cultural image of what this society understands by 'family'. Family photography is a strongly regulated activity, and so is the display of family photographs. Its severity lies hidden in an apparent naivety and in a feeling of 'naturalness' in which pictures are made and shown (Antúnez, 2008). The rules for the arrangement and organisation of the exhibition of family pictures (where, how and when a picture, and of whom, can be on display or taken away) are the common thread of this chapter, as they state how the families build their image. It is through the analysis of these rules that we can see to what extend the depiction of family photographs is a family assemblage and how this process works.

The first part of this chapter is thus devoted to the analysis of the rules organising the visual presentation of the family. The definition of the public and private spheres operates through the rules about the depiction in each space of the house. Here, the uniformity under which certain rules of presentation are applied raises the question of the cultural model that lies beyond the particular interests or styles of the families. Part two deals directly with the depiction of family pictures as family assemblage through the rules that state who belongs to the family. Furthermore, the form of presentation, the place and the size of the different people represented in the pictures depicted in the dwelling give a clear sight of who is who in this particular family. The relationality perspective is here the key to analysing the importance of identity in the process of family assemblage. The third part is devoted to the analysis of how the family practises through the process of depiction and organisation of the photographs. The display of family photographs is also another way to display family relationships, or to 'do' family (Finch, 2007: 65). In our case, photographs are the material through which negotiation and exchange between family members take place as part of a continuous and conscious process of assembling. The reorganisation of the collection of family pictures, which is the subject of the last part of this chapter, also shows this dynamism. Through the photographs, the family displays itself as a social entity through its own history. The biography of the family is represented through the pictures exhibited, which are changed, added and removed at the same time as the changes in the course of life take place.

Data and methods

The present study has been set up from fieldwork conducted from January to June 2008 with members of three different generations of five family groups living in ten different dwellings in Majorca. These people have let us take a deep look into the public part of their families, although with it and through their explanations and discourses about the photographs we have entered the private space of the emotions, feelings, souvenirs and memories that make us aware of the meaning individuals give to the family group and how they express it through images.

The families were asked to show us all the pictures exhibited in their dwellings and to tell us the story of each picture: who are the characters, when it was taken, the meaning of the moment in which the picture was taken and so on. The discourse about the pictures was far richer than the sight of the picture alone, but it had also to be followed by a large knowledge of the genealogical links of the family members and the social networks they built in their particular configuration.

The number of times every person appeared in the photographs, and the type and style in which they were presented was counted. Nevertheless, the process of 'counting' was difficult as a common pattern had to be found for classifying the number of times and the type of photo in which a given person appears, which is not an easy task when taking into consideration that the way in which (the position) this person is in the picture might also be relevant.

The photographs show marked differences in the way generations, social groups and family structures (forms) are represented, but they also reveal that common patterns and common rules define the terms of this exhibition. This leads us to raise the question about the persistence of a cultural model of the family – ideal and idealised – which becomes active when a family thinks about itself and shows itself to the outside world. With this idea in mind, we were also interested in paying attention to absences and incoherence.

Some of the informants went beyond our demands by showing us the pictures they had removed from the public scene and the photographs they store in albums or boxes. During the period of fieldwork, some of the dwellings were visited several times and we could see some significant changes. Photographs which had been replaced by more recent ones, old frames that were broken . . . nonetheless, we could see little changes in the logic of the exhibition, confirming the solidity of the rules.

Assembling families through pictures

The arrangement of the spaces addressed to introduce the family members shows the division of the family imaginary into an internal–private and an external–public sphere. In its public dimension, the goal is not showing 'who we are' but instead 'what and how we want others to see us' (Bourdieu, 1977). The arrangement of the photographs in the walls and furniture of the house is regulated by specific rules sorting out persons, events, objects and places of special relevance in the family biography according to an established hierarchy. Where it is placed, how it is presented and who is presented is a calculated strategy for an image placed by the family, which expresses a way of structuring the domestic space and the personal relations within the family. The exhibition of family images is made through the patterns given by the image that the family has of itself and the one it wants to project to the outsider. However, if the rules governing the public and the private spheres are different, the boundaries between them are not well defined. The public image shows the present and the past of the family, the individuals that are and have been part of it, and the events that have built the family biography. These events are presented through two different groups of pictures – of ritual events and of daily life – which are also distinguished by different formats. The ritual photograph shows the events that have marked the different stages of the life courses of both the family as a group and of the individual: weddings, births, first communions, graduations, birthdays. According to Bourdieu, ritual photographs have the 'function of making the important moments of the family life more solemn and eternal and also, to embed the group members making them reassert the feeling of identity and unity to the group'. These photos, although different from those representing domestic and daily life, have similar functions and representations, but are exhibited in a completely different form and in different places.

The introduction of the cameras as a daily object in family life changed the meaning of family photography and became an opportunity to turn daily family life and the domestic into images. Before the 1960s, taking a photograph was a ritual in itself. It took place once a year or at the special events only. It was normally taken in the studio of a professional photographer and people were dressed for the occasion. Nowadays, people can take pictures with their own cameras and mobile phones at any moment. This dynamism clashes with the solemnity of the family photograph in the past. In a certain way, the ease with taking pictures and the amount of them has made the process and the pictures vulgar – even ritual ones. There is no need for pride of place anymore. Images can be exhibited on mobile phones, computer screens, fridges or spice shelves, all of which have become suitable places to show the family. Furthermore, the digital technologies of the image have brought more dynamism to the image, not only in the process of taking photographs, but also in showing them (digital frames, videos, DVDs and so on) and exchanging them. Actually, a focus of interest in the process of digital media and the use of the image are rapidly growing towards the exchange of images and the emergence of social networks through such exchange. The use of the Internet in these processes makes them more fluid and dynamic, creating new practices and new visual languages for giving meaning to social relations.

However, to what extent do these new practices involving the definition of the family and the differences in the formats and ways of presenting the family images imply new meanings and new forms of conceiving the family? To a large extent, these changes remain at the formal level. Nonetheless, besides the format chosen and despite different family styles in the forms of exhibiting the family according to social group, generations, family structure or even aesthetic preferences, the way people and family events are presented and placed in the domestic sphere are not fortuitous and 'every image has its place and a particular form of being exhibited' (Belleau, 1996: 125).

Looking at the different dwellings, we realised the existence of common patterns and rules guiding the organisation of the domestic exhibition of family photographs. Pictures of ritual events follow the traditional patterns: they are generally made by professionals, people pose for them and they take place in a pre-arranged setting. Also because of the solemnity of the moments in which these pictures are taken, they are usually of large size, richly framed, and very often we can find them on the walls or furniture of the public spaces in the house: the living room, the dining room and the main entrance.

Just on the other hand, family daily life is shown in a simple format, not always framed or with cheap frames (plastic, colourful and so on), frequently hooked on other frames, fridges, mirrors, etc. and they swamp almost all the corners of the house. Exhibiting pictures on the walls has a very different meaning from exhibiting them on a piece of furniture. Placing a photograph on the wall shows the intention of permanence and, therefore, only the pictures that have an important meaning in the family biography are placed there. Nonetheless, the idea that the eventuality of a divorce could distort the production of the family image, is a reason why a picture of the couple at their wedding day seems too risky and is not very often in this place. The piece of furniture on which a given picture is placed is not free either. The type of frame chosen, the size of the picture, even the room in which photographs are placed show the place of the person in the domestic group and the moment chosen to represent the process of construction and re-construction of the family biography.

The private sphere has other representative functions. It is not (so much) about showing an image to the outsider than about remembering and reaffirming to the family members the basis under which the family is constructed. If we wonder about the people who appear in the photographs in the domestic sphere, we reach the conclusion that they are beloved people, those who are meaningful for our lives. The emotional dimension of the family has multiple forms of expression and photography is one of the material objects through which this is done in the most explicit form.

Nonetheless, if, as Bourdieu says, the public exhibition of family photographs asserts the continuity and the *cohesion* of the domestic group, photographs in the private sphere show the affective links between individuals and between generations. Bourdieu thinks that taking pictures is in itself the expression of feelings (1979: 53) and that they also play an essential role in the personal integration and identification within the group. The place, the amount of images and the forms in which a given person is exhibited have a particular meaning in the affective and relational environment of the family members (Halle, 1991; Belleau, 1996) and, therefore, in the place this person has in the family group. Bedrooms are, then, the individual spaces of the family as a group, the place for the intimate life of the couple, the most loved people, the fondest memories and also, the exhibition of oneself. The rest of the house has to be negotiated according to – more or less respected – standards defined by the generation of the head of the family, the attachment to traditions, the importance of the extended family and the fashion style of the decoration.

In a certain way, the formats of the display of family pictures in the domestic sphere recall domestic shrines. In many cultures shrines are placed temporarily or permanently to venerate deceased family members. However, in these 'modern family shrines' past and present, individuals and the group melt in a profusion of images showing a particular configuration of one's family. These 'secular shrines' are always in the living/dining room or in the entrance, both the public spaces of the house *par excellence*. They are a sort of 'visual summing up' of the most representative aspects of the family (mainly people but also places and objects). Apparently there is not a specific rule about who should be in this place and who must not. They are not necessarily linked with the genealogical line, as many of the photographs do not show the ancestors, but the children and the couple, and siblings may be there, especially if some of them are already deceased; siblings, parents and children, a lot of children, mixed under apparent chaos.

Nevertheless, rules of exhibition may emerge when we wonder why these people and not other family members. We can ask, then, whether the unbalanced profusion of the children (also grandchildren) and the couple – together and separately – are, in fact, a way to get around the rule of equality between the genealogical lines that is required when ancestors and siblings are exhibited. We will return to this point later on, as rules of depiction are far more tangled than they seem at first sight.

Visual technology has provided a new form of exhibition of family images, both in public (digital frames etc.) and private spaces (mobile phones, personal computers). Mobile phones have come into family life in their multiple forms. They shape the practice of social and interpersonal relations in new forms, affecting the daily organisation and coordination of the family members, thus fostering new forms of expressing feelings and of communicating between people affectively linked (Castells et al., 2006; Matsuda, 2007). The pictures on mobile phones have not yet replaced the traditional pictures of the beloved ones carried in wallets and handbags, but they have the same meaning and they present advantages as one can carry more pictures in less space. Mobile phones as personal objects are, therefore, linked to the person and not to the family group. However, they cannot come off from it, because these images are shown in public as a form for expressing a personal identity built from the links with close family members and beloved people (Smart, 2007b: 46).

In the case of personal computers and mobile phones, images are halfway between the public exhibition and the private/intimate space. Pictures can be seen by anyone once the mobile phone or the computer has been turned on, but the images are for him- or herself. Looking at the picture, either while showing it to somebody else or not, has the function of remembering the beloved person and, consequently, of identifying and reaffirming the affective links. Digital formats have also given other dimensions to photographs, such as the amount of images and the ease of taking and erasing them. This mediation also affects the exhibition of images in the domestic place: the great amount of pictures and their exhibition in audiovisual screens contrasts with the scarcity of photographs on walls and pieces of furniture in their homes. A third dimension is the possibility of 'repeating' the same image several times, exhibiting it in multiple places in the house or distributing it among relatives.

Who belong to us?

Presentation rules organise the ways photographs can be exhibited. However, whenever looking for the meaning and the intention of the exhibition, the question of *who* the main characters in these images are has to be the focus of attention.

Family photographs focus on the nuclear group and the direct descendants of the extended family (collaterals, siblings) and ascendants (Belleau, 1996: 124). The 'rule of genealogical proximity' as a selection mechanism in the disclosure of the family configuration (Jallinoja, 2008: 3) applies well to the photographic display in the domestic realm. In the Majorcan dwellings analysed, pictures of the nuclear family group (parents, children and grandchildren) dominate the scenes. Furthermore, there is a great difference in the exhibition of one member or another of the nuclear group. Children and grandchildren, generally in their childhood, appear twice as often as other members, and they appear in the multiple forms: alone, with parents, with other people and so on. As Gye (2007: 2) ironically remarks, Kodak Eastman knew it when launched his product in 1904 with the slogan: 'Where there's a child, there should be a Kodak'.

Without forming a general pattern, the proximity and the frequency of contact and the intensity of social relationships between parents, adult children and young grandchildren often affect the amount of photographs exhibited. Those who live far away or with whom there is no daily contact are more present in the pictures than those who live in the dwelling. However, this is not a general pattern, as we can find other dwellings with a large profusion of images of those with a strong contact and relations and even those living in the house. In this last case, it is normally a child (an adult son or daughter still living in the house) and almost all the pictures about him/her will be from his/her childhood. In any case, the descendants are more represented than other family members. Actually, despite the idea pointed out by Bourdieu that family photographs represent the unity and the cohesion of the group, the group's public representation is not achieved through the pictures of it; instead, the group is represented by the children.

Beyond the 'aftertaste of enthusiastic parenthood' seen by Belleau (1996: 142) in the photographs of children, their representation has an essential role in the reinforcement both of the integration into the group and the public image of this embeddedness. 'If taking pictures is strongly linked to the presence of children in the house (and even more if they are younger), it is because the appearance of the children reinforces the integration of the group and, at the same time, the tendency to look at this image of unity will work to reinforce this integration' (Bourdieu, 1979: 64).

The exhibition of the 'family children' – joint or individually – is completely different from that of the adults and, above all, from that of the elderly. Apart from the few ritual photographs that state the main social events of the children (baptism, first communion), the presentation of children is mainly made in everyday life scenes and in a simple format (on cheap or plain frames or without them). The simplicity and profusion of images of descendants contrasts with the scarcity and solemnity in which the ancestors are represented (parents, grandparents and remote ascendants). The exhibition of the photographs of ancestors in the public space of the dwelling is regulated by the principle of equality and genealogical proximity, which implies a negotiation in the exhibition of the members of each genealogical branch. The equality not only affects the number of pictures shown, but also the place and the format in which they are shown. There is a good example in the house of M and C: a couple in their seventies, with two children and four grandchildren living outside the island. The main entrance is the place of the past generations. Two big same-sized black and white studio-framed photographs of the father of C (mayor of the town in the 1930s) and of the grandparents of M flank the big mirror and the table of the hall.

The genealogical stock of two traditional Majorcan families and their social position is clearly established throughout the introduction of the 'founders' of the family. The pride of the exhibition shows the importance of an identity defined by national and cultural roots but also by a social position. These pictures show social roles (Bourdieu, 1979: 62). The relevance of these ancestors in the identity of the group rests in the sumptuous way they are represented. Deep inside the house, in the living room, we find a sumptuous representation of the father of M, on the wall above the chimney. In this case it is not a photograph, but a painting made by a famous painter from the town where both the father and the daughter were born.

The sumptuous presentation of these pictures in the entrance and living room contrasts with the large profusion of small-sized pictures of the couple, their children and their grandchildren spread in the other rooms. Once again, the solemnity in which the past generation is exhibited shocks against the 'familiarity' in which the current ones are presented. The emotional and biographical content the pictures of ancestors have for the eldest generation dilutes in the next one and it is rare to find them in young couple's houses.

Parents and grandparents appear in group pictures, almost never alone, and they represent meaningful moments for those living in the dwelling either in formal or semi-formal situations (birthday parties, scenes of the wedding day of the young couple, the baptism of grand-children and great-grandchildren, or informal happy moments (a day on the beach, an excursion, a meal on Sunday and so on). The framing of these pictures is not sumptuous, and they do not take up relevant places in the house. Elders are not represented in the public spaces. In contrast with childhood, elders belong to the 'private', having meaning only for the family members and not for the outsider. These pictures are located in small tables in hidden corners, in the bedrooms or put away in albums.

Identity and affection

The identity and embeddedness of a person as a family member is defined by the links he/she has with the other family members, but also by the public acknowledgment of this membership. This is exactly one of the functions of the exhibition of family photographs. This fact explains the sadness that one feels at the absence of pictures of oneself at one's parents' house, or the extreme equality in the number of images of the children and grandchildren, or in the fact that adult children offer their parents pictures of themselves to be exhibited at the parents' house.

The exhibition of oneself in one's own dwelling is not necessary (you do not need to remember yourself) but it might have sense in certain contexts (we will go back to this point later). They can be important in the process of appropriating the domestic space (the residential dwell-ing) as a personal space for its inhabitants. This function makes sense when it is an ambiguous or new house, so frequent in cases of remar-riages or living in other's houses.

The 'rule of genealogical proximity' and the 'verticality' of the fam-ily links in the display of images are applicable as an abstract general pattern. It is, in fact, affection and love relationships that define, at the particular level, *who* are exhibited. Therefore, if co-laterals (siblings and cousins) and other kin (nephews and nieces) tend to disappear from the public domestic space, their presence increases in specific cases in which the affective and relational links are or have been especially strong. This is the case of, for example, godchildren, mentally ill siblings, uncles/aunts who have played a substitute role as parents, and cousins and siblings with whom the relation has gone beyond what is considered a 'normal' relationship with this kind of kin. The intensity of the relationships (of exchange or care, for example) is not, in itself, as relevant as love and affection links in the configuration of the visual representation of the family.

Practising the family: Grouping the pictures

In the logical basis of the exhibition of family pictures as a representation of unity and embeddedness, the individual has little space. Although it cannot be considered a taboo in the exhibition of adult pictures, as Halle (1991, quoted in Belleau, 1996: 124) says, it is possible to detect some regular patterns. Even if it is frequent to find individual pictures, they are never placed alone. With the only exception of large pictures of the first communion, individual pictures are generally grouped, surrounded by images of other family members. The 'domestic shrines' are a clear image of the family assemblage. Individuals are somehow 'grouped' in these symbolic places of 'recognition of belonging'. Pictures showing the professional or academic status of a person are usually group pictures, in which the individual is surrounded by classmates or colleagues. Most of the individual pictures representing the adults of the domestic group refer to their childhood and youth, and, therefore, to a period before their own domestic group was created. We also have the same pattern in single dwellings, where it is difficult to find pictures of oneself as an adult in the public spaces of these houses.

However, if the individual (as an isolated entity) has little space in the visual representation of the family group, the same holds when organising the process of exhibiting photographs in the public domestic space. The process of displaying images aligns with the actions and decisions of the process of family assemblage. How? As family memory is plural, the links, experiences and discourses each member has of a specific event and with other kin members might be different. To find balance between the identity needs of each member requires negotiation. The rules guiding whose photograph is placed, where it is placed, when it is set up, when it is removed and how it is framed are collective decisions that must be agreed among the group. Beneath these rules lies a process of negotiation based on the principles and values that define a particular family model.

One of these principles is the absence of preference for particular children and the acknowledgement of the *equality* between the couple in the family construction. The balance and equality is evident in the same number of pictures of the kin relatives of each member of the couple and the same number of pictures of each child and each grandchild. The double dimension of the space in the organisation of the exhibition (inside/private – outside/public) allows a greater margin of negotiation among the family members. This is clearly seen in case of divorces.

On the other hand, it is well known that the exchange of visits and presents also include family pictures. They are material and symbolic objects which flow across kin members and, thus, help to reinforce the family or according to Morgan's approach (Morgan, 1996, cited in Smart, 2007b), actions through which family practises itself. If digital technology enables an increase in this exchange – pictures can be enlarged, copied, modified and printed as much as we want – they go a few times out of the hands of the domestic group, but the exchange is restricted to those with whom the exchange of 'favours', presents and services are flowing. Only ritual pictures (mainly baptisms and first communion) go beyond the domestic group to the extended family.

Reorganising the collection of family pictures

The photograph is also a dynamic familiar object that allows the 'construction' of the family through the recreation of the family biography. Actually, as Bruno argues: 'In a post-modern age, memories are no longer Proustian madeleines, but photographs [. . .] we claim our history by means of its reproduction' (Bruno, 1990: 183). The huge profusion of photographs of children at different moments in their life cycle, of main events and of those people who have marked the family biography evoke how important memory and the reconstruction of biography are in the process of the theoretical building of the family. But photographs, as extremely dynamic objects, change and move from one place to another in the house. Home photographs are renewed and changed as the family is developed, according to the incorporation of new members or the disappearance of others. But also, home photographs can change according to the aesthetic canon over the decoration of every generation. Just so, the internal and external divisions of the family imaginary are not watertight compartments. Photographs are moved from one part of the house to another, depending on time, on suitability or on the desire to hide or bring to light (that is, show) feelings, people, facts, memories and so on.

Showing the family's development is one of the functions of the photographs exhibited in more public places: the birth of a child or grandchild, the marriage of a child or grandchild, significant birthdays, a graduation and so on constitute moments that shall be remembered with the exhibition of the main characters' image and/or with the updating of exposed photographs. The rituals that indicate special events in the family biography are exhibited in a more sumptuous way, but the photographs that have a dynamic movement are those little daily life scenes, those that definitively show these facts that let the family define itself.

Old photographs from previous generations are established as an emblem that identifies the family and this is why they are quite static: they hardly ever have their frame or the place changed. Conversely, modern photographs of the descendants are more capable of being changed in their frame, on the wall, on the piece of furniture or in the room in which they are placed. Moreover, modern photographs can be replaced by more modern ones or by those of new members, which show how the family is growing and developing. Photographs of the grandchildren take the place of those of the children in main and more public rooms (living room, entrance). Meanwhile, photographs of the children when they were young are taken to the secondary and private places of the house, such as the bedrooms. In the same way, photographs from childhood and youth stay in the older generation's dwelling when a new one is founded. Memory space remains at parents' homes while the new home is opened to the establishment of its own biography.

The death of a family member also implies a 'moment' to exhibit a photograph of him/her. It is a way to keep alive not only the physical presence of that person through their image but also the affective bonds. Moreover, it is a public acknowledgement of that person's significance in the life path of the family members. The acceptance of a new member (through a marriage, for example) implies the incorporation of the new person's image in the family space or, even so, the replacement of other members that are not in the group any more. Photographs are the graphic evidence in the dynamic process of family building. In fact, family biography is built over both the events and over the relations and emotions. Therefore, what we show is as relevant as what we put away, hide, tear up or throw.

Tearing up or throwing away the photograph of a person is not a usual action. In fact, however bad the affective relationship with the other person is photographs are usually kept hidden or given, instead of torn up. This fact has a very strong significance and it represents the virtual 'death' of the photographed person: the real and definitive extinction of that person from the other's memory. In other situations, photographs are erased because memories, and not the people, want to be forgotten. Some passages or critical events in the family biography which were photographically registered are carefully hidden or removed not only from the public places but also from more private ones.

6
Obituaries as Family Assemblages
Riitta Jallinoja

Obituaries or death announcements in newspapers are examined as the traces (cf. Latour, 2007) of rules that guide the formation of family assemblages, which in turn are thought to mark social bonds between assembled persons. Connectedness manifested by obituaries does not necessarily mean emotional closeness; instead its essential element is the genealogy that generates social bonds. This is examined here with the rule of genealogical proximity, but also with other rules that organize these ties, some to such an extent that they intrude into the workings of the rule of genealogical proximity. The rule of monogamy is such a rule and so is the rule of equality. These are the three rules that are examined in this chapter.

Compared to other assemblages caused by the death of a community member, obituaries are fairly recent forums of assembly. In Finland, they began to appear in newspapers at the end of the nineteenth century, first among higher and middle ranks, and by the end of the 1930s among the rest of the population (Kemppainen, 2006: 113). Specific to obituaries is that assembling does not occur face-to-face, but persons involved make their appearances in names and categories only. They are set in the strictly designed frames of obituaries, shut in small, fenced-off areas, side by side with other obituaries on a newspaper page reserved for this very purpose. Thus, obituaries are strongly stereotyped and regulated public performances. The functioning of the rules are analyzed with an analysis of the people present in the obituaries and their ranking on the list of mourners.

After the introduction of my data I move on to explore how the lists of mourners in obituaries are arranged in ranking orders. First, I draw attention to the most common ranking order, which I call the elementary genealogical order, apparently framed by the rule of genealogical proximity. The outline of this rule draws its inspiration from Lévi-Strauss, Bourdieu, Schneider and Carsten, above all. After this more theoretical delineation, I return to the data to take under scrutiny the rule of monogamy, which dictates the location of spouses in obituaries. Then I go on to see how divorce complicates the workings of the rules of genealogical proximity and monogamy. After that I examine the backstage of obituaries, what is behind the rule-governed front. Its investigation brought to light the third rule, the rule of equality. To close, I consider death as a cause for assembling and the specification of the three rules: after all, they organize the relationship between families in two generations, the family of origin and the subsequent families of procreation and the relationship that the death of a member of the family of origin revives.

Data

The analysis is mainly based on obituaries published in *Helsingin Sanomat*, the Finnish newspaper with overwhelmingly the largest readership (about one million daily) in Finland. I started to collect the data four years ago, unsystematically at the time, to see the variation in the ranking orders of the lists of mourners, in all its scope. After that I collected the principal data, consisting of 1490 obituaries published on Saturdays and Sundays (a vast majority of obituaries are published on those two days), from August to December 2008.

The feasibility of the data is dependent on how frequently the mourners in the obituaries are categorized. Kin categories absolutely dominate categorization, but friends are also mentioned, most often by bundling them into the phrases 'other relatives and friends' or 'relatives and friends', nearly always in this order. Regarding kin categories, a sufficient amount of information was obtained, as 44 per cent of the obituaries denote the mourners according to their kin relationship. For 15 per cent, information in this respect is imperfect, but the obituaries contained many illuminating hints that made it possible to infer the missing kin categories reliably. In most of these cases, some kin categories are mentioned, while the missing categories can be concluded on the basis of the names (they are very often generation-based) and the layout, that is, how the names and rows are located on the lists. Naturally, the assumptions can most easily be made based on the most common ranking order. In some cases the deceased were well-known persons whose close relatives are also known, or the information was possible to derive from *Who is Who*. In addition, I included in this group obituaries where the deceased were personally familiar to me. Thus, all in all, kin categories could be deduced for 59 per cent of the obituaries. The remaining 41 per cent were largely or completely without kin or other categories, the mourners performing as non-categorized persons, primarily by first name only.

The data consist only of private obituaries, that is, the mourners are family members, relatives and friends. Obituaries submitted by employers and nursing homes are thus excluded from the data. I obtained additional data after I was interviewed in *Helsingin Sanomat* (8 March 2009) about my obituary research. At the end of the interview I asked readers to send me accounts of their experiences with obituaries. As a result, I received responses from 50 readers: 15 from men and 35 from women, mostly by email. All in all, these accounts contained stories about 68 obituaries. Adding the oral accounts I received from some 30 acquaintances and friends, the total number of personal accounts near 100.

The elementary genealogical order

Life expectancy very much determines who from the kinfolk are included on the lists of mourners; today the majority of deceased are old, in my data most were born 70–90 years ago. In these cases, the most common ranking order of mourners gives top priority to the *spouse*, if there is one. After her or him, in the next row, are the *children*, most often with their spouses if they have them. In all those cases where the ages of children were available, seniority determined the ranking of the children. This was also confirmed by some respondents as 'natural'. The *grandchildren* appear after the children, either in the same row as their parents or in their own rows. If the deceased was very old, there are often great-grandchildren on the lists of mourners, too.

In the obituaries of the younger deceased, who have descendants only in one generation, the following ranking order prevails. If the deceased was married, the first row on the mourner list is reserved for the *spouse*. The *children* follow next. So far the order is the same as in the most common pattern described ahead, but two kin categories appear to be too few, as in the majority of cases other kin categories are added. Most often these are the *mother* and *father* of the deceased (or mother or father alone), but there seems to be a tendency to include the *siblings*, too, if the mother and father appear in the obituary. In this pattern, the family of procreation precedes the family of origin, but both families tend to perform in their entireties. This is sometimes emphasized by grouping the names into two sets of rows.

For the deceased who were younger, single and childless, the *parents* are at the top of the list, even if the deceased were not so young, say in their fifties or sixties. In most cases other kin categories are again added. For the single young deceased the lists are typically extended by the *siblings* (after the parents) and after them by the *aunts* and *uncles*. Godmothers and godfathers are sometimes mentioned. In the case of the elderly deceased, if no parents, siblings, aunts or uncles are alive, kin categories genealogically next to them are adopted; most often they are *nephews* and *nieces* but also *cousins* appear on the lists of mourners. All these cases show that it is very common to present one's family in an extended form and that this whole most frequently comprises three to four kin categories.

It is not at all insignificant that, in most cases, there are three to four kin categories on the lists of mourners. The number of categories seems to demarcate the proper realm of kinship; it never comprises all possible kin categories, but neither is the list wished to be very limited. Some respondents told about the sadness they felt when reading one-mourner obituaries. The elementary genealogical order of three to four kin categories indeed models the realm of kinship seen as appropriate to present circumstances, but this model allows variation according to personal conditions and tastes, as the accounts of obituaries prove. It is not at all rare for obituaries to have wider than three- or four-kin-category ensembles on the mourner lists, whereas the shortest lists contain one single kin category, which may range from mother/father or daughter/son to cousin, in one case even to second cousin. One respondent enlightened me in his account that he had seen obituaries where not a single mourner was mentioned, which aroused many kinds of reflection on the deceased's fate.

The kin categories as they have been ranked in the obituaries persistently tend to follow a certain order: the spouse appears first, after this the children, then grandchildren, (or parents and grandparents), siblings, aunts, uncles, nephews, nieces, and cousins. This ranking order should not be taken as a statistical regularity (cf. Schneider, 1980: 5–14), but as a signifier of something more significant, namely of a rule that compellingly guides the survivors to take their proper positions in the obituaries. This is also affirmed by the respondents. One respondent refers to the 'culture of customs'; others talk about the 'right order', 'orthodox order', 'civilized manner', or 'established custom'. These statements manifest that when making a public performance in an obituary one must follow the rules. If this is not done accordingly, 'shame', 'guilt', 'wondering' or 'offence' will result, as the respondents explain. I call the 'right order' the *rule of genealogical proximity*.

The rule of genealogical proximity

As the description of the lists of mourners in obituaries show, kinfolk dominate the forum and they are ranked genealogically. In exploring the logic of ranking orders in obituaries I adapt the double-character of kinship as an analytical tool, as outlined by Lévi-Strauss, Bourdieu, Schneider and Carsten; all of whom have made the distinction between kinship as a system and as practice.

At the most general level, the system of kinship articulates the criteria of kinship, that is, what relates certain people to each other as relatives. Schneider (1980: 21) concludes that the Americans explicitly define relatives as those who are related by blood and by marriage. These people are *relatives by definition*, but kinship is also considered through practice, for which Schneider (ibid.: 59) reserves the expression '*relatives as persons*'. Schneider (ibid.: 64–5) reserves this term for those kin between whom interaction and transactions of different kinds occur. Interaction, whatever kind it is, turns relatives by definition into 'real relatives', as Schneider's American sources demonstrate.

The distinction made by Schneider is equivalent with the one Pierre Bourdieu (1989: 33–8) makes in his analysis of kinship. Bourdieu substitutes the terms 'kinship as a system' for '*official kin*', but in principle they mean the same. Schneider's 'relative as a person' Bourdieu replaces with the term '*practical kin*'. To define the difference between official and practical kinship Bourdieu (ibid.: 34) states: 'Those uses of kinship which may be called genealogical are reserved for official situations in which they serve the function of ordering the social world and of legitimating that order. In this respect they differ from the other kinds of practical use made of kin relationships, which are a particular case of the utilization of *connections*' (emphasis in the original, Bourdieu). Bourdieu (ibid.: 38) emphasizes the significance of practical kinship. In emphasizing its significance Bourdieu (1976: 39) widens the scope of practical kin beyond official kin: 'A network of practical relationships which comprises not only the sum total of genealogical relationships kept in working order, but also the sum total of the non-genealogical relationships which can be mobilized for the ordinary needs of existence'.

Unlike Schneider and Bourdieu, Claude Lévi-Strauss represents the view where, instead of practice, great emphasis is placed on the system of kinship that structures the relationships between relatives in a highly regulated way. In explaining what is behind incest taboo, Lévi-Strauss (1969: 32) refers to a rule as 'completely independent of its modalities'; for him, 'the fact of being a rule is the very essence of the incest prohibition'. This means that a person cannot do just what he pleases (ibid.: 43). Lévi-Strauss (see ibid.: 52–83) must be credited for understanding that the rules differ in respect to generality and abstraction. As he claims, the incest prohibition and the exogamic and endogamic rules must be seen as aspects of a more general rule of reciprocity. Thus, Lévi-Strauss supplements the skeleton of kin system with obligations that the kin relationships inherently entail. For him, the kinship system is not only a system of categories but, in addition and inseparably, a system of obligations defined by the rules (see also Finch and Mason, 1993).

Although Lévi-Strauss has been strongly criticized for placing too much emphasis on the 'logic of culture rather than how societies function or what the actual practices are' as Carsten (2005: 12) expresses it, Lévi-Strauss (1969: 75) also admits that a principle of organization is 'capable of widely varying and, in particular, of more or less elaborated, applications'. Carsten (2000b: 1–14) goes much further: it is practice that, after all, is decisive in determining one's kinship. For Carsten kinship comes true in *'lived experience'*, as she calls practical kinship. She is even inclined to substitute the concept of kinship for the term 'relatedness' that is meant to encompass all those relationships that 'carry particular weight socially, materially, and affectively'. This corresponds with Bourdieu's view, as stated earlier. Carsten's view coincides with those of contemporary researchers like Morgan (1996: 189–92), who point out the significance of practice, in which a sense of doing and action as well as what is regular and ordinary, should be of primary significance when analyzing present-day families. By family and kinship practices, researchers mean all kinds of interaction and transactions that are transferred between relatives and that lay the ground for the formation of family configurations (see Widmer and Jallinoja, 2008).

Regardless of conceptual differences, the four scholars share the distinction between kinship as a system and as practice. On the one hand, we consider kinship as a system or structure, as general rules or principles, or as official or theoretical kinship, while on the other, we have kinship in practice, as lived experience, as practical kin relationships or as relatives as persons. The terms 'system' or 'rule', and 'practice' have been sensitive to criticism, some finding fault in too much abstraction and hence an escape from reality, and others blaming them for going too far into details of practice, which prevents us from seeing what is common in a variety of practices. Instead of taking one or the other of the competing strands for an analytical instrument, we should pay more attention to the interrelation of the rule and practice. This is what Bourdieu has done, according to Carsten (2005: 49; cf. Smart, 2007b: 22), when providing 'a bridge between an earlier structuralism and a more phenomenological approach that pays more attention to how people experience living together'. This kind of bridging is the step to be taken next.

Let us start with the most general level: kinship as a system of categories and relationships. This very general systemic rule is not visible in the obituaries as such, but its existence can be concluded on the basis of a rich spectrum of kin categories listed in the obituaries and by the fact that in a vast majority of obituaries at least one kin category is in use. When looking at the kin categories included in individual obituaries, we notice the difference Schneider discerns: in practice the number of kin categories in the obituaries is more limited than the whole spectrum of kin categories. This must be seen as 'practical kinship': the presence in the obituaries would then be dependent on the intensity of interaction between the relatives, particularly with the deceased. However, appearance in the obituaries is not only dependent on the 'lived' interaction (cf. Carsten, 2000b), as the analysis of the obituaries and the accounts testify. The rule of genealogical proximity has much say in whether relatives are present in or absent from the obituaries.

The rule of genealogical proximity is not as abstract a rule as the one that affirms the whole system of kinship. The rule of genealogical proximity directs interaction between the relatives, which means that this rule regulates 'practical kinship'. When observing practised kinship Schneider (1980: 21) adds a 'modifying element': the distance to kinship as a system of categories and relationships, in order to indicate on what grounds relatives are selected for interaction. One form of distance is genealogical; the other two are emotional and physical. Instead of Schneider's term 'distance' I prefer the term 'proximity'. Logically, they are equivalent but proximity captures better the essence of the incorporation of kin people into family configurations. Thus the rule of genealogical proximity is as follows: the closer the relatives are genealogically the more likely they will interact with one another.

The rule of monogamy

All that has been said so far about the functioning of the rule of genealogical proximity hold true for blood relatives. It was quite easy to recognize ranking orders for them, even when only parts of the kin categories were visible. Genealogy thus functions so logically in obituaries that even scant hints unveil the genealogical order. However, there is one kin category that repeatedly appears to break the rule of genealogical proximity – that category is *spouse*. The position of the spouse in the obituaries was the key that led to the discovery of the second influential rule, the *rule of monogamy*.

The decisive question is: how spouses are placed in the obituaries. If the rule of genealogical proximity solely assigned the order, then priority would always be given to the blood relatives over the relatives by marriage. This could, for example, mean that the in-laws would perform as a specific ensemble of their own at the end of mourner lists, perhaps ranked according to a rule of their own, but this does not hold; instead, spouses are systematically associated with their conjugal partners and children. The spouses are placed in-between their partners and common children, that is, in-between two blood relatives of the deceased. Hereby, kinship by marriage (spouse) takes priority over blood kinship (grandchildren of the deceased). This is contrary to the rule of genealogical proximity. The ranking order of the spouses is totally dependent on how genealogically close their companions are to the departed. Although spouses are regularly present in the obituaries, the category 'spouse' is only mentioned for the deceased's widow(er). The term primarily appears in the headings of the obituaries ('my spouse'). Practically all the other spouses on the lists are mentioned by name only.

The main effect of the rule of monogamy is that the spouses perform together, side by side. This rule is deeply rooted in the Western cultures, to say nothing of the influence of the Christian church's position on monogamous marriage, founded as it is on the unity of husband and wife (Cott, 2002: 10). Irrespective of what the arguments and reasoning over the course of the institution's century-long history have been, whether biblical, natural, utilitarian or romantic, the common perception has been that husband and wife form an exclusive and solid union, bound to each other 'till death do they part'.

The rule of monogamy not only ties the spouses together in the obituaries, but also organizes the mourners into families. Although the deceased's grandchildren are sometimes lumped together in a row of their own, family-wise performances are much more common. When looking at these performances it is easy to observe that the rule of genealogical proximity first determines the ranking of the blood relatives, that is, the first name in each row, and that the rule of monogamy casts the spouses in their proper places with their children. As a result, family-based rows are prevalent in the obituaries; single relatives are listed individually, each one in a row of their own. In the same way, the deceased's sisters and brothers, in addition to aunts and uncles, nieces and nephews, and cousins are placed family-wise in the obituaries, most often following the model 'Sister Ester with family' or 'Sister with family'. The rules of genealogical proximity and monogamy create two essential structures in the obituaries. The former structures the mourners into *lineages* that descend (or ascend) from the deceased, while the latter organizes the mourners into *families*.

Divorce complicates the functioning of the rules

Divorce complicates the workings of the rule of monogamy and makes the reading of the obituaries much more difficult, because ex-in-laws are never included in the categorization. Therefore, conclusions were of necessity made on the basis of a handful of cases which are known to me and the information I received in the accounts sent to me. All these cases testify that divorce puts the rules of genealogical proximity and monogamy to the test; rules as exact as the two previously described have not yet emerged for divorce-cases.

Schneider (1980: 23) determinedly states that ex-spouses are 'out' of kinship. In saying this he means that in-laws are out of kinship by definition, that is, kinship as the system of categories. Divorce terminates an in-law kin tie that marriage once established. The total absence of ex-spouses from the obituaries demonstrates this, but absence also indicates strict compliance with the rule of monogamy: people can only have one spouse at a time and this is signified by omitting other spouses from the obituary. However, as obituaries also demonstrate, ex-spouses are not categorically ostracized (cf. Castrén, 2009a): in many cases there are two spouses mentioned in the same obituary, the widow(er) and the ex-spouse. By being present in the same obituary, the two spouses break the rule of monogamy in its strictest sense, but the ways in which the co-presence is designed proves that yielding to this rule is obvious, after all. In most cases, the ex-spouse is ranked far off from the widow(er), typically at the end of the mourner list, in his or her own row. The inferior position signifies the ex-spouse's status in terms of the rule of monogamy. Yet the deceased's second spouse can sometimes lose his or her privileged position. In my data the following arguments were most frequently referred to. If the second conjugal (or cohabitation) relationship had been childless and established at late age, the children from the first marriage may occupy the topmost rows on the mourner lists. This is seen as 'natural' by the respondents, that is, the deceased's adult children. The same order also results from the adult children's reluctance to accept their late parent's second marriage. In both of these rankings, the rule of genealogical proximity surpasses the influence of the rule of monogamy.

Divorce also affects the ways children appear in the obituaries if the deceased had children from two marriages. The rule of monogamy compellingly organizes the children into two distinctive sets, although the children have genealogically equal status to the deceased. The most common ranking order is that the children from the second marriage come before the children from the first marriage, although the principle of seniority would in fact require the opposite order. In addition, it is only the second spouse's children who appear family-wise with their parent, whereas the first spouse's children most often appear without their parent, who may be left out altogether or put at the end of the list, alone in her or his own row.

The rule of monogamy also affects how the mothers and fathers of young people who have passed away perform in the obituaries. If they are married they appear together in the same row, but if they are divorced they have the rows of their own. The point again is that the marital tie is signified very concretely by placing the parents either in the same row or in successive rows. If the mother or the father has a new spouse, he or she is referred to be his or her first name and in connection to his or her spouse ('Father and Sara').

Backstage

Goffman (1982) divides the performances of the presentation of self into 'front' and 'backstage'; front refers to 'that part of the individual's performance which regularly functions in a general and fixed fashion to define the situation for those who observe the performance' (ibid.: 32), whereas backstage Goffman defines as a 'place where the suppressed facts make an appearance . . . where the performer can relax' (ibid.: 114–5). Obituaries can be considered as a front; they are public performances *par excellence*. Obituaries would thus be places where the role of the rules is decisive. It is tempting to assume that there is also a backstage where the rules do not function. This can be examined through the accounts of obituaries sent to me. Some respondents emphatically highlighted the inconsistency between the obituaries and 'reality', for example, in the following manner: 'By and large, obituaries are conventional in their intention (pretending to gather the kinfolk together), but what is really behind them?' This attitude inspires readers to guess what is 'behind' the presented story, as many respondents told me they do.

In the majority of the cases, the most evident motive for sending an account to me was a deviation from the 'right order', which was also described, interestingly, in the same way as I had concluded on the basis of the obituaries. Backstage really appears to be the scene of deviations. In the following, the character of backstage is elaborated through a few selected examples picked up from the accounts of obituaries.

The breaking of the rule of genealogical proximity cropped up in a surprising context, and it proved to be highly valuable for finding still one rule that remained concealed in the obituaries. When reading the obituaries, I supposed, as I think most of us do, that the lists of the names in each blood kin category are fully complete; for example, that all the deceased's children are mentioned. This assumption is very strong and gives as such testimony to the existence of the *rule of equality*. It does not require that all relatives should be given an equal status in the obituary, it instead merely requires that all relatives in each kin category are treated equally, that is, included in the obituary. As the accounts verify, breaking the rule of equality needs a really good justification, otherwise the omission of a family member from the obituary is indefensible.

When explaining the dropping of the names of relatives from the obituaries, respondents mostly cited disputes over money or inheritance, or severely improper conduct including alcoholism. The omission of a relative is most severely criticized in the case of the closest relatives (the deceased's children, siblings and parents). Here the rule of genealogical proximity determines the surest scope of the rule of equality; whereas with the rule of monogamy, the rule of equality is totally irrelevant – as a matter of fact, the spouses and ex-spouses are said to deserve different statuses in the obituary.

The accounts reveal that it is the breaking of the rule of monogamy that particularly causes dispute. In these cases, writing up obituaries is a controversial process, sometimes requiring negotiations, sometimes not, but always giving rise to concern about who are put on display and in what order. The divorce cases indicate that attitudes towards the ranking orders on the mourner lists are greatly dependent on the quality of the relationships, particularly between the spouses and ex-spouses, but also between them and the two sets of children, although other relatives are also allowed to take a stand on the matter. For instance, if the widow(er) and the ex-spouse are not able to reach an agreement on the order of the mourner list or on the presence of the ex-spouse in the obituary, the dispute may lead to the publication of two obituaries. In these cases, the divide between the kindred becomes clear. The constellations of the mourner lists are dependent on how the relatives have taken their sides for and against the two spouses. Side-taking easily divides family lineages into two branches, as a number of accounts testify. This challenges the idea of lineage-based kinship as one whole.

Death as a cause for assembling

Morgan (1996: 194) correctly states that 'the occasion of death, together with the subsequent funeral and disposal of property, routinely and effortlessly brings to the fore questions of family'. One of the major consequences of death is the assembling of those people who are related to each other. Throughout history, death and gathering together have actually been inherently associated, as witnessed in the memorial mortuary rites. Although part of them has vanished, the rites that have survived represent what is today regarded as 'good death' (Pleck, 2000: 197; Miettinen, 2006: 97–106; Howart, 2008: 132–53). The essence is the *intensification of interaction*. Because the deceased are elderly persons, in the majority of cases, interaction is intensified between the grown-up children and the dying parent. They come from the same family of origin, but have since then lived apart, the adult children in their 'own' families, which are now their families of procreation. The obituaries bring to light the unification of these families.

Memoirs and biographies bear a lot of witness to this unification. Eira Mollberg (2008), daughter of a well-known Finnish film director, writes in her memoirs that she terminated a ten-year estrangement from her father when she heard about his incurable cancer, starting an increasingly intensive interaction with her father that continued until he passed away. An entire body of literature and media stories follow the same scheme: the common ethos is *reconciliation*. This procedure functions like a catharsis. If this is not done, for example due to a sudden death, it is common to regret that it was not possible to clear up the relationship with the deceased. Death also stimulates recalling the shared past and the rummaging of family archives (Smart, 2007b: 39). All these activities that death mobilizes focus on the family of origin, the family that just lost or is losing one of its members.

We have to take death as a particular type of event; even though get-togethers caused by death resemble other family assemblages, they are also different (cf. Latour, 2007: 36). Because death is irrevocable, it is capable of strengthening the feelings of togetherness between the family members, even in entangled relationships. In Durkheim's (2001: 299) words: 'The origin of mourning is the impression of diminishment that the group feels when it loses one of its members. But this very impression has the effect of bringing individuals together, putting them into closer contact; making them participate in the same state of the soul . . . we never value our family as much as when it has just been tested'. These occasions are favourable for rule-bound practices, without fear of losing one's personal autonomy.

Death, like other motives for familial assembling, still has one aspect to be kept in mind and that is the fact that the get-togethers are always of a short duration. In everyday lives the members of the family of origin live scattered, in their own quarters, but at the moment of death those who once upon a time belonged to the same family feel once again attached to each other. Yet these get-togethers are only intermittent. It is common to say that get-togethers of this kind reaffirm the unity of a community (Bourdieu, 1990: 19), but in the case of the family of origin this is not the major point, rather the point is that death causes a *revival of the lost past*. When intensifying interaction it makes the family of origin, for a while, look as it used to look in the past. Death always revives this interaction and, in doing so, it reorganizes the structures of family configurations as long as there are members left from the family of origin. This is why the members of the family of origin have a dominant position in obituaries.

Conclusion

Finch (2007: 66–7) correctly states that '*families need to be displayed as well as "done"*' (emphasis in the original). By 'displaying' she means 'to emphasize the fundamentally social nature of family practices, where the meaning of one's actions has to be both conveyed to and understood by relevant others'. [There] are 'actions which confirm that I regard these people as part of 'my family'. To become understandable the actions 'need to be linked in a sufficiently clear way with the wider systems of meaning (to borrow Morgan's phrase) to enable them to be fully understood as such'. Obituaries are such actions or practices and they are fundamentally social by nature; the rules of genealogical proximity, monogamy and equality represent the wider systems of meaning, which frame the making of obituaries, likewise the making of families. The rules mediate our understanding of who belong to 'us' as a family in the context of obituaries, within the nucleus of the family and beyond.

The rules have evolved in a long process of habitualization, which gives them a sense of objectivity, to apply what Bourdieu (1990: 4–6; see also Berger and Luckmann, 1981: 70–84) says about the social nature of photography. The range of templates to be used in the drawing up of obituaries is defined by implicit models, having come to our knowledge via obituary-making practices, that is, via perpetual repetitions, not only visually but also in substance. It is this fact that rationalizes maintaining control over these practices, not by purely personal preferences but by particular rules, to a considerable extent. The accounts of obituaries in turn show that objectivity also conveys subjective experience, but it is at this level where variation steps into the world of rules.

In essence, the rules that I have discussed here are practice-bound rules, that is, they are tightly interwoven with practice, which reveals that the rules are not only obeyed but also applied and broken. For those who apply the rules their collection appears as a kind of repertoire of principles from which the most suitable principle can be chosen, as the accounts of obituaries verify. They also show that family members and relatives may be at variance over which principle should be relied upon, and they may even ground their views on personal likings and dislikes, without regard to other kin's personal affections. The very character of obituaries is that, as such, they are 'still life' presentations, hiding all those disputes and negotiations that have preceded the drawing-up of the obituary and that, in many cases, will follow its publication. For this reason, it is not so far-fetched also to see obituaries as reduced to pure signs (cf. Bourdieu, 1990: 27) which, for this very reason, are a natural place for the performances of the rules. However, these performances and the accounts of obituaries give additional evidence for strong social bonds that still tie together the family of origin and the subsequent families of procreation (see also Bengtson, Biblarz and Roberts, 2002).

Part III

Setting up Families with Significant Others

7
Couple Formation as a Transition between Families

Laura Bernardi and Anna Oppo

It is relatively accepted that family boundaries are a matter of definition. Some of these definitions are institution dependent, marked by residential, vital or legal events (like co-residence, descent, marriage, adoption). Some other definitions are non-institution dependent and rather based on transient and subjective exchanges (like material and emotional care, shared identity). When we use non-institution dependent definitions, the timing when individuals become 'a couple' or 'a family' – or cease to be one – is fluid and its definition is relation-dependent. The purpose of this chapter is an invitation to rethink our conceptualization of 'couple' as a process and one that is relational and distributed through people.

We begin with the consideration that *coupling is a process with different phases*, involving a progressive commitment of the two partners (Reiss, 1960). Demographers, and some sociologists, used to study unions, in particular first unions, by considering mainly living arrangements: people passing from one living arrangement (living alone, at parents' home, sharing with peers, or living with a different partner) to the living arrangement 'in union'. What defines the couple boundaries before this residential transition has rarely been considered. However, coupling and living together are not necessarily happening at the same time, nor does one necessarily imply the other. When marriage was the exclusive path to cohabitation, there were a number of more or less institutionalized passages – like courtship and betrothal – intended to prepare the couple for the marital union. Nowadays, despite the heterogeneity of forms of union, living together is still often the result of a coupling process made up of different phases. In some contexts, like in southern Italy, the time lag between the beginning of a partnership and the moment in which partners leave their family of origin to move in together lasts on average a few years. These years of committing partnership often involve not only the pair but also relationships among their families and friends.

This leads to a second consideration: *coupling is a process shaped by relationships beyond the dyadic partnership*. It is often assumed that in post-industrial and individualized societies, partners control to a great extent their transition to couplehood. They are the ones who negotiate and decide when their transition begins, which statuses they will pass through (exclusivity of the relationship, frequency of contacts, common activities, public exposure, having children together and so on) and how long they will spend in each state. Even the vast socio-psychological literature of structural-functionalist inspiration dealing with premarital dyadic formation and based on the US 'dating system' of the 1960s and 1970s, mainly focuses its attention on the partners' dyads, even when coupling is seen as a developmental process (Lewis, 1972).[1]

Drawing on the idea of interlinked lives (Elder et al., 2003; Macmillan and Copher, 2005), we challenge this 'dyadic' perspective by arguing that coupling and its timing are also defined by the recognition of the couple by salient others. Even when union formation does not create legal or formal obligations between the partners' families – as in the case of cohabitation – a new couple almost always means creating affective and moral bonds with family members and friends as a specific new entity. Being involved in the process, these social circles may acknowledge, ignore, support, resist, be excluded by or even deny a new couple. They may do so on the basis of affection, interest, values, commitment and so forth.

Here we intend to explore how the couple comes to be recognized in advance of the partners' cohabitation or marriage, and while the two partners each reside at their parents' home. This is a particular form of living arrangement for being in a union that we shall call, by analogy with the LAT (living apart together), 'LATAP' or 'living apart together at parents'. The questions we ask are: what are the different stages in the process which makes the couple socially visible? What issues are at stake when partners' expectations towards their own couplehood have to meet those of their relevant others? At which stage are families expected, willing or reluctant to redefine their borders to include or exclude a new possible relative? We will see how many intimate relationships confront families with challenges: not only are the borders of family inclusion and exclusion redefined, but often also the meanings attributed to coupling and family relationships.

We argue that studying pre-cohabiting intimate relationships may be crucial to defining the process of subsequent co-residential union formation, its timing and the choice of union. Our analysis focuses on young adults who enter steady relationships while they are still co-residing with their parents. This situation is far from rare for young adults between 20 and 30 in the Mediterranean regions, and southern Italy among them. Such co-residence means a constant exposure to relevant others' expectations, evaluations and behaviour towards the new forming couple. The choice of a partner as an individualized sphere of action is less self evident under these conditions and makes southern Italy an extremely interesting case study. In particular, we address the tension between individual and relational choices, the progressive recognition of this tension by the involved subjects themselves, and its implications for the current debate on mating and family choices.

In the next pages we first give an overview of the data and the chosen analytical approach. We then reconstruct the constituent phases of pre-residential couple formation, paying particular attention to the turning points which transform two individuals into a new couple, while at the same time making them new members of two existing families. Similarly, we analyze 'uncoupling' dynamics and mechanisms – partnerships' interruptions and failures. The chapter concludes with a discussion on how studying couples during their pre-cohabiting phase could help in family theorizing.

Data

We rely here on a qualitative study conducted with women aged 20–45 in southern Italy. The analyses are based on 75 qualitative narrative interviews collected between 2005 and 2006. In one quarter of the cases we have also interviewed the woman's partner, if they were cohabiting at the moment of the interview (not if they were living with their parents), and the woman's mother. All interviews contain a detailed subjective reconstruction of the respondents' life course development from adolescence to adulthood; of the respondents' family of origin and peers' group, with attention to major events and transitions related to employment, partnerships and unions; and family formation.[2] The women were residents of the two cities of Cagliari and Napoli in southern Italy, and were selected through personal contacts gained by a complex indirect snowballing procedure with multiple entries (independently selected initial contacts) to avoid a clustered sample. The interviewers were trained anthropologists with whom the authors regularly interacted before and during the fieldwork over a two-year period.

The sample includes substantial variation in respondents' ages, social background characteristics, education, employment, couple and parity statuses, relationships and careers, as well as the kinds of living arrangements. Of the 34 women who are still living with their parents (ten only with their separated mother or with siblings) at the moment of the interview, 20 are engaged, only five were never engaged, while the remaining ten had been engaged but had more or less recently broken up with their partner; thus, the sample covers an wide range of engagement experiences.

We are interested in women's narrations of their non-cohabiting intimate relationship as well as the conditions and the values that informed their developments. In particular, the analyses focus on the material contained in these heterogeneous biographies with the aim of abstracting and theorizing the process of 'becoming a couple', that is the process of getting involved in a romantic relationship as individuals and establishing a couple unit as members of a larger network of family relationships.

An important feature of this dataset is the rare information on intimate relationships developing in LATAP residential arrangements. The analysis is based on interpretative content analysis of the women's narratives. We employ the initial concepts of partnership and coupling as orientation concepts to search for the sequences in the narrations in which the interviewees reconstruct their partnership biographies and their phases until they move out of their parental home. Particularly, we focus on the *social birth* of a couple, the transition from the status of an intimate relationship involving exclusively the partners to a socially recognized couple embedded in a larger net of relationships. Our first exploration of this material will, therefore, explicitly include a gender perspective. We chose to limit ourselves to women's accounts of the coupling process while living with parents in order to give justice to the richness of the data; men's vision of the development of an intimate relationship needs a separate account which would go beyond the ambition of this chapter. Similarly, we do not discuss the same sex coupling process.

Transition to couplehood

Nowadays, as in the past, transitions are extremely revelatory moments to focus on for social researchers, because they bring to the surface the tensions – and the corresponding strategies to solve such tensions – which shape individual and family biographies. When two partners recognize themselves as being a couple, a crucial transition is potentially occurring in terms of family configurations. On the one hand, the couple represents the potential birth of a new nuclear family; on the other hand, such genesis requires the redefinition of family relationships and configurations from the partners' family of origin. But when is a couple called or considered a couple? Love relationships typically develop before, may continue after, or simply may exist beyond co-residence, as the growing literature on living apart together has underlined (Levin, 2004; Haskey, 2005). The complexity, diversity and uncertainty of the coupling process have increased with modernity; diversity is omnipresent in the objective behavioural trajectories, in the subjective perception of actors, and in the institutional contexts affecting private relationships. The increasing entropy affecting traditional sequences of family-formation-relevant events makes union and couple formation a more undefined process than in the past: its timing is open and its place in the course of life is negotiable (Corijn et al., 2001; Elzinga and Liefbroer, 2007).

Some scholars underline the rising individualization of the coupling process. They claim that the increasing diversity and individually tailored definition of what a couple is seem to have the consequence of making the construction of an intimate relationship an exclusively recursive and individualized process (Sennett, 1998; Hall, 2002). In addition, the meaning of what constitutes a couple is seen as a moving target on which actors need to negotiate (Giddens, 1992) if they aim at achieving some convergence in their biographic trajectories (residence, education, employment, for instance). Yet they engage in these negotiations since the search for a partner has retained all its attractiveness as a source of intimacy, solidarity, emotional security and affective commitment, in contrast to the uncertainty in other domains of life (economic, political and social contexts). From this perspective, aspirations to a fulfilling intimate relationship remain high, while the likelihood of realizing it decreases (Beck and Beck-Gernsheim, 1995).

While the individualization perspective is appealing and offers an interpretation of recent partnership dynamics characterized by instability, its focus on choices and individuals leaves open the question of the forces which shape the preferences underpinning such choices. From the point of view of family theory the challenge is to understand these choices by analyzing the negotiations involved in the making of the couple in the everyday practices of dating, having sex, going steady, moving in together and eventually, for some, marrying and having children. Two such forces are (a) the strength of family ties and

(b) family culture. Carol Smart refers to individual choices as always being relational choices and proposes that we 'think in terms of a continuum along which degrees of attentiveness to kinship structures and parental wishes fluctuate', and as well as a continuum 'envisaged as stretching from a point where there are very strong kinship ties and arranged marriages, through to a mid point where kinship and family culture provides the context for choice, and on an end point where elements of individualization are more clearly evidenced' (Smart, 2004: 495–6). Another way to think of this continuum is to stretch it along the time axis and think of the individual dimension leaving room for the relational dimension of choices while the process proceeds through time. Enduring romantic relationships bring along, in most cases, a quest for social recognition; social recognition is conditioned on the evaluations and expectations of others; the anticipation of the criteria for social recognition enters the process and makes the most individual and intimate choice – that of love and partnership – soon profoundly relational.

We illustrate the continuous hypothesis by accounting for the process by which young adults enter steady relationships and form couples before cohabiting, and particularly when they are still co-residing with their parents.

Living at parents' homes until age 30 and beyond is quite common in Mediterranean countries; therefore young adults often experience long-lasting romantic relationships while living separately, at their parents'. In Italy, young adults stay at their parents' home longer and longer, well after the end of education in their late twenties and mid-thirties, and the great majority of them leave home only when marrying (De Rose et al., 2008). This pattern seems to be a shadow of the past, a culture-dependent answer to the growing uncertainty in employment and housing conditions, originating in the late-home-leaving tradition which historically distinguished Southern European regions from continental and Scandinavian Europe (Barbagli and Dalla Zuanna, 2003; Reher, 1998; Jones, 1995). The perception of both parents and children is that this practice increases their chances of social success or at least some certainty in adult life (Menniti et al., 2000). Especially in southern Italy, where labour market conditions are worse and the infrastructures weaker than elsewhere in the country, family solidarity provides protection for individuals and a private substitute for public social security. In particular, downward intergenerational transfers of resources are crucial. Comparative studies on intergenerational transfers have shown not only that adult children in Italy receive 'much higher proportions of support, higher than those in the Continental and Nordic countries', but also that 'co-residence is the Southern European way of transfer- ring resources from parents to children and vice versa' (Albertini et al., 2007: 17).

While some scholars have stressed the necessity-driven nature of co-residence (Esping-Andersen, 1999), others claim that Italians, and particularly southern Italians, have not (yet) been permeated by proc- esses of individualization, and therefore by values like individual auton- omy and personal responsibility (Banfield, 1958; Esping-Andersen, 1999; Dalla Zuanna and Micheli, 2004; Rosina and Rivellini, 2004).

This interpretation does not account for the fact that the meaning and practice of co-residence and family solidarity are subject to change. These may have different significance in Italy than elsewhere because of the Italian welfare system which favours the older generations (Ferrera, 1996) and the distorted labour market which discourages new entries (Sgritta, 2002). It is a fact that relationships between parents and adult children have evolved in the direction of losing much of the hierarchi- cal characteristics they used to have in the past; in contemporary family group, self-realization, self-expression, and autonomy of children are encouraged and supported (Allegra, 2002; Facchini, 2002). Therefore, while parents and children prolonged co-residence is certainly an indicator of children's economic semi-autonomy or dependence, as Goldscheider and Davanzo (1989) call the necessity of living with par- ents for young adults in the US, it does not hinder the promotion of individually shaped life projects. Quite on the contrary, paths of emanci- pation and individualization are paradoxically built into the framework of strong networks of family solidarity. Middle-class parents are ready not only to agree with most of their children's educational, vocational and partnering choices, but also to invest personal and familial resources to make them possible (Oppo and Ferrari, 2005). The long co-residence between parents and adult children may produce a conscious sense of solidarity and deepen sentiments of mutual affection. After the tumul- tuous period of early adolescence, relationships usually transform into relationships among adults, so that it is not unusual to find a new kind of friendship and complicity (Facchini, 2002; Oppo and Ferrari, 2005).

In such a relational context, adult children entering into steady sentimental relationships, multiply their family membership: they are simultaneously children and siblings in their family of origin, they are partners in the new intimate relationship, and they are children's partners for the partner's family of origin. As members of a couple in its pre-cohabitation phase, they are living-apart-together-at-parents'

(LATAP) – the southern Italian version of the LAT that is common in regions where children leave their parental homes earlier. According to the most recent ISTAT data, the duration of pre-cohabiting engagement in Italy has been steadily growing in the last cohorts: on average it lasts five years for the marriage cohort of 1993 (ISTAT, 2006), which means that a considerable number of LATAP living arrangements may last ten years or more. In this life stage, typically, affective and economic bonds may be created with the partner's parents and, on the other hand, conflicts and divergences may also emerge. We focus on the process which binds individuals in families and the negotiations between family obligations and family bonding, inner and outer constraints, values, and identity which are characteristic of this process.

Although the interviews display variation in biographies and narrative styles it is possible to identify dimensions of shared regularity. First, these are narrations of autonomy and choice, for both younger and older women. Coupling is the sphere of life in which they have room for initiative, either because they encounter no pressure or because they feel entitled to resist any pressure they may receive; yet it is also a sphere in which one is required to take initiative and to decide. Second, the narrations of sentimental biographies include a number of internal and external obstacles that women encounter along the partnering process. Internal obstacles include doubts about the partners' 'fit' to their ideas of an undefined 'right partner', to their expectations of intimacy and understanding or to their ideas of a harmonious life together. The external obstacles are due to difficulties in the educational and employment biographies or interference from the relevant others of both partners, which often challenge the intimate relationship and its stability. Parents and siblings, in the first place, but also aunts and uncles, friends and neighbours, who each, to a different degree, actively contribute to the construction of the new couple. Not surprisingly, their influence is particularly strong during the pre-cohabitation phase. This is the phase in which young adults' double membership (on the one hand being a child or a sibling and on the other hand being a partner) engages them in daily negotiations of intimacy and commitment. The family of orientation of each partner needs to be redefined, since almost paradoxically each of the two families simultaneously acquires a member (the partner) and partially loses one (the child or the sibling).

Third, evident in the narrations is the effort of progressively harmonizing the values and norms of different families of origin. Successful or unsuccessful coupling processes could be ultimately distinguished on the basis of this accomplishment.

Steps into couplehood

The encounter. Encountering a partner is always coincident with falling in love in the narration of the couple biography, whether falling in love is a matter of a moment or the consequence of a slow construction of intimacy built over months or years of frequentation. And the encounter is experienced as one of the most personal choices. However, as all studies on the marriage market continue to confirm, homogamy remains high in post-industrial societies (Aldous, 1996). Cupid does not shoot randomly (Berger, 1963); men and women who start an intimate relation often belong to the same social circles – school, working place, associations, church, music and sport clubs, the public square where the usual *comitiva* or *compagnia* meets, or the disco where chains of friends introduce each other. In Italy, individuals often form very cohesive friendships in their teens and regularly meet many years thereafter; these groups are often these groups *are* often *privileged* to spend free-time together, also in couples. During this period of experimentation, later normalized by the same individuals as 'teen-like relationships', parents and family are not expected to be informed. Occasionally, this occurs with siblings and cousins belonging to the peer group, or with older relatives acting as confidants (Milardo, 2008). Parents' intervention consists more in giving general guidelines for behaviour than in evaluating or interacting with the specific partner. Individuals vary in the extent to which they feel committed at young ages, but all have the perception that commitment grows with duration.

The encounter is only one phase of a path, which may be more or less short and may or may not be accompanied by sexual intercourse. Hesitations to go steady depend mostly on doubts concerning the affective dimension of the relation (on its reciprocity, complicity, disinterest and solidarity), on advancing on what Reiss calls the 'wheel of relationship development' (Reiss, 1960: 143). Hesitations may be overcome, more or less quickly, and at times accompany partners over months. In this initial phase partners are not alone: the best friend, the sister and the peer groups are witnesses to the infant relationship. And their attitudes, comments and advice, often requested, challenge the conclusions reached by the partners. If peers' role is not crucial, except in critical cases, certainly it brings to consciousness the way in which the relationship is perceived and evaluated from outside the couple.

The couple disclosed

A further step in the process is the public disclosure of the non-cohabiting couple, particularly the disclosure to the family of origin. Only rarely, and in the lower social strata, does disclosure still happen as a formal introduction of the partner to parents 'with flowers and cakes', as one interviewee described the first visit of her boyfriend. More typically, legitimization of a relationship is actively provoked by casually letting the partner meet the parents as a friend, as a special friend, and by agreeing to get to know his family. As a consequence of this disclosure, partners get invited to family events, from Sunday meals and festivities to celebrations involving the extended family and joint summer holidays; they are allowed to pop up in for a visit without warning, and are treated as the parents' 'own children' or 'part of the family', as we are repeatedly reminded by the interviewees. It is not rare that even when the sentimental relationship breaks up, the family-like relationships with the parents or the siblings of the previous partner are maintained, in a fashion reminiscent of the relationships among relatives of post-divorced partners.

Here the interviewee reasons on the continuation of her relationships with the family members of her ex-boyfriend:

> The relationship between you and him is one thing, and the relationship between you and the family, and other people is another thing [. . .] maybe one does not maintain relationships with ex-boyfriends, but with the [their] family, yes. They always treated me nicely [. . .], at Christmas, Easter, I call them, I make my season greetings, without having to think it over twice.

Inclusion also means that the partner's family engages its almost-new member in exchanges of reciprocal support and occasional presents. Reasons for the 'coming out' of a relationship are affective, strategic or simply related to the duration of the relationship or events which act as turning points, such as an unforeseen pregnancy. Affective reasons include the desire to share one's affection. Strategic reasons related to parents may be directed to obtaining permissions or to giving reassurances; strategic reasons related to the partner may signify the wish to increase the commitment of an ambivalent partner.

In some cases the expressed approval of the partner's family may mitigate a complex coupling process and reconfirm the partners themselves about their fit, as in the case of Natalina, who had initiated a relationship with a work colleague who is legally separated from his wife and children, and who reports about her mother-in-law's expressed comments:

> The mother, who had known the previous wife since forever, always told me 'I have always seen him as a different person with you',

because he comes close to you, he hugs you, he kisses you; he had never done these things before.' So I think that the fact that they [his parents] saw him so happy and close to me lead them to pass over everything.

There are, however, situations in which disclosure is not desired, is purposively avoided or the relationship is hidden. This may happen because the partner does not meet the essential requirements to be accepted without creating discussions (they do not meet the criteria of a 'good boy', are too old or too young, are of the wrong sex, do not have the right education and job perspectives, do not hold the right political or religious faiths, is divorced or still married, or lives too far away) or because of the fear that the relationship is going to be intruded on and/or limited (time for family visits, invitations for joint holidays, shared obligations). Family attachment to a previous partner may also be a reason to keep a new relationship silent until chance and frequent contacts between the partners are 'discovered'. In most such cases the existence of a steady relationship may be known, but a relatively common tacit agreement exists to pretend it is not. Such compromise allows at the same time the parallel existence of the new relationship and of family solidarity; it is a temporary best solution while hoping that incomprehension will gradually be reduced and that apparently incompatible positions will get closer or be reciprocally tolerated.

When recognition occurs, it is the beginning of a fusion process in which the family configuration around the partners starts changing families: from the perspective of the couple they both open to the partners' families; from the perspective of the partners' families, they recognize a stranger as potential kin and welcome (or not) the possibility of having new family bonds. This is a turning point in the coupling process. Yet only when the partners start making explicit efforts to construct a common biography can the affection and the exchanges between the family of origin and the partner become economic support and reciprocal obligations that involve the couple as a distinct new entity.

The couple as a project

From the project-less phase of falling in love, *going steady* marks a step towards a couple's life project, which, however, has not been defined in time and form. When reciprocal commitment is there, the usual frame of reference is a relatively traditional life course trajectory in which the transitions are sequentially ordered: end of education, stable job, living together, having children. Such a schema is also shared by the large majority of parents, who see as a personal success their daughters' transitions. However, since the majority of partnerships at this stage are between young adults busy with making transitions in domains other than partnership, the project of a life together is only a draft, legitimized by relatives and friends, intertwined and often conditional on parallel goals. This is a life phase normatively devoted to 'being young', which means cultivating one's friendships and hobbies, and during which couple commitments should be 'light' (Buzzi et al., 2002). This period is hardly identifiable with a given age, but it is not rare that women in their thirties consider themselves 'immature' or 'too young' for heavier commitments like marriage and family, even when marriage and children are seen as desirable aspirations. Generally, for younger women in higher education, when the uncertainty of the timing of other life course transitions is high and the potential life course trajectories are still numerous, romantic relationships do not easily become concrete projects. The normative sequence of life course transitions below a certain age suggests caution towards commitments. Such is the case of the 22-year-old Irma, a university student who occasionally works in order to pay for her studies. Irma had a romantic involvement, but she withdrew when the partner started delineating marriage intentions. She preferred a lighter relationship, in which she did not yet need to plan a common life. Her family and his family are aware of the relationship and accept its remaining open to the future. At the moment, in agreement with the partner and her mother, Irma has set the priority of getting her University degree and take timing off from her relationship:

> A university degree is something my mother has always insisted on, having a higher education . . . because she would have liked to study herself and my grandparents did not allow her to go on, so at least I would like to give her this satisfaction . . . yet, if I felt it was the right moment, if I felt that what I wanted in that very moment was a serious couple relationship . . . that we were really convinced, I know that my family and his family could help us to start up.
>
> (Irma, 22 years old)

The couple life project has less foggy borders when, in addition to the affective certainty, educational and employment projects get coordinated, with implicit and explicit negotiations. Negotiations are often directed to the restriction of women's aspirations towards vocational careers which enhance compatibility of work and family life. Regularly time-scheduled jobs and teaching are often also the direction for those women who chose a scientific specialization. This is also the phase in which minimal conditions for life as a couple are considered, and often the evaluation is made against the life experience of the parents. Highly educated women display a high degree of reflexivity and caution in evaluating both the quality of the relationship and in anticipating its future. Often, still in the early thirties, there is a hiatus between the internal security about the achieved stability of the relationship and the lack of the external conditions needed to proceed with the project:

> We are very close . . . and we also have a project, anyway, not too far in time, I hope . . . we often talked about marriage, but it does not seem to be close neither. He has a job as an engineer, self-employed, he still earns little still. And I just got my degree; I am looking around for a job . . . I hope that not too many years will pass by . . . after ten years of engagement, friends and relatives see us as if we were one unit . . . my friends are friends of both of us . . . We really wish to live together, to have our stuff, to have a family, above all to start a family . . . But the job, at least in my case, is a problem . . . for a woman in general it is difficult . . . I had various interviews and I have been told that preferably one should not have family engagements.
>
> (Cristina, 28 years old, looking for a job)

> [Without money] we can have all the intentions of this world, but neither is so crazy as to make a step which would risk making us go back in the family of origin.
>
> (Sara, 27 years old, university degree)

When the partner has reached a satisfying employment situation, women in their early to mid-thirties are ready to delay the end of their education or the search for employment and realize the project of moving in together with him. They are supported by their parents, who often provide the children with appropriate housing if they can afford to pay, or contribute towards buying or building one (Del Boca, 1997; Barbagli, Castiglioni and Dalla Zuanna, 2003; Poggio, 2005). Only occasionally disappointment may be expressed, as in the case of Ilaria, 31 years old, with a degree, who married while enrolled in a specialization course:

> My family was not happy, they were rather surprised when I told them, because I was in the middle of the specialization, and my mother, when I told her, was like stoned: 'What? How comes? Get your specialization first . . . why now?'

Women with a lower social background, who had a shorter educational history, generally enter the labour market earlier. However, this does not mean that they realize their couple project earlier, because the partner, usually of the same age, may also be in precarious employment like themselves; for them it is a phase of saving money for the house and the furniture that their parents cannot afford and which should be there before the formation of the union. Efisia, a part-time dental assistant, married at 27 after a 10-year official relationship with her current husband:

> During the first years (of engagement) I did not enjoy much freedom . . . I had to respect schedules etc . . . But then, when I finished school and I started working, they understood that he was a hard worker and a serious boy. Then there were no problems anymore. We preferred to wait and buy the house and some furniture before marrying.

The couple project, even if its realization is only a far distant prospect, is nevertheless sufficient for the partners to be considered part of the families of origin and at the same time as an independent unit. The daughter's partner is treated as a son on whom one can count and of whom one can ask for and receive help and advice. The son's partner is generally invited, even also when he is not present, to share a meal, to make a conversation or to help with caring for the future in-laws. Giovanna, 27 years old, who is still looking for a job and waiting endlessly for her marriage, says:

> Every Sunday we have lunch at his place, the mother [. . .] may invite me also alone, 'come and eat at home' . . . In my house he has been welcomed very well, he comes every evening to eat with us . . . During the summer holidays he comes with me, with my parents [. .] imagine that if there is a problem to solve, they call him, because he is smarter, more intelligent, he solves all their complications, he provides them with what they need.

Whatever their social background and their contingent situation, our women under 30 all report their active role in defining their relationship trajectory as making choices, constrained but nevertheless reflexive individual choices. Constraints are important in a difficult economic context; however, choices are perceived as such and are presented as personal choices shared with the partner, but also supported by the salient relatives, parents and siblings in the first place. Underlining the need to share choices within the family (many women mention their mothers as their best confidants, in some cases ranking her before the partner) is a very interesting feature of relationships developing in LATAPs: there seems to be a process of convergence of values and visions related to partnership, a sort of reciprocal socialization between parents and children. As one interviewee puts it, 'I had to educate my mother'. Sometimes re-socializing is the result of hard difficult negotiations, a process of estrangement or of compromises; however, there is a collective effort to preserve, on the one hand, individually defined couples and, on the other hand, family solidarity. Religious or 'traditional' parents (the word 'traditional' is a dominant term of the discourse on family matters and often mentioned by the interviewees) accept civil marriages and cohabitations, as well as a pregnant daughter at home who delays her union transition in order to allow her boyfriend to complete his working trajectory.

Daughters also play their part in this convergence process: they postpone the realization of the project to take care of ill or poor relatives, accept a ceremonial celebration of their transition so as not to disappoint their relatives, encourage their divorced mother to find a new partner, even though they may be attached to their father. In only one case was a non-approved marital cohabitation the cause for a serious estrangement of the couple with the woman's parents. The interviewee suffers tremendously from the situation, and yet maintains her claim of having the right to decide; she maintains her family bond through her siblings and hopes that the birth of a child will bring her parents back to her. Generally, parents and children recognize the reciprocal right to make choices, also including partnership choices, and they agree that solidarity is not the same as uniformity of opinions and life trajectories. In Southern Europe this change of perspective represents a major cultural shift.

To sum up, the idea of a couple being based on long-term commitment achieved through long-lasting pre-cohabitation unions and paralleled by the achievement of a relatively satisfying education and employment status is undoubtedly part of the contemporary Italian imagination. Of course, the idea of partnership in our imaginations (and hence the framework through which we interpret experience) remains an idealized conventional story. Actual partnerships may take a variety of shapes and may be relatively discordant or unhappy. Yet a cognitive map made up of this ideal and the meanings which constitute it functions as a guide to the vagaries of real life. Ideas of what a proper couple process should be often mediate actual experiences. These ideas are built together by partners and their relevant others all along the coupling process we have described so far.

So far we have stressed how values, norms and practices with regard to the way in which partners become recognized, in the larger group of relatives, as a couple structure pre-co-residential unions. However, the very coupling process in turn modifies family values, norms and previous practices in order to allow, on the one hand, individual agency in the choice of the partner and, on the other hand, the maintenance of family cohesion and affective ties. Within the boundaries of the specific family cultures, the actors involved partially share and partially negotiate the meaning of the three transition markers we described. This interpreting activity produces changes in the meanings, values and norms attached to each of the particular markers.

The coupling process is not immune to delays, interruptions, and failures: long lasting pre-cohabiting relationships may never make it to the final residential or legal step, the 'union transition' that we usually measure. One third of the women in our sample report having had more than one serious relationship, where serious is generally an attribute used for relationships which are certainly well advanced in the phase of disclosure and often already in the project phase. We do not have the space in this chapter to elaborate on uncoupling, but we would like to underline that also during the process of uncoupling, family members are involved in the non-co-resident union dynamics: they are either witnesses of the difficulties and the sorrows caused by disagreements or they are providers of support and advices, and only rarely do they become direct and explicit decision makers. Inevitably, uncoupling, like coupling, accounts for family members' attitudes and expectations.

Conclusions

This chapter is devoted to the study of a frequent and socially recognized form of union in many (Southern) European countries, the LATAP, or living apart together at a parents' home. We focus in particular on the developmental process of union formation, its phases and the role of relationships beyond the partners' dyads in the process. We analyzed the role of family relationships in shaping the stages of the coupling process, as well as their timing. We have shown how, at each stage, a relational perspective is useful for interpreting the way in which the partners frame their choices: there are choices, indeed, in terms of preferences, but these are linked with commitments and compromises with relevant others in the family (mainly parents, but also siblings). A 'free' choice, which does not take into account the feelings and expectations of relevant others, meets high costs in terms of redefinition of belonging, acceptance and social recognition.

We have highlighted how the timing of the transitions involved in the coupling process is partially defined by the partners, but also partially dependent on others' reception of the forming couple. Relationships define the couple's trajectory by modulating the timing and the context of its transitions. If 'trajectories are constituted by transitions and transitions are embedded in trajectories' (Hagestadt, 1991: 23), couple transitions are certainly embedded in the partners' individual trajectories and social relationships. Although perceived as active processes in which partners shape their present and future relationship, coupling is often influenced by external conditions. We show how these external conditions may be relational conditions – that is, conditions due to relevant others in the family – which act by directing preferences during the encounter stage, the timing and the forms of the disclosure, and also the negotiations of commitment and compromises during the project phase.

Not only does LATAP deserve attention as a form of union, but it also represents a privileged observation point in the process of family making. The appearance of a partner and therefore of a new couple questions the existing family configuration and may, but does not necessarily have to, result in its enlargement. Focusing on couple formation as a family process (interaction by which families make up and maintain their unity, manage their conflicts, achieve socioeconomic integrity and model the social and emotional personality of their members) means focusing on moments of intense elaboration of the meaning of coupling and family.

Moreover, given the net of expectations and commitments built into a LATAP, as well as the timing role it has in the couple's life course, it is reasonable to assume that including LATAPs in the study of union formation and dissolution is crucial to the understanding of union and family dynamics (low fertility, late marriage and low divorce, for instance). This focus is particularly relevant in southern Italy, where young adults, students or the employed, leave the parental home at comparatively later ages. Reliable data sources still need to be produced in order to test these hypotheses on a representative sample, leaving room for promising future research in this direction.

8
Social Networks and Family Formation

Sylvia Keim

Postponement of parenthood, a low number of children and a certain level of permanent childlessness are characteristic features of Western societies. Current research on family formation on the one hand points at processes of modernization and individualization leading to a pluralization of living arrangements, including various forms of living temporarily or permanently without (biological) children – stressing that having children competes with other life goals and that the traditional model of the family as a permanently married couple with its own children has lost its self-evidence. On the other hand, presently most individuals still become parents at some point of their lives, and most children grow up with both of their natural parents (and not with lone-mothers/lone-fathers or in patchwork families) – at least in western Germany, which is at the centre of our research. This tension between the emergence of 'new' living arrangements and the reproduction of rather 'traditional' patterns of family formation stands in the focus of our article.

One central argument in the individualization thesis is a weakening of traditional bonds, that is, kin relationships and rural communities, which sets individuals free from conforming to traditional norms and gives them the opportunity to choose how to arrange life (Beck, 1986). This increase in individual autonomy leads to a decrease in traditional living arrangements, together with an acceptance of a variety of different ways to organize one's life. As a consequence, having children is not self-evident anymore, but is a matter of choice. The connection between the bonds in which individuals are embedded and their attitudes and behaviour is central in social network studies. Modernization and individualization processes have already been translated into the terminology of network research with Wellman's (1979) community study focusing on how personal bonds influence individual integration into society and personal well-being. Wellman hypothesizes that modernization processes implying a weakening of traditional bonds can have three outcomes: (1) the dissolution of traditional living arrangements, such as family and neighbourhood, leads to social isolation (sparse networks consisting mainly of weak ties) and a lack of social support (community lost); (2) solidary communities continue to be relevant; accordingly, personal networks are dense, based on strong and supportive ties to kin and neighbours (community saved); and (3) although communities are changing structurally, they continue being solidary; social networks are sparse and spatially dispersed; they include strong as well as weak ties and are prevalent sources of support (community liberated).

In research on family formation the relevance of social interactions and social networks has been increasingly acknowledged in the last decades (Bongaarts and Watkins, 1996; Bühler and Fratczak, 2007; Kohler, 1997; Kohler and Bühler, 2001; Valente et al., 1997). However, related studies have been conducted mostly in developing countries and in countries in transition (Central and Eastern Europe); in Western countries studies focusing on social interactions in order to explain late childbearing and growing childlessness are rare. One could assume that an individualistic perspective on family formation in modernized societies is sufficient, because these societies are built on a strong welfare state and a functioning market economy. However, it has also been argued that in the case of developed countries including social effects can offer new insights into reproductive behaviour (Kohler, 2000; Montgomery and Casterline, 1996). Additionally, research on intergenerational support (Aquilino, 2005; Mandemakers and Dykstra, 2008), on intergenerational transfer of fertility patterns and the transmission of family values and ideals (Axinn et al., 1994; Murphy and Wang, 2001; Steenhof and Liefbroer, 2008), and on peer influences on teenage pregnancies (Arai, 2007; Billy and Udry, 1985) in Western countries indicate the relevance of personal relations in fertility decision-making and related behaviour (Van Putten et al., 2008). This research, however, considers specific relationships and does not take an explicit network perspective focusing on the *patterns of relationships* that provide or constrain opportunities for individual action (Wasserman and Faust, 1994). One important step towards analyzing network effects on reproductive behaviour in Western countries was taken by Bernardi (2003) in her qualitative research on Italian couples. Analyzing the influence of personal relationships on family formation, she identified influential relationships (stressing the relevance of parents and siblings as well as peers and acquaintances) and four mechanisms of social influence: social learning, social pressure, social contagion and subjective obligation. However, this study also does not confront network structure with attitudes and behaviours related to having children. In this chapter, we therefore endeavour to analyze how young adults conceptualize family and formulate their intentions on having children, and aim at exploring the role of social networks in this.

Data and Methods

Our empirical analysis is based on a set of 50 semi-structured, qualitative interviews with young adults conducted in western Germany. This includes 35 focal individuals (egos), and up to three of their network partners (alters), who were egos' partners or friends. The focal respondents were men and women between 28 and 32 years. We chose this age group because the median age of first births for women in western Germany lies in this age span. Therefore we presume that at this age family formation is a salient topic. Our focal respondents have grown up in the same town in the northwest of Germany; most of them have attended the same school class, either at a secondary school or a high school. Because some friendships from school-times were persistent, we were able to collect several interviews with egos who are befriended of each other. We limited our sample to respondents with secondary or higher education. Most of our respondents are childless; some have one and very rarely also two children. They are either married, cohabiting, living apart together or single. The interviews were collected in the frame of a comparative mixed-methods research study on social networks and family formation in eastern and western Germany (cf. Bernardi et al., 2006, 2007).

The interviews cover the respondents' educational and professional trajectories, partnership histories, attitudes and intentions concerning parenthood and childlessness, general values and life goals, as well as their social relations. Additionally, the respondents' social networks were collected with the help of a network chart (Kahn and Antonucci, 1980; Antonucci, 1986) and a network grid. The respondents were asked to place into the network chart the persons they are in contact with according to their 'importance'. The chart consists of six concentric circles corresponding to different degrees of importance (cf. Bernardi et al., 2006, 2007). Along the way the respondents were asked to provide detailed information on their network partners and their relationship with them. In order to learn more about the relations between network partners, the network grid collects information on the strength of relations between ego's ten most important alters. The information from the interviews was complemented by a short questionnaire asking about the respondents' socio-demographic characteristics (for example, education and profession), their partnership characteristics (for example, duration of partnership) and the characteristics of up to eight of their most important network partners.

Our analysis proceeded in three steps. First, the interviews were analyzed based on the open coding procedure developed in Grounded Theory (Glaser and Strauss, 1999; Strauss and Corbin, 1990). This enabled us to explore in detail how respondents conceptualize family as well as the accounts of social influence and selection of network partners they give. At the end of this process we had built a typology of family conceptions, identified four mechanisms of social influence and analyzed processes of network partner selection. Second, the network charts were analyzed regarding the bonds of which they are composed (traditional or individualized) as well as according to other structural features that are either connected to being engaged in traditional bonds (for example, density and share of kin, local distribution of network partners) or seem to be relevant for family formation as we have learned in the interviews (for example, number of young children in the network). In a third step the network structure and the conceptions of family were brought together and discussed and three network types were identified that correspond to the types of conceptualizing family.

Thinking about family formation

We identify three different types of conceptualizing family, which include a different perception and evaluation of what having children means and what other life goal would be worthy of pursuit. Each type coincides with certain values, attitudes and behaviours, for example, concerning the intention to become parent.

Type 1: Traditional family conception

When respondents of this type use the term family and think about their family of procreation they imply a married couple with at least one child:

> Basically, this has been clear, that we both would marry and have a family. Well, he only wants one child; I always wanted to have more children . . . We will have to see how this develops. But the basic aim has always been there.
>
> (L17ef, female, 29, married, 1 child: 18 months)

This respondent uses having a family and having children as synonyms and shows how self-evident this conception is for her by designating that this 'basic aim' has always 'been clear'. This formulation is found in various interviews, here another example of interview extracts with a couple:

> For us, it was clear, we both wanted to have children; we wanted to have two children. And this after the marriage.
>
> (L50, male partner, 31, married, 2 children: 6 and 3 years)

> For me, it has always been certain that I want to have two children, and for him it was the same. I don't remember if I really imagined how my future life would be, somehow having children simply belongs to how I conceptualize my life.
>
> (L50, female partner, 34, married, 2 children: 6 and 3 years)

They could not imagine and never thought about remaining childless. Respondents of this type report that establishing a family consisting of a married couple with children has been their basic life goal. Other areas of life such as the job or a career are considered as subordinated (mainly by women) or as a means for family formation, that is for providing the economic basis (mainly by men). To have children is so self-evident, 'clear', 'normal', that respondents only rarely give reasons for their desire to have children. Respondents who express this view are mostly already parents or intend to become parents soon. This type also prefers a gendered division of tasks in the household and orients on the male-breadwinner-model. Because of the conceptualization of family as married couple with children and the traditional values the respondents hold, we have labelled this type *traditional family conception*.

Type 2: Individualized family conception (with children)

Respondents of this type also conceptualize family as a couple with children, but they do not feel that having children is self-evident (for others as well as for themselves); they perceive alternatives to having children and do not feel that a marriage is necessary before having a child:

> I have never been a real family type and it has never been my greatest desire to marry, to have children, to be a mother – never. I rather wanted to do my studies, my education, to conquer my world and then see what comes.
>
> (L11, female, 29, cohabiting, pregnant)

As alternative life goals they mainly indicate a fulfilling partnership, self-fulfilment in the job, a career, self-fulfilment based on friendships and leisure time activities and personal freedom. They feel that it is difficult to combine these goals with having children. They also perceive various risks that may prevent them/others from having children (for example, lacking a stable partnership, experiencing economic uncertainty, mobility demands of the job, health-related problems). Differently to those respondents who find it self-evident to have children, they openly discuss the costs and benefits of having children. During the interviews they explicitly talk about what 'family' means to them and why they would like to have children, as this male respondent does:

> Without children . . . at some point something is missing. You maybe have fun for five years, 10 years, but then, at some point it becomes lonely. Children mean to me: vitality, zest for life, reason for living.
> (L12, male, 29, married, childless)

The reasons for having children mostly centre on children as providing a 'reason for living', preventing loneliness and as 'personal enrichment'. Emotions also play a role and children are described as 'cute' or 'beautiful' or the warmth and safety a family with children may provide is indicated. Additional to these positive meanings of a family as a couple with children, there are negative views on children: children are perceived as a burden on personal freedom, on the quality of the couple relationship, on the career and on the couple's income and standard of living, etc. Many respondents experience a large uncertainty about when and how they should realize family formation, trying to minimize its negative effects. Respondents of this type are mostly childless. While some of them feel ready for parenthood and intend to have a child soon or are currently pregnant, the vast majority postpone[1] having children. Respondents of this type do not prefer and do not currently enact a gendered division of tasks in the household, but rather both partners share their chores equally. They find it difficult to imagine how they will organize their life with children satisfactorily. Because these respondents are open to alternative concepts of family and base their personal conception of family not on traditions, but present a very explicit and personal reasoning mostly connected to their partnership situation or professional life, we have labelled their family conception as *individualized*. However, despite different intentions on the timing of parenthood, they mostly agree that they would like to have a child at some point, while the third type of respondents – with a similar openness for alternatives and personal reasoning – comes to the conclusion that they intend to remain childless.

Type 3: Individualized family conception (without children)

Compared to the other two types, it is a small group of respondents that forms this third type. They are men and women, often engaged in a stable partnership, who intend to remain childless and conceptualize their family rather as consisting of their partner and selected friends, as this respondent does:

> We are three friends [the respondent, her boyfriend and another close friend]. We've said that some day we will buy an old farm and live there as artists. I don't know if you can consider this as a plan . . . but concerning family and children I have no plans. My boyfriend and I, we are together since two years, but marriage and children? No! I think I would blow! I still want to travel too much and keep my independence. That I could say one day: 'oh, I like it here, I would like to stay here.' To establish yourself at another place, this is very difficult with children. Actually it is not really feasible.
>
> (L54, female, 31, LAT, childless)

Most of these respondents are or have recently been engaged in steady relationships. If they are engaged in a partnership they state that they are very content with their partnership, as well as with their job, their leisure time activities, their personal freedom, the egalitarian division of tasks in their partnership, their life as a whole; and they do not want to give up any of this in order to raise a child. They consider parenthood as incompatible with their interests and activities and name various negative consequences of becoming parents. In one case we were able to interview both partners. They indicate that they both fear that at least one would have to give up their full-time job; both fear a loss of flexibility, partnership quality and personal freedom. They are not career-oriented, but would like to continue as a dual-earner couple and enjoy the financial benefits of having a double income as well as achieving self-fulfilment in their jobs. It is not that these respondents dislike children – some are very happy to include their nieces and nephews into their wider conception of 'family' and to spend time with them – but they feel that this is just enough children they need.

Correspondence between network structure and conceptualization of family

Among our 50 respondents we found a very clear correspondence between network structure and conceptualization of family. As a consequence in accordance with the three types of conceptualizing family, we can identify three types of social networks. Respondents holding a traditional family conception are embedded in dense networks including a large share of kin (for example, parents, siblings/cousins and their partners and children, aunts and uncles, grandparents and godparents, parents-in-law, and other relatives of the respondents' partner). Kin and neighbours are often rated as (very) important and the respondents interact frequently with them. The networks are perceived as very supportive. In most cases, many among the respondents' young network partners have children. The network is rather homogeneous, containing network partners with similar educational/professional backgrounds, partnership status, parity and hobbies. Many or even most network partners live in the same city, often in the same quarter. Due to the high share of kin and the high share of young persons with children we have labelled their networks *family centred*. The network structure corresponds to Wellman's (1979) hypothesis of 'community saved', indicating that despite modernization processes social networks can have a rather traditional composition and structure.[2]

One example of a *family centred network* held by a male respondent, who intends to have a child soon, is provided in Figure 8.1. This displays the respondent's (ego's) ten most important alters (mainly kin and close friends with young children) and the relations between them. The lines designate relations between alters rated (from ego) as 'know each other well' or 'are in close contact'. The graph displays one densely knit clique and two befriended couples tied to ego's partner.

Ego's network partners are rather homogeneous, especially in partnership status and educational background, including many friends from his former school-class. Parents, parents-in-law and the sister-in-law belong to the ten most important network partners.

In contrast, respondents holding an individualized family conception are embedded in networks that are in most cases sparse and include a low share of kin. Among the (very) important network partners friends dominate (and the respondents often give reasons why they have been chosen, for example, based on similar interests, personal affection, and mutual support). The kin included into the network are often rated as less or not important. The network consists of persons located in the

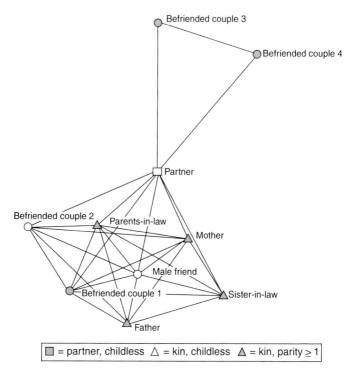

Figure 8.1   Example of a *family centered network*

same city as ego, but also persons rated as (very) important who live in other parts of the country or abroad and with whom contact is held via telephone and the Internet. In most cases the networks are large and contain many strong ties that are perceived as supportive (corresponding to Wellman's hypothesis of 'community liberated'), but there are also cases, in which a fertility relevant form of support cannot be provided (support in childcare by parents/parents-in-law who for example are considered as problematic or live too far away to offer regular support) and very rarely the respondent can be considered as socially isolated ('community lost').[3]

We have found two interesting differences in network composition between respondents who include or exclude children in their individualized family conception: the former hold networks that are very heterogeneous, regarding their educational/professional background, partnership status, parity and hobbies. Often they include at least some young network partners with children. In contrast respondents who

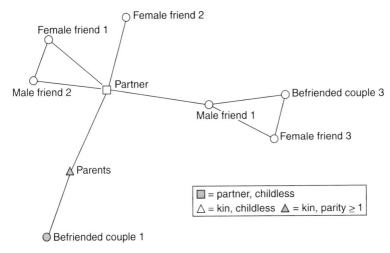

Figure 8.2 Example of a *heterogeneous network*

intend to remain childless are embedded in networks composed mainly of persons who are homogeneous in their interests (professional or hobby related) and in their intention to remain childless or at least to consider family formation as far; while they are heterogeneous in such aspects as educational background and partnership status. Additionally, they include no or very few young persons with children into their network. Due to its heterogeneous composition, we have labelled the networks of persons with an individualized family conception including children as *heterogeneous networks*. One example is provided in Figure 8.2, displaying the network of a childless female respondent who is uncertain about becoming a parent. The graph shows ego's ten most important network partners (among which there are very few kin) and the rather rare inter-relations between them. Most network partners are somehow interconnected (mostly via ego's partner), but there is also one befriended couple which is not in close contact to any other of ego's network partners.

Ego's network partners are heterogeneous in parity, partnership status, age and educational background. She does not include any relatives apart from her own parents among her ten most important network partners.

The networks of persons who conceptualize family without children are labelled *childfree by choice* and one example is given in Figure 8.3. The network is held by a 31-year-old female respondent living apart together

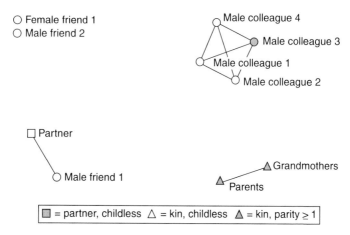

Figure 8.3   Example of a *childfree by choice network*

with her partner. The graph displays ego's ten most important network partners, who are, except for a group of colleagues, hardly interrelated. One female friend and one male friend are not in close contact to any other of ego's network partners (upper left corner of the graph).

The only person with children in her network (apart from her own parents and grandparents) is a male colleague, but she stresses in the interview that their contact is restricted to their working time and that she does not meet with him and his family in her leisure time.

For a better overview, we have summarized the network characteristics and network types corresponding to the different conceptualizations of family in Table 8.1.

Processes of social influence and self selection in establishing conformity

How does the strong correspondence between family conception and network type come into place? We found two seemingly contradictory processes in the heart of establishing conformity. On the one hand individuals are influenced by their network partners to behave in a conforming way; on the other hand they select network partners who conform to their own attitudes and behaviour. These two processes are not exclusive; our interviews show that our respondents experience both: incidents of social influence and selection. The opportunities for choosing network partners as well as the ways social influences are

Table 8.1 Family conception, fertility intention and network structure

	Traditional family conception	Individualized family conception including children	Individualized family conception excluding children
Network characteristics	• dense • high share of kin • many young network partners with children • homogeneous • mostly local ties	• sparse • low share of kin • heterogeneous • local and dispersed contacts	• sparse • low share of kin • no/few young network partners with children • homogeneous in interests and childlessness, heterogeneous in other living arrangements • local and dispersed contacts
Network type	*Family centred network*	*Heterogeneous network*	*Childfree by choice network*

exerted (and their effectiveness) strongly depend on the type of network the respondents are embedded in.

Accounts on social influence have been provided by all respondents, and we have identified in line with previous research on social networks (Burt, 1983; Marsden, 1987; Mieneke and Midden, 1991) four main forms of social influence (for more details see Keim et al., 2009):

- Social learning: the experiences and observations individuals make, as well as the information they have access to, shape their attitudes, intentions and behaviour. In dense networks redundant information is exchanged and the present conforming/homogenous attitudes and behaviours are reinforced, while in sparse networks 'new' information is transmitted more easily. Therefore in the identified dense *family centred networks* of persons following in conformity with traditional values, the traditional conception of family remains unchallenged. In contrast, in the sparse *heterogeneous networks* of persons with individualized family conceptions, 'new' information on alternatives to marriage and parenthood, for example, enters the network and traditional conceptions lose their self-evidence. However, being confronted with a variety of options may also make it difficult to take a decision and lead to uncertainty and fertility postponement.
- Social pressure: social networks are the space wherein personal orientations and moral values are discussed, enforced or questioned, where deviance may be sanctioned and compliance rewarded. Social pressure is especially effective in dense networks and produces conforming/homogeneous attitudes and behaviour. We found that in dense *family centred networks* traditional conceptions of family are ubiquitous and childlessness is valued negatively or ascribed to medical problems. In contrast, in *heterogeneous networks* there is little conformity and more variety in respondents' attitudes on marriage and the timing of birth, for example; postponement of parenthood and voluntary childlessness are tolerated.
- Social or emotional contagion: individuals can spontaneously pick up emotional states and behaviours of persons with whom they come into contact and as a consequence alter their behaviour. Respondents embedded in networks containing small children or pregnant women often report that observing these families has induced their considerations about having children and fuelled their desire for an own child. A special form is the cascading of events: the experience of more and more persons in a dense network beginning to talk about having children and becoming pregnant fosters ego's

own thinking and decisions about having a child, which – if ego talks about this with her friends – again has an accelerating effect on ego's friends. In dense and *family centred networks* this mechanism adds to the perception of the self-evidence of having children, while it is less powerful in sparse and *heterogeneous networks*.

– Social support: through social interactions individuals gain access to specific resources provided by other persons. Most relevant regarding family assembling processes are financial support and support in childcare, mainly provided by parents and parents-in-law. Respondents value these types of support highly and (expect to) receive them when they are embedded in *family centred networks* and in some of the *heterogeneous networks*. However, respondents embedded in *heterogeneous networks* very often do not have access to these types of support (for example, parents/parents-in-law cannot provide childcare because they do not live close by). The provision or refusal of social support is also one means of sanctioning and therefore links the influence mechanism of social support to the mechanism of social pressure in establishing conformity. One example is parental support in childcare: respondents who need their parents' support in childcare in order to combine family and job,[4] mostly arrange their life in a way that their parents approve of.

In addition to processes of social influence, selection effects can also be found in most of our networks; however, some *family centred networks* especially have – as the respondents retrospectively report – been very stable and the ties involved have been held for many years. In such dense networks ego finds it difficult to exclude one network partner without having to exclude the whole clique and at the same time it is difficult for new persons to enter the network. As a consequence these networks tend to be very stable. In contrast other *family centred networks*, and especially the *heterogeneous* and *childfree networks*, often include more recent ties and the respondents report various persons having joined or left their networks in recent years.

From the interviews we were able to identify two major selection effects: selection centred on having/not having children and selection coinciding with decisions in other areas of life. With planning to become or becoming parents many respondents describe that their networks have changed: contacts with kin and other persons with children have increased, contacts with childless friends have decreased. The respondents provide three explanations for these changes: (1) their interests have changed with becoming parents, they enjoy talking about child-related topics or spending their leisure time with other families with children, which brought them closer to kin and friends with children; (2) they feel as parents they often cannot join their childless friends in their activities (for example, going out spontaneously in the evening, travelling to exotic countries etc.), which leads to a decrease in contacts with them; and (3) they profit from or depend on financial support and support in childcare, mainly provided by parents/parents-in-law, which leads to increased contacts. As we have learned from our respondents' accounts many networks have changed with the transition to parenthood from a more heterogeneous to a more family centred structure. Our interviewees report that this retraditionalization in network composition has coincided with a change in values and/or the division of tasks in the couple. One example is the attitude towards gender equity. Although these respondents had not organized their educational and professional careers in a gendered way, when it comes to family formation and family life they hold a strongly gendered image of parenthood: the mother as carer for the children and the father as the financial provider. Although they do not formulate this image as a self-evident fact, they state that they have realized that a gendered division of tasks is the only way they personally would be able to organize their family life.[5] This retraditionalization effect has been variously described in literature (Rüling, 2007). While this selection effect centres on planning/having children, we also found a selection effect centred on not having children in the interviews with respondents who intend to remain childless. They report retrospectively that network partners who had become parents have left their networks, while new childless network partners with similar interests have entered in recent years. By this selection process the respondents manage to establish themselves in *niches of acceptance of childlessness* in the background of a society in which traditional living arrangements with children dominate.

The second major selection effect is connected to decisions taken in other areas of life than family formation. This is mostly the case for respondents who have decided to pursue further education after being trained in a job and are therefore currently enrolled in education or have started their first job only recently. While their former school-mates have established themselves in work, they have enrolled themselves at university. At university they made new friends with similar interests and over the years reduced contacts with their former friends. As a consequence, when their former friends became parents they were not in close contact with them anymore, but rather had found new friends who – as themselves – do not consider family formation until they have finished their studies.

These results show that the selection of network partner can be on the one hand induced by life course transitions related to family formation; on the other hand it can also be the outcome of decisions taken in other areas of life. Hence, social networks and their effects are not static but dynamically evolve over the life course.

Conclusion

As network theory suggests, we can show a correspondence between network structures and composition and the way individuals embedded in these networks conceptualize family. Persons embedded in *family centred* networks composed of mainly traditional ties (kin ties and local ties) conceptualize family in a traditional way, as a married couple with children, and – as our interviews show – they hold in correspondence with their network partners rather traditional values, for example, regarding gender roles. In contrast, persons embedded in *heterogeneous* or *childfree* networks, composed of mainly individualized ties (friendship ties, dispersed ties) conceptualize family in a more individualized way, as a couple with or without children, and hold individualistic values. This sounds very well in line with the individualization hypothesis that relates traditional/individualized bonds with certain types of traditional/individualized (fertility) behaviour. Our analysis, however, shows that the relationship between social bonds and individual behaviour is more complex. Social networks not only influence how individuals think and behave, they are also the result of individual behaviour. The concept of conformity encompasses this dualism: first, conformity is produced by processes of social influence, processes ego is not necessarily aware of; and second, conformity is the outcome of ego selecting network partners that fit to her/his present life situation, interests and needs. What we perceive at the time of our interview as traditional bonds may therefore be on the one hand social ties forming a social network that has indeed been rather stable for many years and has been transmitting and reproducing traditional values; but on the other hand the social network may also have undergone a process of retraditionalization when ego became a parent. Here a longitudinal research approach would be necessary to gain further insights. The sources of this retraditionalization process are difficult to disentangle: (1) experiencing the transition to parenthood may be a life event that induces changes in values, which in turn lead to changing relationships. These value changes can be fostered by social policies, labour market conditions and gender roles that encourage the traditional male breadwinner model for parents. (2) Looking at social ties, we found evidence that in a societal context in which public childcare is only inadequately available, kin ties gain relevance with the transition to parenthood based on a need for support in childcare. This increase in kin ties may in turn lead to an increased transmission of traditional attitudes and values, as for example the male breadwinner model.

Coming back to the tension between the emergence of new living arrangements and the prevalence of traditional patterns of family formation, our data confirms a polarization: most of our respondents are either childfree and singles, live apart together with their partner, cohabit without being married, or they are part of a married couple with children. Although most opt for gender equity in general, when it comes to having children they mostly seek orientation in the male breadwinner model. This orientation is fostered by such macrostructures as social policies and labour market conditions, reproduced in social networks and enhanced by a dependence on kin support in childcare.

Acknowledgements

This chapter is part of the project 'Social Influence on Family Formation and Fertility in Northern Germany'. The project was funded by the Independent Research Group 'The Culture of Reproduction' at the Max Planck Institute for Demographic Research in Rostock, Germany and the 'Max-Planck-Landesgraduiertenstipendium des Landes Mecklenburg-Vorpommern'.

9
Exclusivity and Inclusivity in Transnational Adoption

Riitta Högbacka

There has been an unprecedented rise in the popularity of transnational adoption in Western countries in the twenty-first century. Although on the global level annual numbers of intercountry adoptions have recently decreased from around 45,000 to fewer than 38,000 (Selman, 2009: 580), demand in the West continues to rise. As adoption involves biogenetic as well as ethnic and national dislocation, it also provides a lens through which to examine who is included in and who is excluded from the family. The family here refers to both the adoptive family that is assembled and the birth family that is disassembled within the process.

In this chapter I explore the familial realities and narratives of Finnish adoptive parents and South African birth mothers concerning parenthood and the family. Are there differences between them in the principles of family formation and in the maintenance of family boundaries? First I will present two logics of family formation that help us to understand the narratives of adoptive and birth mothers (and some adoptive fathers). I will argue that the prevalent exclusive logic of family formation in transnational adoption collides with the more inclusive understanding of South African birth mothers. Pressure to move towards inclusivity also comes from the lived experience of adoptive families.

The chapter draws on thematic interviews with 15 Finnish adoptive families (19 parents altogether) conducted in 2005 and 2006, and with 31 South African birth mothers conducted in 2006 and 2008. I used a list of broad themes rather than a fixed set of questions in the interviews. My interviewees included seven married women, one man, three couples together, and four single women. Between them they had adopted children from China, Guatemala, the Philippines, Thailand, Russia, South Africa, India, Colombia and Romania. I also used one interview

129

with an adoptive father conducted by a student (Päivikki Akpi), with the interviewee's permission. The parents' ages varied between 33 and 55. The majority of them lived in the Helsinki area, but some were from smaller towns or rural areas.

From my extensive body of South African material I will use the interviews I conducted with black birth mothers: eight pregnant women who had made adoption plans and 23 women who had already relinquished a child for in(ter)-country adoption. About half of those who had given up a child had done so several years previously (some more than ten years previously), whereas for the other half the relinquishment was more recent. The ages of the women varied between 14 and 43, the majority being between 19 and 25. In all except three cases I conducted the interviews in English. They were held at four different locations in South Africa (Durban, Cape Town, Johannesburg and Pretoria). I also refer to interviews I conducted with ten adoption social workers.

In 2007 the four biggest countries of origin of adopted children on the global level were China, Russia, Guatemala and Ethiopia, and the most common countries of destination were the USA, Spain, Italy and France (Selman, 2009: 580, 579). Adoptions to Finland started to increase relatively recently, towards the end of the 1990s, and never reached very high numbers. In 2007, 176 children were adopted to Finland, the majority coming from China, Thailand, South Africa and Russia (Finnish Board of Inter-Country Adoption Affairs, 2008.) South African children are mainly adopted to the Netherlands and the Nordic countries (data provided by the author). In 2007 a total of 186 South African children were adopted abroad (Selman, 2009: 588).

Two logics of family formation

The logic of exclusivity

Historians have shown that the informal fostering of children by relatives and others was very common in Europe in the nineteenth century, and that it was not customary for a family to look after or be responsible for all of its children (Gillis, 1996, quoted in Howell 2006b: 149). Fostering in private homes rather than adoption or institutional care was the main solution throughout the nineteenth century in Finland. The situation changed during the first decades of the twentieth century with the emergence of a single acceptable way of life, that of the nuclear family. 'Proper' family relations were now emphasized over fostering. The first adoption law in Finland was passed in 1925. The aim was to establish a parent-child relationship that would be as close to the 'natural' one as possible. However, the adoptive relationship could still be revoked if the child turned out to be 'unsuitable'. This was amended only in the new law of 1985 whereby adoption became irrevocable. At the same time, all ties with the child's previous family were cut (Pylkkänen, 1995: 138–40).

Adoption as it has been practised in Western countries since at least the 1950s is based on the as-if-genealogical model of a nuclear family with strong boundaries (Modell, 1994). Parental ties are exclusively created between the child and the new adoptive parents, at the same time as there is a 'clean break' with the past and the natal family (HCCH, 1993; Finlex, 1985; Bowie, 2004: 9; Yngvesson, 2007: 564–5). The Finnish law states that after adoption 'the adoptive child will be the child of the adoptive parents and not the child of its previous parents' (Finlex, 1985, Chapter 2). Adoptive parents are told that after the signing of the adoption papers 'it will be as if you had given birth to this child' (data provided by the author). Birth mothers are told that after adoption 'it is no longer your child' (data provided by the author) or 'it will be like the child is dead to you' (Yngvesson, 2003: 20).

The adoptive family is supposed to be just like a 'normal' family with one set of parents who have exclusive possession of and rights to their children (Modell, 1999: 53). There is also a common understanding that the family should be protected from interference by third parties (Strathern 1995: 352). This type of thinking is prevalent in the forming and regulation of other non-orthodox family types such as those created with the help of reproductive technologies (Hirvonen, 2007) and post-divorce family arrangements (Théry, 1986; Castrén, 2009b). The goal of family-making in these forms and in adoption is the creation of a completely new, exclusive family unit (see also Allen, 2005). In step-families, for instance, the other birth parent of the child was previously regarded as a potentially disturbing influence or even as harmful to the new nuclear family, the birth parent and that parent's new spouse (Théry, 1986).

The fact that adoptive families are not quite like other families is the source of much ambiguity in their everyday lives, however (Högbacka, 2009). Yngvesson (2004, 2007) refers to the exclusive, clean-break model of adoption as legal fiction. Traces of the past can never be totally erased. Even adoption laws and the Hague Convention make some allowances for this fact, reflected in the requirement to give 'due consideration' to the adopted child's 'ethnic, religious and cultural background' (HCCH, 1993, Article 16).

The logic of inclusivity

Family making is understood differently in the countries from which adopted children come from. According to research, Oceanic societies, various parts of Latin America, Asia and Africa tend to follow a more inclusive logic. Informal fosterage and child circulation are common, and social parenthood does not have to replace birth parenthood. Rather than substituting or cancelling each other out, the various 'parents' are simply added to the child's kin group. A child can be raised by another member of the extended family or by non-kin, yet ties with the natal family are maintained and the child will at some stage usually return to it. (Bowie, 2004: 3–17; Scheper-Hughes, 1992: 104–5; Siikala and Siikala, 2005: 146–8)

Informal fosterage is also a mechanism whereby poor families place some of their children in families that are at least slightly better-off. There is an expectation in Oceanic societies of a close bond between the giver and the receiver of a child. Adoption and fosterage are social endeavours. Modell (2002: 183), Fonseca (2003: 115–22) and Hoelgaard (1998: 207) give examples from Latin America of 'multiple' parenthood, of child sharing and how a child may have many 'mothers': not only the birth mother, but also whoever brings it up (Fonseca, 2003: 120). Children are regularly circulated among kin in Africa, but permanent rupture from the birth parents is unusual (Goody, 1982; Howell, 2006a: 50).

Informal fosterage (children with living mothers staying with relatives elsewhere) has typically been high among the black population in South Africa. Young urban couples or single women might leave young children in rural areas with grandmothers, and rural families might leave their school-age children with relatives in urban areas so that they will be able to go to better schools. (Makiwane, 2003: 58) In fact, 27 per cent of children (of non-orphans) (and 35 per cent of paternal orphans) in South Africa do not live with their birth mother (Africa's Orphaned Generations, 2003: 13). Over 60 per cent of South African children who have lost one or both parents live with their grandparents (ibid.: 14–15). The tradition has been to take the child home and the extended family will look after it. At some stage the children usually return to the birth family. This extended-family system is currently under great pressure due to extreme unemployment and HIV/AIDS (ibid.).

Intercountry adoptions from South Africa started in the twenty-first century when there was a sudden increase in the number of black children entering children's homes. The principles of the Hague Convention (1993) were followed early on, and South Africa also promptly ratified the treaty. A new Children's Act was passed in April 2010 that also regulates adoptions. The legislation refers to the Western model of exclusive adoption in which previous legal relationships between the child and his/her biological parents are terminated. The field of adoption in South Africa is still predominantly white. According to statistics from the central registrar in Pretoria (Department of Social Development), there are still more than a 1000 white domestic adoptions every year, compared to about 200 intercountry black adoptions.

I will now turn to my empirical material. I will analyze (1) adoption stories, in particular how adoptive parents talk about their family and the child's previous family; and (2) stories of relinquishment, in particular the birth mothers' understandings of motherhood without a child. The focus is on two questions in both the adoptive-parent and the birth-mother data: family formation (reasons for adoption/relinquishment) and family boundaries (striving towards a clean break from past relationships/ continuity). The aim is to discover whether different family-formation logic (exclusivity or inclusivity) can be discerned from the mothers' narratives. Together, these provide insights into broader questions concerning how families are being made and unmade.

Adoptive parents' familial realities and narratives

Making a family of one's very own

Intercountry adoption is strongly connected to family formation. My data revealed three slightly differing paths to adoption: through couples having trouble conceiving (the majority), single women, and a few families with an interest in adopting from abroad but with no history of infertility (Högbacka, 2008). However, the most dominant theme in all the adoptive parents' narratives was the desire to have a child, and thus an exclusive family, of one's own.

Foster parenting, which would have provided a quicker route to having children, was not what they wanted. This came out emphatically in the interviews. 'I wanted a child of my own. If you're a foster parent, the child is never legally yours', as Vivian remarked. Parenting entails an exclusive and permanent tie with the child. One cannot experience the parental role to its fullest if the child can be taken away. Eva's story is instructive. 'They [the social workers] said they had a one-year-old that should be placed in foster care. [. . .] The child's father was going to prison. [. . .] But afterwards he will be free I said, and then I'd have to give this one-year-old back. My heart isn't that big. [. . .] I would want that child as my very own'. Another side of exclusive parenting is that the parents make decisions concerning their child without interference from others. The existence of possible other carers is problematic in this context. Jenny and Mike explained: 'Our conviction that the children must be ours so that no outsider could have any say in the matter was strengthened during the [adoption] preparation courses'.

Obtaining a child had been a long project for most of the adoptive parents, and the waiting periods had been uncertain and nervewracking. Mike described his family's actions and feelings as resembling those of an athlete practising for the Olympics, their only goal being to obtain a child. In Mike's case it took ten years to achieve that goal. It seems that all this waiting, hoping and imagining builds an overflow of sentimental feeling in and around adoption. This, in turn, helps the parents in making the child their own on the emotional level. Peter explained: 'The child felt like your own straight away. [. . .] Even if the process was long and uncertain and you weren't sure of the outcome, it also prepared you to think of the child as your own'. A lot of emotion and affection are directed towards this child of one's dreams. Isabella, for instance, had strong feelings towards their child-to-be even at the beginning when she and her husband were just starting the adoption process and did not know anything about the actual child. She said: 'I loved my child even when I didn't know her, even when I didn't know from which country she would come or who she would be'.

If the idea of the child evoked feelings, the moment it was assigned was very emotional. Jenny recalled her experience of being told that a child had been referred to them. She knew from following the situation via the Internet that their turn was approaching, so she was expecting a phone call from the adoption agency within a few days. She told me: 'I was already crying before the phone rang'. It seems that strong emotions help to make the child one's own, but also that it is specifically the thought of having a child of one's own that has the power to evoke these feelings. This is exemplified in Isabella's words: 'It is the most wonderful thing in the world. There can be nothing better in life than being told that you own, I mean that you have become a mother'.

The adoptive parents mentioned that feelings for the child tended to come very quickly after they first set eyes on it. Ann: 'Attachment to these children, my husband says this as well, attachment comes within 24 hours. [. . .] Very strong feelings of attachment'. The overwhelming happiness and joy of being new parents was tangible. They remarked how proud they were to be parents. This is captured in Mike's account: 'At first, the first months you're just so proud and glowing in all directions'.

In another interview Steve told us: 'At first I was just so proud. I was surprised to realise how proud I was to walk in the street with my child. I didn't expect to feel like that'. The new mothers, too, felt this way. Eva: 'I think I would be a lot more selfish if I weren't a mother. [. . .] Somehow this is for me, and I'm so proud that I'm a mother. Now I'm in the category of mothers'.

The motive for adopting, the wish to have a child, is in many ways connected to the idea of an exclusive family of one's own. It seems that for adoptive parents only exclusivity guarantees the proper and enjoyable role of a parent.

The impossibility of having two sets of parents

Birth mothers of adopted children have generally been cut out of the picture. A survey conducted by the Finnish Adoptive Families Association among its members in 2005 revealed that of the 33 families that had adopted domestically and the 278 that had adopted from abroad only three per cent reported that the child was in contact with the birth family. 53 per cent of the respondents had some information about the birth family, whereas just under half said they did not know anything. In my interview data three adoptive families had been in some contact with the birth mother, either through letters mediated by the social worker or having met her when they collected the child. A few families had a photograph of the birth mother.

The birth mother aroused ambiguous responses. Some adoptive mothers were angry with her, or had heard of others who were angry, for having 'deserted' their children. One adoptive mother I interviewed agreed with what another had said: 'Only I am the mother, you can't be a mother if you're not taking care of the child'. Some put the birth mother out of their minds: 'I never think about her. Terrible'. The most common reaction seems to be compassion, however. They understand how difficult it must have been for the birth mother. The difficulty is that 'someone else's misfortune is my happiness' as one adoptive mother said. Another said: 'What a pity she could not keep this lovely child'. The adoptive mothers seemed to have one wish: 'If only she could somehow know that all is well with her child'.

The question of how to deal with the subject of the birth parents in the everyday life of an adoptive family was fraught with difficulties. How should you tell a young child? Some parents said that it was 'surprisingly easy to forget', and that they had to make a real effort to tell the child. This is understandable as adoptive families have to incorporate the child fully into their lives and make it their own.

The point at which the child starts to call the parents mother and father is significant. The interviewees said that they meant to talk about this later but 'not now'. As Ann put it, 'I don't think he's capable of think-ing there's another woman somewhere'. Another said: 'We have told her that she was born there. But I always talk about the parents from that country. At the moment I find it very hard to talk about the father and mother from that country [. . .] father and mother are now reserved for us'. According to another adoptive mother: 'We have told her the basic stuff [. . .] that she was born there [. . .] but that she has a mother and father somewhere else, no [. . .] and about her [biological] sister, we have not said a word'. The parents would only talk about the birth kin in the future, when the child is an adult. The worst scenario was that unknown birth parents would suddenly appear in the lives of adoptive families with small children. The birth parents clearly could never be totally erased from the adoptive family, but they could be put on hold, at least for the time being, as long as the children were small.

One of the problems is our culture's exclusivist understanding of the family, which is connected to biogenetic understandings of exclusive necessary ties. Adoptive parents therefore fear that the 'real' mother will exclude or replace them (Yngvesson, 2003: 23–4). The fear of actu-ally losing the child was explicit in my data. One mother stated: 'I do have fears [. . .] what if she suddenly appeared saying it's my child and I want him back'. Another mother told me that some time ago a rumour was going around on the Internet that birth parents could reclaim their children. She said: 'I thought about it for weeks [. . .] Even the idea of it was absolutely terrifying'. Parents also remarked that it was a 'relief' or 'safe' that the birth mother was far away. An exclusive understanding of the family makes it very hard to deal with the idea and existence of possible other parents.

Birth mothers' familial realities and narratives

A better life for the child

I will now consider the motives and circumstances of black South African birth mothers giving their children up for adoption. In general, at the time when the adoption decision was made the situation of my informants was desperate: most were struggling financially and many did not have a roof over their heads. The majority were unemployed at the time of relinquishment, and came from families or extended families in which others were unemployed as well. Many came from rural areas to look for work, and they actually sent the little money they managed to earn back home where they had other children cared for by grandmothers or female relatives. There were two illegal immigrants from Zimbabwe among my informants. Poverty, unemployment and destitution were thus the reality for most. The unemployment rate for African females in 2005 was 56 per cent, compared to 39 per cent for African males and 10 per cent for white females (South Africa Survey, 2004/2005: 176). Of all children in South Africa 66 per cent lived in poor households (South African Child Gauge, 2006: 69).

Most of the women I interviewed had been deserted by the father of the child at the time of relinquishment. The destruction of the African family that began during apartheid has been documented in several studies. Strict pass laws allowed only men to enter cities as workes in the mines, while families (women and children) remained in the countryside. This caused a lot of strain on family life (Thomas and Mabusela, 1991). African women have low marriage prevalence. Nevertheless, childbearing is almost universal, and it is usually the woman who carries the sole responsibility for the children. (Swartz, 2003: 15–16) At the end of 2004, 37 per cent of all households were women-headed (South Africa Survey, 2004/5: 190). I also had four HIV-positive women in my data, and in their case this fact combined with poverty and unemployment constituted the background for the adoption decision. South Africa currently has the largest number of HIV-infected people in the world (State of the World's Children, 2007: 114–17).

Mary was 34 years old and had given her child for adoption about a month previously. She had joined in a support group for birth mothers and was able to earn some money from temporary employment in a weekly sewing and baking project organized by the adoption organization. Other than that she was unemployed with no fixed abode. She came from a poor rural area, where her other three children were being taken care of by her aunt, who was also unemployed. A recurrent theme in the interviews was that the women did not want their children to suffer as they had, and that the child should have 'a better life'. They also said how much they loved their children. It was because they loved them that they gave them away.

> They asked me the same question that why are you want to give the child for adoptions. I say that I want my child to live better life. I don't want my babies to suffer, so that is why I want do the adoption. Because for now I, I'm homeless. I'm not working.
> [. . .] My other children at home don't even have shoes to go to school.

[. . .] I love him so much. That is why I chose a better life him. I don't want him to suffer.

(Mary)

I looked for parents who make sure that he gets better education and a better life and gets love that I didn't have. And that where he would be happy. Because I didn't want to see him suffering like I did.
[. . .] Sometimes I think about it every night. It's sad. But I wanted to give my child a better life, a better future.

(Cindy)

Others said the same thing: that the decision to give the child away was painful but they felt they had 'no choice'. 'No choice' and 'a better life for child' were mentioned frequently in the interviews. Most of the women (21 out of 31) had other children apart from the one given for adoption, and they were trying to support these children as well. In Hope's case the grandmother was looking after her other child in Zimbabwe. Hope herself was in South Africa illegally, looking for work and sending whatever money she managed to earn to support her own mother, her other child, her older brother's little child, her younger brother, her 18-year-old sister, and the sister's boyfriend and their baby, all living together at Hope's mother's place. In other words, love for one's child meant separation and not staying together (see Beck-Gernsheim in this book for a parallel case).

And then I tell them that I'm not working, and then I don't have place to stay, and then if, uh, if I have a baby where I'm going to stay with this baby because I don't have place, I don't have money, I'm not working. [. . .] I discovered I'm pregnant when I was five months. And then I don't have money to support this child 'cause I have one child.

RH: You have another child?

– Yeah.

RH: In Zimbabwe?

– Yeah.

[. . .] Cause I don't have choice. I don't have anything to stay with this child. If there's someone who gonna take care of this child I must give her.

(Hope)

That they probably did not have a choice was confirmed in my interviews with the social workers. The options were: either keep your child (which because of your economic and other circumstances you could not do) or give it up for good. There was no viable third possibility. Foster care was not really an option for these women as it was only granted in cases of severe negligence or abuse of the child. The social workers commented: 'There is a real sense of despair in the moms that we work with because we can't offer them what's needed most'. There were no programmes or support for poor women to help them keep their children. Other social workers said that they actually saw a lot of changes in the women's circumstances after six to twelve months or two years, so if there was a way to support them or to have the child taken care of for a while, many would find a job or otherwise improve their situations and would be able to take back their children. I also met birth mothers who came back after two or more years saying that their situation had improved and they wanted to have their children back. Many would, in fact, have preferred some sort of temporary care. Thapelo's case is not an exception. She had given up her child two years previously. She had just learnt at the maternity clinic that she was HIV-positive, and that her other, older child also had HIV. Her husband left her when she told him this.

> I just asked, I found out, I was sick and I thought, I wanted to do, what do they call it, not adoption but I wanted them to take the baby for awhile and then, yes, foster care so they told me it's not possible.
>
> RH: Oh, why?
>
> – Because they said I can work, I'm not that much sick and my CD-count is still good and I'm still working so there is a big ground that I can keep the baby, so. That's why they said it's not possible. And adoption is possible. It was so sad. I'm still missing her.
>
> (Thapelo)

The force with which the women voiced their lack of choice also reflects another convention, against which they were feeling defensive. There was considerable stigma attached to giving a child up for adoption in the black community, and in fact it was almost unknown. A woman who did so would commonly be called 'a bee, 'cause she's giving away her child', or it would be said that she was 'throwing away' or 'dumping' the child, or even 'selling the baby'. There was also a saying that

'Even a dog knows where its puppies are'. Most birth mothers would therefore try to keep the adoption secret. The expectation was rather that you take your child home and *gogo* (the grandmother) will take care of it.

In other words, the family composition was very different, mostly comprising the woman and her children and the grandmother (the woman's own mother). Circulation of children was common, but only within the extended family, and the expectation was usually that they would eventually return to the birth mother. Most of the birth mothers in my data had at some point been raised by someone other than their birth mother, and many of them had other children who were being looked after by grandmothers, aunts or paternal grandparents, for example. Lucille, for instance, described her current situation as 'coming full-circle', as one of her sons was being returned to her after having lived with his paternal grandmother and aunt for five years. Lucille was also wondering if it would be possible one day to have back the child she had given up for adoption.

In a cultural situation in which less permanent, informal child circulation is common, and is sometimes just a way to help the mother through a desperate financial situation temporarily, relinquishing a child for adoption may not be viewed as the total breaking of ties it turns out to be.

'At the end of the day, it's my child'

Wanting to remain in contact with and to receive information about the child was very common. Only four of the 31 women who were interviewed thought they would not want any information. Of these two were still pregnant, and two had given birth just a few days previously. It is therefore not known how they would feel later. The social workers confirmed that the birth mothers 'come back asking for news on their children a lot'.

In some cases the birth mothers were able to receive information about the children they had given up for adoption. The adoptive parents might send photographs and sometimes letters to the social worker, who would then forward them to the birth mother. In some cases the birth mothers were involved in the choice of adoptive family and could meet them. These mothers were happy to know where their child had gone. Receiving information on how the child was and seeing for themselves in the photographs how it was developing and whether it looked happy were important to them.

This is better than not knowing anything. You know, it, it will hurt that uh, I, I gave the child away, I don't know, I don't know how he, he's doing, how he's coping. Maybe he has problem, uh, even though I'm faraway, but I can help. Even though you don't know how, but you, you feel that, you know, if he has a problem I can help. Even though you know that there's nothing you can do.

(Natie)

RH: Is there anything you want to add that is important?

– Mm. No, I can't think of. I'm just glad I know where my child is.

RH: Yes, that's the main thing.

– And I get information and I still see him through photos, how he is growing, so.'

(Meg)

The agencies had adopted a policy according to which information could, in some cases, be sent for a period of two years. The practices varied, however. Sometimes it stopped coming, and in other cases it might continue if both the adoptive parents and the birth mother so wished, although the recommended period was two years. Some adoptive parents I met in South Africa thought that it had to stop then for legal reasons, and some birth mothers I talked to did not know it would stop. In other cases the birth mothers were unhappy about the breaking of the connection, and would have liked more information.

RH: Do you get pictures of the child from adoptive parents?

– I did. But then, it's, ever since I haven't got any. And it's (inaudible). So I don't know what's going on. Because they told me that I'm gonna get letters and pictures every after four months for period of two years.

[. . .] And then I mean, uh, a two year period that's nothing, I mean, look, the year's already gone. And then I'm only left some few months. And then they haven't done any. So sometimes when I, uh, think about that, I just get angry. That why are they doing this to me? Why aren't they sending me pictures anymore? They, are they, have they forgotten about me, you know? All those kinds of things.

(Molly)

There was a very strong wish and a strong belief that one day they would meet up with their child and that the child would come back. Children given up for adoption were still thought of as part of the birth family. They saw them as their children. The clean break of Western adoption clearly does not happen in reality, not in the minds of the birth mothers.

> RH: Do you think you will one day tell your daughter that she has a sister?
>
> – Yeah. 'Cause that baby, she will come maybe after eighteen years. She wants to see me. So I, I think I must tell them that there's another baby. 'Cause if they see that baby there is gonna difficult now to explain that then. As long I didn't throw him at dustbin it's not a problem.
>
> (Hope)

> I hope that in five years, uhm, now, from now, I will be running my own business. Uh, raising my child in a proper way. I will save, saving money for, for him, that even though he will come on the eighteen, when he's eighteen I'll take him to the universities, and then graduate. Everything that he need and a good home. Everything.
>
> RH: So for, for this child who's now adopted?
>
> – Mm.
>
> RH: When he's eighteen?
>
> – Yeah. Because I won't say I can't save anything for him (inaudible) because he's not with me. Still he, he is my blood, I must, I must, uh, put something for, for him.
>
> (Elsie)

Many of the birth mothers used the metaphor of a gift or of giving someone a child 'whole-heartedly' (10 women used it spontaneously). They had probably been told by the social workers that there were many well-to-do parents who could not have children but who very much wanted a child. My interviews with the social workers seem to indicate that this was the case. Nevertheless, the fact that the birth mothers were so ready to use the analogy means it was pertinent to them for some reason. As anthropologists have pointed out, giving implies an ongoing relationship between the giver and the receiver (Modell, 1999; Yngvesson, 2002). Making a gift or giving something with all one's heart also implies that it is something of value and such a gift, i.e. the child, should be appreciated and well taken care of. It also implies that the child is the birth mother's to give. More than anything else, a gift implies reciprocity, and this creates a bond between the adoptive family and the birth mother. Lerato put into words what was implicit in many other birth mothers' narratives. She indicated a wish for a wider-ranging, inclusive sort of arrangement or bond, and sharing with the adoptive family. Lerato was one of the birth mothers who did not know anything about the child she had given up for adoption until several years later, when her situation had changed. She told me that she had passed the office of the social workers so many times before, but never had enough courage to go in or she felt that she did not have the right. She now received photographs of her child.

> But if it is not possible that I can get him back, just he must be in my life, coming to visit us, we must be together, you know, something like that. Yeah, like I know his family, I know those people and they know me, coming to visit like one big family, you know, like be friends with his mother, you know, the woman who adopted him. If I can be friends with her, you know, that's the things that I want, that can make me happier.
>
> (Lerato)

Conclusion

Twentieth-century Western ideas, practices and legal understandings regarding the family, child welfare and adoption have until recently been governed by the logic of exclusivity. 'Proper' family relations, that is one mother, one father and their children, have been the goal in child welfare and for step-families. The twenty-first century has brought a clear shift towards greater degrees of inclusivity. It is now recommended that children maintain relations with both birth parents after divorce, for example. Post-divorce families may thus contain several 'parents' (Théry 1986: 354–7; Castrén, 2009). Likewise, Western domestic adoptions are now in a process of change. Open adoption means maintaining some kind of contact between the birth and adoptive families. This may involve regular meetings between them, or just the exchange of letters and photographs mediated by social workers (see Hollenstein et al., 2003: 44). Some form of open adoption is now widely regarded as good practice in Western domestic adoptions (Neil 2006: 3; Safeguarding the Rights . . . 2007; Reamer and Siegel, 2007: 12). The experiences of the birth mothers of internationally adopted children in my data further suggest that adoption does not necessarily disassemble the family. Ties of some kind remain.

The problem with openness and inclusivity in family formation lies in the fact that it clashes with the Western understanding of the family. As my data shows, adoption is characterized by highly sentimentalized notion of having a family of one's own. In the current practices of intercountry adoption, bringing the birth mother into the picture would seem to shake our view of being a parent, being a family. It would extend the boundaries. Would such a constellation still be called a family?

Part IV
Families in the Remaking

10
Money and the Dynamics of Intimate Relationships

Caroline Ruiner, Andreas Hirseland and Werner Schneider

Since the mid twentieth century a lot has changed in the way couples live together. The employment rates of women have increased dramatically and the male-breadwinner/female-housekeeper-model regressed. Compared to the bourgeois ideal of the family (Parsons and Bales, 1955) the question of how to live together in intimate relationships has become one of individual reflection, choice and decision (see Giddens, 1992; Beck and Beck-Gernsheim, 1995).

Against the background of this progress this chapter attempts to illuminate the dynamics of intimate relationships, the processes between the partners and the development of couples over the course of time from a micro-sociological perspective with regard to the couple's dealing with money and its effects on (designing) the biographies of the (individuals-in-)couple.[1] For this purpose, some results that stem from a qualitative panel study of dual-earner couples will be reported in this chapter.[2]

Especially when both partners are employed and earn their own money, the synchronization of two lives (and related schemes of life) will end up being a challenge for the (individuals-in-)couples. Within this process money receives a particular task: while money is not merely an economic resource, but rather attributed with manifold meanings (Zelizer, 1994) according to its origins, its purposes and the specific situation of couples, it influences the development of the intimate relationship.

The development of couples – a relational view

The present times of individualization (Beck, 1992; Beck and Beck-Gernsheim, 2002), social transformation processes and increasing uncertainty do not leave intimate relationships unaffected. Blueprinted biographies and schemes of life (Macmillan and Copher, 2005: 859) are no longer adopted unquestioned. Life events such as finding employment, getting married or having a child will be anticipated and coordinated according to personal timetables (Feldhaus and Huinink, 2006: 5).

This requires considerable efforts, especially for intimate relationships: individual biographies will be 'shaped' and have to be brought into agreement with the partner's biographies; life courses have to be 'co-organized' (Blossfeld and Drobnič, 2002) to enable commonality and continuity. Due to the interdependency of the individuals-in-couples, modifications in the life of one partner subsequently affect the relationship and thus the other partner. Hence, for example, interests and life plans are influenced by intimate relationships[3] because these are important reality-building and reality-confirming institutions (Berger and Kellner, 1970: 50). They emerge from the actions and interactions of the individuals-in-couples, which are interrelated and mutually affected (Blumstein and Kollock, 1988: 468). Accordingly, the intimate relationship can be seen as a dynamic interactive connection of two 'significant others' (Mead, 1934) (re-)constructing their own reality/realities (Berger and Kellner, 1970).

Money in relationships – and what's love got to do with it?

The interactive construction of the relationship is deeply interwoven with the handling of money. With regard to the interaction processes money has a social meaning beyond its economic value: it is not just money or simply 'household money', earned by one or both partners and spent with more or less consensus. The decline of the male-breadwinner/female-housekeeper-model opened up for manifold attributions, symbolic meanings and practical arrangements which are negotiable and have to be negotiated between the partners. Money is symbolically loaded in a specific way and therefore causes effects in everyday life through interaction. This specific symbolic meaning – attributed by the partners – affects the way money is dealt with in intimate relationships. According to this, money in intimate relationships can be seen as 'relationship money', or in other words: money in relationships can be differentiated between 'my money' – 'your money' – 'our money' (Wimbauer, 2003; Schneider et al., 2005). The handling of money in everyday life of couples and the attributed symbolic meanings appear in their monetary arrangements. And because of the symbolic meaning of money – manifesting the partners 'construction of reality' (Berger and Kellner, 1970) – it is inadequate to concentrate only on the amount and the availability of (own) income, bank accounts and their allocation. Monetary arrangements rather implicate specific meaningful attributions to money as well as the chosen ways of dealing with money in the relationship and the principles for which purpose it should and can be used (Schneider et al., 2005: 212).[4]

For example, individual income on one side can be labeled as 'own' money reserved for the interests and purposes of one partner or on the other side can be regarded as 'joint' money which serves the couple. This money defined as 'our money' might not be used entirely for 'own' interests like hobbies or for example further education of one partner. Thus the monetary arrangements confine specific eventualities or even facilitate them, which is why they are closely linked to the partner's biographical development.

As a conclusion, it is a matter of attribution of the (individuals-in-) couples how money is regarded, symbolically loaded and therefore causes effects in everyday life through the interaction of the partners. Thus the handling of money in intimate relationships is deeply interwoven with the interactive construction and assessment of the entire relationship by both partners, which is why the monetary arrangements can only be understood against the background of the relationship concepts which structure everyday life in couples.

The relationship concepts

The relationship concepts implicate ideas about 'good' relationships, respectively what constitute and maintain intimate relationships.[5] Ideal-typically (Weber, 1985) two relationship concepts can be distinguished: the collectivistic and the individualistic relationship concept (see Figure 10.1).

In 'collectivistic' notions the couple is perceived as overarching both individuals. The continuance of the relationship is strongly prioritized over individual opportunities and seen as permanent and unquestionable. Reciprocity ('giving and taking') is rather generalized and the partners strive for balance over the life course. Within collectivistic relationships money is primarily seen as joint money, is often pooled and spent to a larger amount on the behalf of the relationship. Individual spendings or the availability of own money is less important (Allmendinger and Schneider, 2005; Schneider et al., 2005).

The 'individualistic' relationship concept sees a couple basically as something that is produced and maintained by the individuals through interaction and negotiation. Therefore the continuance of the couple is

Relationship concept	Collectivistic	Individualistic
Values	Prioritize the couple	Prioritize the individuals
Reflexivity	The relationship is seen as permanent and unquestionable	The relationship can be cancelled (in principle) at will at any time
Reciprocity	Generalized reciprocity	Exchange of equivalents
Money	Primarily seen as 'joint'	Primarily seen as 'individual'

Figure 10.1   The relationship concepts

not taken for granted as the relationship can be ended (in principle) at will at any time. The relationship itself is rather like a contract between the two individuals and the continuation of the relationship depends on the contractual 'terms and conditions'. Subsequently the notion of reciprocity is oriented towards an exchange of equivalents in order to keep the 'relationship account' in balance at any time and so prevent any long-term liabilities. Money is primarily seen as individual money that only to a certain amount contributes to the relationship and is spent for joint purposes (Allmendinger and Schneider, 2005; Schneider et al., 2005).

These relationship concepts implicate different notions of temporality; for example when giving and taking is seen as a (dis)balance, which involves effects for the relationship. Thus different enforcements of synchronisation can be identified: Collectivistic relationships give priority to solidarity and enable a mutual 'one after another' over the course of time as long as it serves the wholeness of the couple. In individualistic relationships the partners do not want to owe each other anything and thus they tend to avoid (biographical and other) asymmetries (Hirseland et al., 2005).

The relationship concepts and the related monetary arrangements form the basis for the dynamics of intimate relationships. They clarify the different needs for synchronizing the biographies of the individuals-in-couples. Though any intimate relationship will develop uniquely in ways influenced by and closely linked to specific personal and sociocultural backgrounds, its development also shares characteristics of many other relationships. To analyze this development or, more concretely, how (individuals-in-)couples arrange their everyday lives, a dynamic perspective is required as it is taken on in phase models (Lenz, 2006: 51). In the following the phase model of Lenz (2006) shall be presented exemplarily.

Phase model for the development of intimate relationships

Beyond the many ways that relationships can develop and apart from emphasizing that all relationships have beginnings, middles and endings, Lenz (2006) identifies, referring to earlier phase models,[6] four phases[7] of intimate relationships (ibid.: 56ff.) (Figure 10.2).

The phase of formation marks the beginning of the relationship. The two individuals adjust their patterns of interaction and (more or less) stable routines develop which constitute the everyday-life of couples (ibid.: 61ff.). The intimate relationship enters the phase of continuance as soon as the two individuals define themselves as a couple. The transition can be caused by turning points such as moving together, marrying and starting a family.[8] Moreover, within this phase changes might happen which come along with biographic developments linked to children, (un)employment or others. The phase of crisis occurs when a change is perceived as a burden (ibid.: 101). The crisis might lead into the phase of breakup, but not necessarily: the relationship might either be resolved through instability or it may achieve a new stability after a rebuilding phase.

Phase models classify relationships and their development but do not help to understand how couples arrange their everyday lives in regard

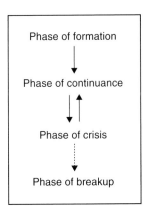

Figure 10.2 Lenz's phase model of intimate relationships

to interdependency and reciprocity. They outline possible careers of relationships, but hardly say anything about the phase of continuance though '[f]or most people, in most relationships, this period of continuous existence *is* the relationship, as they experience it' (Duck, 1994: 45). This is reason enough to inspect the phase of continuance closer.

The continuance of intimate relationships and its dimensions

Dindia (2000) emphasizes that relational maintenance not only refers to keeping the relationship in its present state but also might mean changing a relationship from its present condition (ibid.: 287f.). Also Scanzoni et al. (1989) have been aware that the phase of continuance is nevertheless both a phase of maintenance as well as of development and change. Consequently the phase of continuance is a dynamic process and does not imply that the situation is static.

Over the course of time, different events may become critical for the continuance of intimate relationships, cause changes and/or lead to instability. Initial changes may arise from a variety of sources: for some relationships it can take a change in job, a geographical move, the first child or the arrival of the second child until bothersome interpersonal patterns emerge and the couple begin to reappraise previously established patterns. Furthermore, absent but anticipated events may become critical and can lead the relationship into deterioration or at least to instability, because people internalize norms pertinent to each future stage and then anticipate conforming to them at the appropriate points in time when events should be realized. Already Lenz (2006) highlights the need to refer one's own plans and aspirations towards the other person, to coordinate them and to bring them into agreement with the partner (ibid.: 189).

This effort or process of timing and adjusting the life courses and specific schemes of life can be described as synchronization. Synchronization serves the purpose of having events occur in chronological order or simultaneously and means moreover an adjustment of the aspirations, plans and perceptions of the individuals-in-couples as well as their relationship concepts and their manifestation: the monetary arrangements. Due to the fact that the life courses of partners are interrelated and that trivially some events are only realizable with the partner (for example, marriage), the two individuals-in-couples have to adjust their ideas and synchronize their lives particularly when different perspectives of what constitutes a proper way of living together meet. Thus synchronization plays a decisive role in handling changes, in establishing and maintaining stability[9] and continuity.[10] Especially in times of social transformation processes, which open space for individual configuration, choices and plans, synchronization can be a particular challenge for the two individuals-in-couples as they have to design their own biographies as well as adapt them to their partner's to maintain the relationship.

It requires a closer (micro-sociological) look at the phase of continuance to understand the transitions between the phases and/or the (in)stability of intimate relationships and above all to clarify and detect events that are defined as critical by the individuals-in-couples, which thus cause changes. In addition, almost every biographical event affects money matters which have to be handled within intimate relationships. The question of whether this might affect inversely the couple's definition of their relationship can only be answered by looking at the empirical data.

Data and methods

The empirical findings stem from a qualitative panel of dual-earner couples collected in Germany between 1999 and 2008. In total eleven couples were interviewed in extensive narrative manner at three points in time in joint interviews with both partners together[11] and in interviews with each partner separately (Figure 10.3). The couples were selected by two criteria: first, both partners should have an income of their own and, second, they should define themselves as a 'couple' independently of whether they are married or not, have children or not.

By using a relational account[12] focusing on the partners' perspectives on their everyday practices, the constructed realities and various symbolic meanings of money as well as the effects on the development of intimate relationships can be exposed.[13]

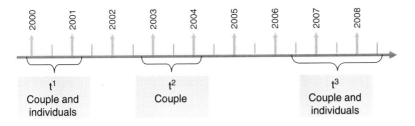

Figure 10.3 Survey waves

To analyze the development of the couples, 'objective' biographical events were focused and compared to 'subjective' events which were made a subject of discussion by one or both partners. Additionally perceptions and evaluations of the development were analyzed as well as causes and consequences of life changes that were mentioned by one or both of the partners. Finally the expected and anticipated trends were compared with the actually perceived development. By relating (missing) 'objective' biographical events to the 'subjective' perceived developments and the meanings the individuals-in-couples attribute to them, the dynamics in intimate relationships can be explained.

The dynamics of intimate relationships

The dynamics of intimate relationships will be illustrated in the following with the help of the development of three couples. These couples[14] and their development were selected because they represent ideal–typically the relationship concepts as well as exemplifying typical patterns of money arrangements influencing their biographies. After a short description of the couples and their particular development, the empirical findings are reflected on theoretically at the end of this chapter.

Couple C: The 'Firm'

Mrs C was born in 1965, Mr C in 1964. They have been a couple since 1982 and have been married since 1988. Their only child was born in 1994.

At the time of the first interview in 2000 Mrs and Mr C were both working full-time as office employees; in addition Mr C was attending further education. In the couple's description of the manner in which they manage daily life and responsibilities, the metaphor of the 'firm' applies in their own words as the supreme guideline: 'Well, we are a team. We have the same goal and we are trying to achieve it in our way [. . .] basically, it's like a firm'. The partners are members of a 'team' who pursue a common enterprise together. The couple's monetary arrangement is presented as giving priority to 'joint money': individual money (one's own earned money) is contributed to the 'company profit' and thus serves the success of the 'firm'. Within this 'firm' Mrs C holds the job of organizing and managing the finances, whereas Mr C, by mutual consent, claims the function of an auditor. In case of irregularities he might impose sanctions against her and at the worst he would have to take away the responsibility of money management from her.[15]

At the time of the second interview in 2003 Mrs C changed her job and consequently adopted a lower salary. Meanwhile Mr C finished his further education and received an increase in salary. The couple again mentioned that they are 'basically [. . .] like a firm'. The income is still seen as joint money, but the question of controlling the monetary arrangement is moved into the centre: every expense is collected and registered in an excel-sheet. Mr C implemented this system and although both argue that they would like to get an overview of their spendings, Mrs C still maintains the monetary administration.

At the time of the third interview in 2006 Mrs C is employed in the same job and Mr C has experienced an occupational advancement. Mr C is doing project work that involves staying abroad for three weeks every third week. The metaphor of the firm is not particularly mentioned in this interview, but still exists implicitly as the couple shows in using business terms like 'brainstorming', 'meeting' and 'making profit'.[16] Smaller adaptations can be found in the monetary arrangement: in contrast to earlier interviews Mr C's role as a controller is enlarged and he is now responsible for the monetary administration, enforced by the excel spreadsheet. This intensification can be seen as a result of Mrs C's spending, which put the 'company profit' at risk.

Mrs and Mr C can be classified as following a collectivistic relationship concept. Reciprocity is informed by the norms of collectivity and is balanced out: it is a giving and taking for both of them, never exceeding a particular amount.

The development of the relationship of the Cs has a high continuity which can be attributed to the specific interplay of the relationship concept and the monetary arrangement. This does not mean that their relationship is static or immutable; it is rather an ongoing project. Though different events in the life course have occurred, none of them have straitened the couple. For example Mr C's business trips would not have been without consequences and changes in every relationship. The relationship is stabilized because the couple construes his lengthy business trips as 'serving the whole' from which both profit. The supreme guideline of the 'firm' implies that the partners contribute as far as possible and whatever one can. The relationship concept as well as the monetary arrangement remains the same, except the monetary administration: the monitoring merely intensified. This was subsequently a modification to keep the 'firm' going and thus to provide continuity.

Couple E: The 'Pure Relationship'

Mrs and Mr E both born in 1968 have been a couple since 1992.

At the time of the first interview in 2000 both were working full-time as office employees. Mrs and Mr E can be classified as both having individualistic relationship concepts. Their relationship can be considered as a 'pure relationship' consisting of two autonomous and equal partners in a democratically structured relationship which is built on principles like equality, mutuality and fairness (Giddens, 1992). For this reason giving and taking is orientated around equality and autonomy, whereby implicit unspoken dependencies should be avoided. The Es attach great importance to their relationship as not being a long-term undertaking, but a daily decision consciously to stay together. As a result, the partners have to maintain their attractiveness and make an effort to work on their relationship. The Es cite this as their reason for not wanting to get married: this would stop the partners from working on themselves and their relationship. The individualistic orientation is manifested in the monetary arrangement: income is seen as unconditional individual money; joint expenditures are paid fifty-fifty. But as a precondition, to be able to contribute the same amount, both partners should proceed from the same amount of available money.

At the time of the second interview in 2004 the couple reports that they moved to another city for new occupational opportunities: Mr E quit his job in favour of being self-employed and so does Mrs E shortly afterwards.

At the time of the third interview in 2006 Mr E is still successfully self-employed, but not so Mrs E. She gave up her self-employment to stay at home and be employed part-time by Mr E. On top of that, the couple surprisingly married after they spoke strongly against that option in the first interviews. The idea of marriage arose because of Mrs E's worries. Consequently they asked a tax consultant about the advantages of being married and decided on the step: they married and subsequently Mr E became the sole earner. This being the case, the Es appear to be a traditional male-breadwinner/female-housekeeper-couple. However, looking beneath the surface, the couple's arrangement is still based on voluntariness and thus on release. For both partners the arrangement is short-termed and terminable at any moment. The exchange is still simultaneous and equivalent, but reinterpreted with altered currencies: while Mr E cares for the economic base Mrs E provides in return a 'quality of being'.[17] She takes care of everyday life, so that time spent together for recreation will be free of stress. Being a scarce resource, time has become more important than money. To keep up the rule of symmetrical exchange, the convertibility of time and money is enabled. By this, the exchange of 'provision and care', which is inherent in the traditional model, is more or less overtly commodified and open to an explicit calculus. Consequently the relationship constellation will be resolved as soon as the scope of benefits is not balanced anymore.

Though the relationship has the form of a male-breadwinner/female-housekeeper-model that seems to be a model of sustenance, the couple can, by analogy with earlier interviews, still be observed as being individualistic. The relationship is still based on voluntariness and seen as a contract which is terminable at any time. The monetary arrangement is adjusted to the occupational arrangement, though money is still being attributed individually: Mr E's income is his income and he agrees to share 'his' money with Mrs E for she is providing a relaxed everyday life. The key to understanding this arrangement is the less rigorous convertibility: the couple (especially Mr E) enables the exchange of money (earned and contributed to the relationship by him) and time (provided with quality by her).

Couple B: The 'Ill-Matched Couple'

Mr B was born in 1974 and Mrs B in 1976. They have been living together since 1996 and have been married since 1998. The first child was born in 2001 and their second child in 2006.

At the time of the first interview in 2000 both were studying. Mr B studied at university, Mrs B had been employed in public service and had just begun an academic course in another city. At the time of the joint interview, the couple was expecting their first child. Mrs B was intending to continue her professional career, whereas Mr B was going to interrupt his studies in order to care for the child. Only a few weeks later, during the individual interviews, this was off the agenda: Mrs B now was planning to take her child with her to her place of study where a childminder would take care of it. She was trying hard to reconcile professional development and childcare while he focused on his career. The joint explanation for this was that his career prospects had to be maintained, which is why she was caring for the child.

The monetary arrangement of the couple based on Mrs B's regular income from her employment in public service and on Mr B's contribution of a varying amount to the household earned by means of irregular jobs in the artistic, cultural area. In conversations between the partners two (symbolic) currencies of different value can be reconstructed: her income seems to be valued as 'ordinary' money, which comes from 'normal' employment and is less valuable. In contrast, 'his' money is some kind of 'special', extraordinary money of higher value as it represents his distinctiveness.[18] These two currencies manifest the notions of the intimate relationship: in Mrs B's (romantic) idea of the relationship the partner is central due to individual characteristics and his high individual relevance. On the contrary, Mr B's concept of a 'love relationship' is marked by more individual-pragmatic aspects. Thus the relationship concepts of the partners are diverging: Mrs B has a collectivistic notion while Mr B can be classified as being individualistic (see also Wimbauer 2003: 149ff.).

At the time of the second interview in 2003 Mrs B had finished her studies and was working part-time. Mr B was still studying and earning money through various jobs. Mrs B's money is still considered as 'ordinary' money, while Mr B's money is 'special' money. In contrast to the first interview, however, Mrs B's money is appreciated as she has the role of the breadwinner. Moreover Mr B's spending on antiques has reduced. Mrs B expects that he contributes 'his' money to the family to realize their aims instead of spending on their 'own' behalf. The interview can be characterized as full of suspense as it was apparent that the couple's living arrangement was causing conflicts. The conflicts spark off money matters which disclose diverging notions of chronology and temporality concerning the joint future. For example Mrs B was willing to have a second child and pass the responsibility of financial sustenance of the family to her husband in contrast to Mr B who comments vaguely on this issue.

At the time of the third interview in 2006, their second child had been born. The couple was pressured over the course of time to change the occupational constellation: Mrs B expected to be on parental leave Mr B the breadwinner. Having this expectation finally fulfilled – Mr B graduated and found a job while Mrs B was on parental leave ('at least with one child') – they characterize their relationship as 'marvellous'. Mrs and Mr B adjusted their life conceptions, whereas Mrs B gained a kind of 'prerogative of interpretation' as her husband can be classified being more collectivistic. Additionally this can be illustrated by Mr B's 'special' money which has been reduced further. Due to Mr B's long lasting study and thus an absence of change in his life, the demarcation of own money became fragile and could not be upheld by him.

Starting from a more or less stable arrangement at the first interview, the situation became instable at the second interview due to different schemes of life, or more precisely as a result of different expectations concerning temporality. At the second interview Mr B's inability to implement Mrs B's perception of a proper life together caused a number of conflicts and crises: Mrs B was willing to have a second child, which was not a possibility due to the lack of a male-breadwinner. The instability was finally resolved at the time of the third interview by an adjustment of his life concept to hers, by the occurrence of the formerly missing events and by modifications to their monetary arrangement. This synchronization of biographical perspectives and practices – which is the modification of the relationship concept (primarily his) as well as the monetary arrangement – leads the couple to stability.

The dynamics of intimate relationships – Similarities and differences in the development of couples

The described development of the three couples, their biographies and the synchronization of their lives' courses give profound insights into the maintenance of their relationships. The way money is handled within the relationships indicates how the individuals-in-couples as modern dual-earners constitute themselves as a couple and, related to this, how they synchronize their life together over the course of time. At this point similarities and differences shall be worked out concerning the principles and dynamics of the development of intimate relationships.

According to the empirical findings within every couple changes or reinterpretations of the monetary arrangement can be found to stabilize relationship concepts. For example the Es enable convertibility to maintain their individualistic relationship concepts, or, more concretely, to provide a short-term exchange and to avoid imbalance. Against the background of their asymmetric biographical development, they maintain the stability of their relationship by breaking their attitude of not wanting to get married and adjusting their monetary arrangement: they provide convertibility so as to maintain their relationship concepts, so they still orientate their giving and taking to a short-term balance but with altered currencies.

A similar development can be found within the collectivistic relationship of the Cs. The monetary arrangement – in particular the regime of monitoring – intensified to avoid financial mismanagement which might lead to a filing for insolvency. This modification serves the purpose of keeping the firm going and providing continuity. The relationship concepts remain the same except within the relationship of the Bs: the diverging relationship concepts of the partners which become apparent in their monetary arrangement were causing conflicts. After

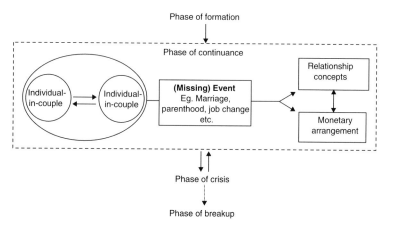

Figure 10.4   The dynamics of intimate relationships – the development of couples

the couple experienced a crisis, Mr B adapted to Mrs B's conception of a proper life arrangement; he became less individualistic. This and the realization of the anticipated but missing events can be found within a rebuilding phase that leads the couple to stability. Thus in the case of diverging relationship concepts, the instability of the relationship is easily conceivable resulting subsequently in a reinterpretation of the relationship concepts.

These couples all being in the phase of continuance show different dynamics in their development. Within every relationship various events happened. Some events and/or anticipated but missing events became critical for the maintenance of the relationship, and others not. This phenomenon – or more precisely the continuance of the relationship – can be explained by the specific interplay of relationship concepts and the monetary arrangements. Figure 10.4 visualizes the dynamics of intimate relationships within the phase of continuance.

The two individuals-in-couples in an intimate relationship have notions of a proper form of living together and of a suitable life course due to internalized schemes of life. When an event (or anticipated but missing event) occurs, this might have an effect on the relationship concept and/or might lead to change or reinterpretation of the monetary arrangement. An absent but necessary adjustment would lead the relationship into instability or at least into the phase of crisis. This phase tends to result either in the breakup of the relationship or in a rebuilding phase, in which the fundaments of the relationship are reinterpreted as well. As a consequence, the synchronization of the relationship concept and the monetary arrangement leads to establishing and maintaining stability.

Finally, in times of social transformation processes the effort of individuals-in-couples increases to adjust their schemes and expectations of life in order to provide an appropriate form of living together. Also in this sense, every (missing) biographical event has to be (more or less consciously) negotiated within the intimate relationship. They have to be construed by the individuals-in-couples to fit in the framework of their relationship instead of getting out of line. The relationship concepts which become apparent in the monetary arrangements are the key to understanding the continuance of a relationship, how the partners establish and maintain stability and which events lead into crisis and/or deterioration. In conclusion, synchronization is more than ever a challenge to be solved by the couples.

Conclusion

In times of individualization, the pluralization of ideas of what a 'good' relationship is and especially the occurring various existing forms of how partners live together lead to the condition that the synchronization of the partners' notions and biographies becomes important for the stability of the couple. In this sense, the obligation of 'synchronization' can be seen as a major rule for the making of couples in individualized modern societies. The process of synchronization can be observed exemplarily by looking at the way money is handled over the course of time.

In this chapter the monetary arrangements of couples in the phase of continuance have been highlighted. We have seen that the maintenance and thus the stability of couples depend on the specific interplay of the individuals-in-couples and their relationship concepts, which include the conception of a proper and satisfied form of living together. They represent the partners' expectations and anticipations concerning the (common and individual) life course. Consequently the partners have internalized norms pertinent to each future stage and anticipate conforming to them at the appropriate points in time when events (such as marriage or the first child) should occur. Some events and/or anticipated but missing events affect the couple's development and will become critical for the maintenance of the relationship, and others not. This is due to the fact that partners might have different plans and expectations. Hence, they have to refer to their notions of a proper way of living together, their own plans and aspirations towards the other person. This process becomes apparent in the handling of money of the individuals-in-couples according to their notions of what a good relationship is or at least should be. Money is symbolically loaded and a medium for the partners to show their prospects. The symbolic meaning of money and its importance for the living together of couples might also be the reason why conflicts in intimate relationships most often are about money matters: it is not just money that is embattled but rather the (common) future of the relationship.

11
Making Families at an Old Age

Dana Sýkorová

The chapter is focused on intergenerational and intragenerational relations in extended family in the later stages of the life course. I will
describe how elderly parents and adult children confirm their belonging
and maintain the limits between them within meetings and exchanges
of support. I will also deal mainly with the situation of the need for
help on the part of the eldest members of the family of origin, which
activates their adult offspring to more intensive getting-together and
providing of assistance.

The specifics of family intergenerational relations are given by
consanguinity and strong emotionality, and the mutual obligations
assigned to them. What is highlighted in this context is the question of
self-(non)evidence of family contacts and exchange of support: is it normatively based exactly on emotional bonds or sense of responsibility,
or is it negotiated, and emotional ties or commitments are not a norm
dictating how to behave, but only a guide-post – *rules*? To answer this
query I apply the theoretical concept of intergenerational *ambivalence*
(Lüscher and Pillemer, 1998; Lüscher, 2002), which refuses to count
definitely upon an influence of obvious cultural norms regulating intergenerational relations, including the scope, level and legitimacy of help
and support, and which also rejects a presupposition of its unshakable
givenness on the basis of the mentioned loyalty and value consensus
of family generations. Thus it clearly contrasts with 'implicitness' or
'unconditionality' of *family solidarity* (Bengtson et al., 1976, 1982, 2002)
on which the structural-functionalist theories of intergenerational relations are founded. The basic terms in my chapter are *assembling*, its role
in the making of families, and *ambivalence*, 'within and round' the *rules*

guiding ordinary family get-togethers and those forced by the necessity of helping the elderly parents.

In the following parts of the chapter I will first describe the methodology of the research, through which the plausibility of the theoretical concept of intergenerational ambivalence or its potential for explaining family intergenerational and intragenerational relations were validated. Then I will present in detail the above-mentioned concept and proceed to the presentation of the results of the analysis of the data gathered. In this 'analytical' part I will deal in detail with outlining ambivalence in family relations, its specifications – mainly the conflict solidarity versus autonomy – and, at the end, the ways of overcoming ambivalences that are used by family generations. In the last subchapter the specific functioning of the rules of genealogy or genealogical proximity and the other identified rules – their concurrence or collision – will be examined.

Data

The qualitative methodology of research project *Seniors in Society. Strategies for the Maintenance of Autonomy in Old Age*, carried out from 2002–5 in the Moravian-Silesian Region of the Czech Republic, helped elucidate the self-definitions of seniors and middle-aged persons as members of the eldest and middle family generations.[1] It facilitates *understanding* the processes of family making – the contexts of family assemblages, their experiencing and meaning ascribed by adult children or elderly parents, including coverage of interdependencies, contradictions and the necessity and rules of negotiating their mutual contacts. Thus the ambivalence of relations within and between family generations clearly emerged from the data.

In the research of *seniors* there were 124 men and 193 women. The age groups of 60–4, 65–9, 70–4 and 75–9 years were represented quite evenly in the sample (approximately one-fifth each), one tenth reached the age of 80–4, and nearly 5 per cent of persons were over 85 years. The sample of *middle-age persons* included people aged 40–60 with at least one parent/parent-in-law alive. The size of this set was 294 people, more than one half of whom was women. The core of the sample was aged between 46 and 55. In the *grounded theory study of seniors* there were 13 women and five men participating, whose average age was 76 years. In the *grounded theory study of adult children* 14 middle-aged persons participated.

Ambivalence in family relations

Consistently with Lüscher and Pillemer (1998), the ambivalence can be understood as the *simultaneous* presence of solidarity and conflict in the relations among family generations. More precisely, on the subjective level ambivalence manifests itself as an emotional dissonance, that is, *parallel* experiencing of both positive and negative emotions. On the level of social structure, that is, on the level of institutional sources and requirements, or statuses, roles and norms, it can be viewed as 'incompatibility of normative expectancy of attitudes, opinions and behaviours', or as opposite normative tendencies contained in the social definition of role (Lüscher and Pillemer, 1998: 416).

According to the authors of the concept, the mentioned *psychological* and *sociological ambivalences* in the relations between parents and children in late adulthood are generated by desire of both sides for frequent interaction, pressure on altruistic support nourished by the 'aura of indissolubility' ascribed to biological kinship (Lüscher, 1999: 5), against which there is an antagonistic tendency to liberation from tying bonds, endeavour and independence, the balance of profits and losses in the exchange.

Lüscher and Pillemer refer to several types of ambivalences imbedded in the family intergenerational relationships: *dependence* versus *autonomy, solidarity* versus *reciprocity* and *solidarity* versus *autonomy*. We can also anticipate the ambivalence developed on the grounds of the clash between adult children's loyalty to the families of origin and their own families of procreation. The incidence of ambivalences probably culminates at the time of a status change. They may also be consequences of the generational distance between parents and children.

Outlining ambivalence

Similar to numerous previous studies, my research proved a relatively high frequency of get-togetherness of seniors and their adult offspring or their families of procreation, positive evaluation of mutual relations and considerable importance ascribed to social bonds to these significant others by them. Both the family generations under consideration show evident continuity of meetings: mutual, emotionally loaded sharing including discussions of family 'problems'. Nevertheless, contacts and relationships between the elderly parents and their adult children are *simultaneously* burdened by tension, stress and contradictions – simply by *ambivalences*.

Thus on the one hand we can see that most seniors feel they are steadily grounded in their families. They usually described with feeling 'what the family means to them'. The strong emotional bound was often concentrated in the laconic statement 'I like them', 'they are my children', 'the meaning of my life', 'they are my closest people, we would breathe for the other'. The presence of the adult children is a 'field of ease and confidence' for the elderly parents – they seek their company. Being in contact, that is, meeting and talking with a certain frequency on common as well as festive occasions, represents an important component of the positive experiencing of mutual relationships for the seniors. The elderly parents' need to meet their offspring is usually higher than the children's declared potentiality. (For example, 'I say if I didn't see them . . . for a long time it would be bad for me. I must see my son every day'.) On the other hand, despite their reliance on their adult children we find at the same time the parents' tendency not to burden their adult children with their personal troubles and also their anxiety about misunderstandings caused by the generational 'gap'. ('There are only few things solved with my family, they are very busy, have their own problems; [. . .] in my age the important things are not discussed aloud, there is no point in it, the young ones don't understand us.') Concurrently the elderly parents do not feel only fine side by side their adult offspring – it was not an exception when they gave their children as a source of their problems. Contacts with these close ones often bother them: 'I like them but I like my peace, a lot of people stress me [. . .] sometimes it's too much for me and they don't understand that one moment I'm talking and laughing and the next moment I'm falling asleep and I'd prefer to be alone. I feel I'm losing my "social stamina"'.

Adult children likewise grant their elderly parents an important position in their lives, again often concentrated in the statement 'they are my parents'. As the wider context shows, it especially means having an emotional hinterland and a source of support in them. In the older middle age, from the age-based perspective over their life course and in particular with their own experience of a parental role, the adult children accentuate yet another dimension of their ties to elderly parents: the parents 'brought them up and sent them into life'. The children talked of relatively frequent and regular meetings with their elderly parents and of their endeavour to see mother and father as much as possible. As a rule, they visit their parents without any particular reason – they meet for a cup of coffee or tea, or a common lunch. From their point of view, the contacts with their parents are most frequently filled with 'talking of anything that comes along': they 'discuss life' of family members, successes and joys, and failures and worries. Impulses to get together are gardening or family trips and an integrating part of family life consists of birthday parties, celebrations of personal or family anniversaries or holidays such as Christmas. (For example, 'on holidays, days-off we take the occasion to meet and it's very nice . . . We visit each other in our spare time, never miss common celebrations'.) The children also express an understanding of the meaning of the contacts for their parents and their demand to see them more frequently. But contrary to this, rather than the parents' presumed expectations, they respect their own capacity and their own autonomy or capacity and the autonomy of their families of procreation ('certainly our meetings should be more frequent. But with regard to their time demandingness it is not possible. I live my life as well; . . . If it would be necessary I could do more. This way it seems optimum to me. I don't force myself into anything unnecessary'.)

The adult children place their present relationship with their elderly parents into the framework of emotional bonds and mutual understanding developed in their life-long interaction. ('As I know them for a really long time I have no problem to cope with them because we understand each other.') Nevertheless they do not base their recent approach to them in explicitly expressed respect and esteem. They love their elderly parents; yet the parents are not an authority whom adult children would grant the right to intervene in their decision making. The children strongly emphasized the unbinding character of their elderly parents' advices and directives. None of them chose their parents to be their confidants. The ambivalence also shows in a way that loving adult children confess at the same time tensions and conflicts in the interaction with their parents. As the source of stress, misunderstanding or clashes are designated to their parents' mental state, their moodiness, character features, opinions – mainly if the parents try to assert them – and their inability or unwillingness to accept the adulthood of their offspring ('we want to be with her but she has her whims; [. . .] it's not always easy because my mum [. . .] frequently requires attention; [. . .] Sometimes mum asserts herself too much and unnecessarily. She hasn't noticed that I'm adult already [. . .] from her good will she asserts organization – of life. She believes that I should also act so. She knows 'better' what and how I should do. These are only petty things but sometimes our cup runs over. [. . .] She tends to give advices and lead by example. She applies the so-called mild psychological pressure. [. . .] Mom doesn't order but suggests! Even ten times until she gets her way. When I do it my way she will probably take offence.'). It is because adult children ascribe great significance to mutual respect – to personal autonomy above all ('it's about mutual tolerance and understanding [. . .] I'm not interested in intervening into my parents' life as well as they don't intervene into mine'). They say they would not dare intervene into their parents' issues and according to their experience the parents would not allow it (because 'they are an independent unit'). The adult children appreciate very much if their parents do not burden them with their own problems, do not favour any of the children, do not remonstrate, and can admit their faults and apologize.

The results of the data analysis support the theses about the ambivalent character of intergenerational contacts and relationships: the elderly parents and their adult children are apparently involved in various get-togethers. Through the assemblages the connectedness and belongingness of both the family generations are manifested. They experience their mutual relations mostly positively as 'balanced', with a high level of intimacy and one's clear interest in the other – despite the realized tensions and conflicts which arise from higher expectations and the reality of togetherness clashing with the individuals' endeavour to keep their personal autonomy. Thus the interactions of both the family generations are characterized by perceived *closeness* parallel to *distance*, *reward* to *burden*, *solidary* behaviour to '*selfish*' respect for privacy, independence, and one's own needs and interests at the same time. This is how they create the image of psychological and sociological ambivalence (Lüscher and Pillemer, 1998). Its specifications will be elaborated in the following subchapter.

Solidarity versus autonomy

The clash of the key values *solidarity – autonomy*, or *dependence – autonomy* visible in 'everyday' family gatherings comes forth in situations of intensification of interactions between the elderly parents and their adult children. As suggested above, there is a considerable scope for real face-to-face communication to open a space for emotional dissonance in the relations of family generations. As well as a higher risk of dissatisfaction, stress and conflicts it also contains limits to independence. As stated by Hamm and Jałowiecki (1990), a certain physical distance allows the control of social interaction.

The seniors from my research relate these risks mainly to receiving help from their adult children. While interaction with adult children and their families presents an important strategy of maintaining their autonomy, for the seniors the threat of its narrowing is also perceived – more or less intensively according to the type and amount of assistance. Although on the one hand the elderly parents see a source of help in their adult children, on the other hand they resist using it. Among other things, the limiting pressure on parents' 'proper' behaviour is present in their children's involvement.

Seniors consider their adult children's 'duties' to them as their parents, but for themselves they emphasize their own personal responsibility. They approach their children as an emotionally strong base that can get mobilized 'in case of emergency'. They do not want to burden their children, do not want to be beholden to them. (For example, 'I don't need help, my wife and me can do all [. . .] it's only about the feeling that if something happens help from the family would be good; [. . .] everybody should take care of oneself first. The family is necessary but one has to start on one's own first [. . .]; [. . .] I ask my daughter or son but usually daughter. But I don't want to burden them too much, they have their own problems; [. . .] I prefer to help myself. It's better than to hear that he or she helped me and then I have to return it'.)

The qualitative study discovered negative emotions related especially to the idea of seniors' total dependence on help from their adult children, and at the same time positive feelings of parents given by the belief that they can possibly rely on such help (and, contrary to it, worries expressed by them about the shakiness of support or, more precisely, its conditionality on the children's limited capacities). Thus the elderly parents' approach is reminiscent of the theoretical concept of *latent matrix* (Riley, 1983) or *rescue, safety network* (Finch, 1989).

When it comes to debates about ensuring exceptionally demanding personal care the seniors' responses reveal vagueness of children's 'commitments' to their parents and parents' 'rights' to their children, or indistinctiveness of values, 'norms' entering the negotiation of both generations very openly: although most elderly parents in fact exclude care from their families, they describe the institutional solution as a way out for 'old people who are alone'. But in the end they admit help from their children, even moving in with them: according to seniors 'the family knows best what their elderly parents need'. ('I wouldn't even be against moving into an institution, it's better than bothering my family – I believe that my family wouldn't put me into an institution; [. . .] I'm not happy that I have to keep asking my daughter for help but I don't want to be looked after by a stranger.')

At the same time that the seniors *implicitly* expect their adult children's openness towards the needs of parents, they *explicitly* acknowledge the priority position of the family of procreation in their children's lives. This obvious ambivalence, which is a clash of the 'norm' of independence and solidarity, nevertheless results in a reduction of parents' own expectations and respect for the borders of their adult children's privacy – what Matthews called *altruistic surrender* (1979). But it seems that the situation of effective total self-insufficiency is absolutely different: the emphasis of seriously ill, very old immobile seniors on the personal autonomy of themselves and their children gives ground to the acceptance of dependence and the requisition of their children's solidarity. Afterwards, for these parents, it is important that their adult children take care and whether they will be able or want to continue in taking it.

The children at the same time appreciate their parents' independence and often interpret effort at it as stubbornness. The parents' adherence to self-sufficiency may be a source of conflicts. Ambivalence is often developed around the clash of the values of elderly parents' autonomy and of protection of their health or safety. (For example, 'sometimes mom complains about her legs aching but usually she does everything for herself without asking us for help and then she's worn-out but she must (!) do it on her own; [. . .] she doesn't even want me to wash windows for her although I keep telling her that she will fall and what will happen then [. . .] she's stubborn'.) The responses of some adult children leak paternalism – a slight, 'considerate' pressure on their elderly parents, shielded by 'the best intentions', imposing of 'their parents' good' defined by the children themselves. Nevertheless, children usually attempt to respect their parents' autonomous decisions when providing help.

Elderly parents' self-sufficiency is a determinant of adult children's own autonomy. Children fear the loss of this value when debating the parents' perspective or real dependency. They agree that 'one should help because they are the parents and it's the children's moral duty' and the majority of them emphatically declared their preparedness to help. But the adult children *immediately* pointed out the limits of their own capacity to ensure wider and regular assistance, mostly pointing out their job duties and in many cases explicitly their own autonomy in their private and family life. Here some other already mentioned ambivalence emerges: adult children's loyalty to the family of origin *versus* loyal relation to the family of procreation. Lüscher and Pillemer (1998: 419) refer to studies that reveal children's deep feeling of guilt of this experienced contradiction.

Although I may conclude on the basis of my research that 'there are always some of the adult children who finally help' their elderly parents, overtaking the responsibility for help and accepting the constraints on their own autonomy is hard to negotiate. The given examples demonstrate a considerable complexity of relations among these closest relatives connected by means of mutual dependencies – *interdependencies* consisting of tension as well as cooperation. A long time ago – at the birth of the 'empty-nest' – the mutual relations of parents and their adult children have shifted to a qualitatively different level: both the family generations have found and developed their own autonomy. The intensification of contacts as a result of their need for help on the part of the elderly parents in the late phase of their life course may bring up the ambivalence as a collision of the established autonomy and lately developed dependency: let us say autonomy and solidarity.

In the following part of the chapter I will focus on the ways how both the family generations cope with the ambivalences.

Negotiation as a strategy to cope with ambivalence

The rules, as implicitly or explicitly (re-)negotiated knowledge of family members as to the ways of acting in certain situations, present guideposts in the context of coping with ambivalence in relations between elderly parents and their adult children; at the same time these guideposts maintain mutual distance and closeness.

Both the generations express their interest in maintaining good relations, which, above all, means *avoiding tensions and conflicts*. Respecting this rule is related to the tactics of willingness and tolerance, readiness to oblige, 'peace offering' and compromises, as well as respect for the others, their self-esteem, well-being and, last but not least, their privacy, independency and autonomous decision making.

So the elderly parents do more or less their best to meet their children's wishes and requirements: if the frequency of mutual contacts is in the end 'directed' by the middle generation, the elderly parents conform themselves to it. They backtrack in the case of misunderstandings and clashes. For example, a *Foster*, a target of rivalling children, is grateful when they at least call him sometimes. Mrs *Hana* tries to 'find her way' to her son and daughter-in-law despite the inconsistency of values and life styles and the perceived disrespect. The adult children try to explain their viewpoints and understand their parents' views, keep 'dispassionate opinions' – they 'nod assent' to their parents' advices or tactfully pass possible tampering, try to 'quietly escape from the situation' etc. Some mentioned respect for their parents' age and dignity ('unfortunately, they enforce their opinion, doubt my independence.

I try not to be bothered – regarding their age. [. . .] We are tactful of our parents and nod approval to them smiling – silently – and do it our way. We try to protect our parents from stress and the feeling of helplessness and not the feeling of that they are no good and use for their daughters. There's always a circumstance when our parents are happy they can give us advice according to their abilities'). Both the parents and children subject the contents of talks and information communicated to selection; they 'conveniently' adjust information ('sometimes I sit with my parents and talk about problems but I don't confide in them – I don't have anything positive, don't tell them about the negative ones, I don't want to stress them'). Clearly they stick to the interaction rules and rituals: according to Goffman (1967) it is in the interest of both the generations not to endanger interaction, to get approval of the other party but at the same time to protect their own independence. The elderly parents must respect their adult children and let them create and confirm their identity; the same applies to the children's relation to their parents. Both the family generations thus participate in maintaining the interactional order.

Also following applied procedures or accepted rules is used both to remove or weakening stress and conflicts and to protect personal autonomy – not only with regard to mutual relations of the elderly parents and their adult children but also to the *identity of Self* in each other: the strategies of reinterpretation of *meaning* or *apologizing* allows the parents and children to acceptably explain a disadvantageous situation, maintain mental distance from it and thus – again also in the given case – to cope with ambivalences of autonomy and personal dependence or solidarity. For example, children describe their parents' occasional attempts to intervene into their decision-making as advices driven by their parents' good intentions as a 'natural part' of parenthood ('Yes – it happens. No success, we know that it's common. Parents will be parents until their death. They feel responsibility for their children and belonging to them until their death'). The elderly parents, for instance, interpret the necessary help from their adult children as a demonstration of strong emotional bonds, point out their hitherto deposit into their mutual relationship. They excuse their possible disappointment at rarer personal meetings due to the children's workload, accentuate their dependability, compare themselves to their peers in senior age who 'don't have family, are alone' and thus are in an 'even worse' situation. The parents emphasize that they 'keep the children's private life in mind'. ('When I feel a need, well, I pop in to my son's. But it's not very often because they don't have time, both of them work, they get up at half past three in the morning so they want to have some rest Saturday and Sunday.')

Parents look for 'substitutive sources of gratification': they get satisfaction from the fact that their children 'turned out well', give them joy, are successful at demanding, ambitious work and from the 'certainty that they think of them, the parents and help them when needed'. The adult children convince the others, and probably themselves too, that the parents are satisfied with their situation and that under the given circumstances the children 'do as much as possible' ('my wife and me work and don't have much time during weekdays. [. . .] After work there's not much time left for my father. Because when you work on shifts of twelve hours you want only to sleep afterward.') These mechanisms remind us of negotiating structured bonds in a family, that is, the *discussion of legitimacy of excuses* (Connidis and McMullin, 2002). By means of them what the relatives can or cannot fulfil in the confrontation with expected or internalized family responsibilities is negotiated.

The strategies or tactics thus described can be interpreted in the context of Mead's concept of Self (1997): they show that even in the parents' old age and the children's adulthood it how they are perceived and whether they are accepted exactly by the significant others has a great significance for creating their Selves. They strengthen the others' consciousness of adequate fulfilment of their fundamental roles of a good parent and a good child.

The next examples reveal both the elderly parents and adult children negotiating maintenance of control over their get-togetherness, help received and provided: many elderly parents try to regulate their social contacts with adult children in the meaning of 'when they (seniors) want and need'. They eliminate or, on the contrary, create opportunities to meet their children and accommodate their expectations. They make an effort to be self-sufficient and independent in their everyday activities, in funding their needs and decision-making. If they cannot get by without help from their children they strive to return it. It is just *observance of reciprocity* in exchange that mostly ensures the management of autonomy in social relations. The elderly parents also act as the main agents of negotiating assistance, its organization and 'parameters'. It is they who not only define the need for help, but who in reality decide about what/when/from which child they will accept it. They limit the assistance to exceptional occasions or specific activities, to such kind and scope of help they do not regard as obliging towards their children and burdening them. Not least the elderly parents combine sources of help and thus diffuse their dependency on children's or others' aid into the social space of informal networks. Adult children, on the other hand, mostly do not force their help and assist 'only when asked by parents', give advice without requiring their acceptance, rely on assumptions that their parents can manage, or that they will eventually ask them for help. Thus the children's engagement primarily develops according to the principle *help only when and as needed*.

Beside rather implicit, 'silent' negotiation of interaction rules between the elderly parents and their adult children, the negotiations among siblings tend to be more explicit or 'louder' and their assistance to parents openly discussed. The siblings control *fairness* of their shares more strictly with regard to time availability, geographical proximity, or competency, sources, gender or real or anticipated share of inheritance. It seems that the siblings' relationships are characterized by rivalry even in their adult age. For example, 'sometimes I'm sorry that my sister doesn't show enough interest in our father. [. . .] Yeah, they think I should visit her more often, 'you should do this and that', they think 'you've got the house so take care'; [. . .] my brother and sister with her family, I feel that they rather bring our mother's grey hairs to the grave. My brother is in debt, hasn't come and seen mother for several years, and when he came he only asked her for money. My sister gets along with her very well, as the only daughter – mother relies on her. But I noticed that rather than her listening to mother it's the other way round.') But the parallel 'counter tendency' is evident: the complaints against siblings are often balanced by the aspiration to 'vindicate' them and debate about the organization of assemblages and help given to their parents usually passes off smoothly, without conflicts. Finally, even from the perspective of the middle generation, the extended family seems to be a relatively dense network of reliable support.

Among the mechanisms for how one generation or the other copes with ambivalences in their mutual relationships found in my research, the patterns of Lüscher's types of strategies can be more or less identified: (1) consensual solidarity, that is, 'reliable support and preparedness to pay or provide services that are not reciprocal' and 'exercising one's authority in the others' behalf' (*to preserve consensually*); (2) legitimization of requirements by means of referring to institutionalized bonds, putting moral pressure on the others (*to conserve reluctantly*); (3) emancipated relations of *equals* within developed social relations (*to mature reciprocally*); and (4) divergence, atomization of relations in extended family (*to separate conflictingly*) (Lüscher, 1999: 18–20).

Conclusion

In this chapter I focused on relations between parents and children, and among children in the later stages of their life course. The research findings prove that they are a jumble of interdependences, a mixture of contradictory feelings and expectations of and tendencies towards closeness and distance. They are also characterized by ease, engagement in personal sharing and willingness to 'pull at the same end of the rope', as well as tension, avoiding the others, family 'responsibility' and the perceived continuity of family generation, and at the same time discontinuity in relationships. Thus let me emphasize, in correspondence with Lüscher and Pillemer, the *ambivalent*, rather than solidary, character of intergenerational or intragenerational relations in the extended family. Cohesion of a family system is *negotiated* in the framework of family assembling, what is especially difficult with providing assistance to elderly parents. Finch and Mason presented relational exchange as a complex process of open, or hidden, latent negotiation, 'not closed in exact and logical schemes'. We can see that in the negotiations the ambivalence between *solidarity* and *autonomy*, especially, is managed through the mostly implicit, 'unspoken' rules guiding get-togetherness and exchange of help and support.

Family ties are organized by the *rule of genealogy* or genealogical proximity. In the words of Jallinoja, 'genealogy generates social bonds'. Nevertheless the rule is not applied unconditionally; the adult children especially do not respect their parents' authority, do not meet them and do not help them not only or just because they are bound together by blood. In the end, blood kinship is not a pillar of parents' expectations about their adult children either. The scope, intensity or content and the experienced quality of mutual contacts and relations are affected by a number of other factors included in the life situation of the members of both the family generations. Elderly parents, as well as adult children, pay regard to their partners, and children significantly also to their families of procreation. In this context a specific influence of the rule of monogamy can be regarded as preference of kinship by marriage to blood kinship (see Jallinoja, this volume) and also the *rule of priority of family of procreation* that brings back the importance of genealogy through the adult child's marriage and cohabitation.

Relations between the elderly parents and adult children are clearly about maintaining their autonomy – not only as individuals but also as constituents of a couple or a family of procreation: the strategy of keeping boundaries is partly based on the *rule of controlling contacts and exchange of support* by means of active regulation of their quantitative and qualitative parameters stated above, but primarily on the *rule of reciprocity*. The importance of reciprocity as a general rule of functioning of kinship was mentioned by Finch (1989) and Finch and Mason (1993), De Singly (1999) and others. The rule applies also to reciprocity of respect to the others' autonomy: the parents' respect to their children and vice versa.

Reciprocal behaviour is a part of the 'strategy of good relations', or avoiding conflicts, applied by both the generations. The *rule to avoid conflict* means, furthermore, to adjust oneself, to reduce one's expectations about the others, to eliminate discrepancies, to be tolerant and to interpret the others' behaviour in a positive way, to excuse them. Overcoming the contradictions is carried out in mutual 'concert' of elderly parents and adult children as partners in interaction. Both the negotiating parties essentially try to 'do what they want others to do to them and not to do what do not wish from others'.

As can be assumed, this is supported by life-long-communicated needs and goals, or by an internalized 'set of attitudes or responses that stands for the group', constituting experiential knowledge (Mead in Carreira da Silva, 2007: 53). The research findings presented can be approached from the viewpoint of Mead's idea that the elderly parents or adult children are able to look at themselves through the eyes of the others – children or parents, to see the world from the perspective of the others. It means that both of them are able to 'import into their conduct a behavioural disposition to respond in a similar way to the other responding to a given type of stimulus' (ibid.: 4, 53). Both the elderly parents and the adult children try, in Goffman's words, to stick to ceremonial codes of deference and demeanour, to contribute to the common interpretation of a situation within the interactional rituals. The result of this – what Bourdieu calls symbolic and practical endeavour, 'complex symbolic alchemy' (and what I have described as functioning of rules) – is, in the end, just that absence of significant conflict of family generations and the presence of confidence as the fundamental feature of their relationship (Bourdieu, 1998: 131).

By means of examples I have proved the potential of the theoretical concept of ambivalence for explaining the merit of sibling relationships in adulthood. Ambivalences become even more evident, 'perpetory', in the interaction of siblings than in interaction between the elderly parents and their children; the rules of negotiation are rather explicit, 'pronounced', respecting the mutual equality (see the *rule of equality*, Maillochon and Castrén, this volume). Through the research findings of the adult siblings it is possible to observe the operation of the *rule of emotional proximity* which is referred to in different contexts by Jallinoja in this book. The siblings point out the elderly parents' different approaches to each child: 'they love one more than the others, visit them more often, help them more'.

To summarize, concerning Lüscher and Pillemer's concept of intergenerational ambivalence, I share the opinion that it represents an important way of understanding the complexity of family relationships. The empirical conclusions we reached indicate the compatibility of the accepted theoretical approach and the configurational perspective, or the concept of relationality. It is not only that the focus on kin 'itself' means to think relationally (Finch and Mason, 1993, 2000) but the data show mainly relations and mutual dependency of the generation of elderly parents and that of adult children as a result of repeated relational makings in the variety of their interactions – informal get-togethers, events, family crisis, etc. – especially in exchanges of help and support.

Let us sum the chapter up with a note: the family of origin consisting of elderly parents and adult children 'revives' in everyday visits as well as joint family celebrations. As one of the grown-up sons concisely said, meeting one's parents 'still brings back memories of one's childhood, a special pleasant nostalgia'. The specific revival induces a situation when the elderly parents need assistance. And it is the organization of help and providing and receiving it that reacknowledges the belonging of parents and children.

12
Reassembling Families after Divorce

Ulrike Zartler

Since the end of the twentieth century, divorce has been increasingly regarded not as a discrete event disrupting family life, but rather as a complex process that reshapes and restructures relationships between family members (Amato, 2000; Smart, 2004). Divorce results, in this conception, not in the dissolution of family life, but rather in a reorganization and transition of the family system. Marital disruption is regarded as a complex process that begins while the couple lives together and ends long after legal divorce is concluded. Research based on this model shifts from a household perspective to a perspective of family relationships and a long-term perspective of family dynamics. The process of reorganization implies changes for the whole family and the macro systems surrounding the family (Cowan and Hetherington, 1991; Fthenakis, 1995).

In contrast to a disorganization model of divorce (Théry, 1988), which is far from being adequate in terms of modern families' realities, I focus on a divorce-stress-adjustment perspective, the family boundary ambiguity model, and reflect on subjective reality construction inspired by the interpretative paradigm in order to develop a subjectivistic approach towards divorce. The divorce-stress-adjustment perspective, based on family stress theory (Hill, 1949), views marital dissolution as a stressful transition for all family members (Amato, 2000; Amato and Booth, 1997; Hetherington, 1999; Pryor and Rodgers, 2001). Events that people experience as stressful – so-called stressors – increase the risk of negative emotional, behavioural, and health outcomes for adults and children. Moderators, by contrast, can be regarded as protective factors and weaken the extent of negative outcomes following divorce.

The concept of family boundary ambiguity refers to a state in which family members 'are uncertain in their perception about who is in or out of the family and who is performing what roles and tasks within the family system' (Boss and Greenberg, 1984: 536). This concept is based on a symbolic interaction perspective and assumes that family boundaries are determined rather by perceptions than by structures. From this point of view, divorce can be regarded as an ambiguous situation of loss and may have an increased potential for boundary ambiguity, which could present a barrier to post-divorce reorganization. Along with other outcomes, the lack of clarity with respect to family membership is associated with family stress, dysfunctional relationships, low quality of the couples' relationship, diminished parental involvement, increased levels of parental conflict and dissatisfaction with parenting (Boss, 1980; Madden-Derdich et al., 1999; Peterson and Christensen, 2002; Stewart, 2005).

Applying the methodological approach of an interpretative paradigm, social actors themselves construct and model social reality, and perception of this reality depends on the perspective (Blumer, 1969). Therefore, family research has to bear in mind the relevance of different family members' subjective experience and interpretation: they are crucial for the perception of a situation, for the perceived chances to act, and finally also for implemented action. Men and women may have different perceptions of their marriage (Gager and Sanchez, 2003). This is the reason why Jessie Bernard (1972) refers to 'his' and 'her' marriage. Consequently, I suggest that we should refer to 'his' and 'her' divorce. Accordingly, the children's perspectives on family change should be integrated. In sum, our subjectivistic approach considers that there is no such construct as 'the' divorce that could be retrieved empirically. Different members of the same family make varying experiences and have varying perceptions. We can only make statements on divorce according to the perceptions of a specific child, a specific woman or a specific man. Post-divorce families, similarly to other families, come into existence through repeated and interdependent relational makings. This chapter focuses on the variety of interactions that construct relationality between post-divorce family members.

Reassembling families after a divorce is a complex process, as the family transition frames the family configuration and the relationships between different family members. Family configurations are, 'to a great extent, built on a bilateral basis, separating relationships further from one another' (Jallinoja, 2008: 107). Personal relationships, especially those with their parents, have been found to play a critical role in children's adjustment following parental divorce (Hetherington, 2003; Smart, 2004, 2007a), and to influence the making of post-divorce family configurations. Therefore, this chapter places special emphasis on the relationships between children and their parents. It is empirically based on a transdisciplinary Austrian study[1] that aimed at understanding the complex post-divorce transformation process for children, women and men (Zartler et al., 2004). The included disciplines were sociology, psychology, therapy, economy and law. Besides other empirical approaches, we conducted in-depth interviews with members of families who had experienced a divorce or separation[2] three to five years previously. Interview partners were the divorced/separated mother, father and their child/children aged 9 to 14; thus, at least three members of each family were included. In total, we conducted 40 interviews in 12 families and interviewed 12 mothers, 12 fathers and 16 children. The interviews were conducted in one urban area (Vienna, with high infrastructural standards and a high divorce rate) and one rural area (southern Burgenland, a socio-economically disadvantaged area with a low divorce rate). The sample did not include individuals from clinical contexts. The partnerships before divorce/separation had lasted between 7 and 20 years. In all families, children lived with their custodial mother and were in contact with their non-custodial father. The interview guidelines were based on open questions covering various pre- and post-divorce dimensions. Therapists, who participated in an intensive training, carried out the interviews separately with each family member. The interview partners' relevance systems structured the interviews rather than the dimensions represented in the topic guide (Froschauer and Lueger, 2003; Strauss and Corbin, 1990). The interviews lasted between one and 2.5 hours. All interviews were transcribed and analyzed in gender-mixed groups by means of an extensive single-case analysis.

The chapter is structured as follows: the following section describes family configurations and matters of inclusion and exclusion after divorce. In the main section, empirical results regarding three family relationships that play an important role in the post-divorce reorganizational process are analyzed, namely the relationships between child, and mother and father, respectively, and the co-parental relationship. The chapter ends with some concluding remarks.

Inclusion and exclusion: Family configurations after divorce

Divorce has a major influence on family configuration and might break down the family composition by including or excluding different members. Post-divorce families are not necessarily well-defined social entities, based on the existence of clear borders. On the contrary, family boundaries stretch back and forth, change over time, and family formation is a permanently ongoing process. A configurational approach emphasizes the interdependencies among different family members regarding dyadic relationships and their families as a whole. Families, in this regard, are conceptualized as 'configurations or sets of directly or indirectly interdependent persons sharing feelings of family belonging and connectedness' (Widmer et al., 2008: 3). Family configurations determine who is regarded as being a member of that family, they shape the boundaries of inclusion and exclusion within the family, and specify members' rights, responsibilities and expectations towards other family members. Divorce can influence these subjective family conceptions, as it questions who is in and who is out of that particular family. Members of the 'original' nuclear family may be excluded, and new family members (such as new partners or their children) may take their place. So we have to look carefully at whether and how transition processes influence processes of inclusion and exclusion.

Empirical evidence suggests that family configurations after divorce are shaped in a very individual way and that post-divorce family construction can be different for every single family 'member' (Ganong and Coleman, 2004; Rosenberg and Guttmann, 2001; Schmitz and Schmidt-Denter, 1999). Each of them 'may share only a small percentage of his or her significant family members with other persons in the household' (Widmer, 2006: 978), and each of them has to draw new lines of inclusion or exclusion with regard to the question: who is (still) part of *my* family? These constructions might result in complex challenges for all involved individuals and might make it difficult to develop a common family identity after divorce. Qualitative interviews reveal that such configurations often vary between family members, in particular perceptions of children and their parents may differ substantially (Berger, 1998; Smart et al., 2001).

This is also the case for our data. We used a free listing technique, asking our interview partners who, in their perception, were part of their family. All mothers and fathers regarded their children as part of their 'new' post-divorce families, also if they had remarried, had stepchildren or children with their new partners. This is in line with Jallinoja's (2008: 115) findings that parents and children are usually the nucleus of family configurations (see also Castrén, 2008). Living in a common household was no criterion for integrating children into the subjective family definition, and in many cases the child was the only connection between the divorced parents (described similarly by Widmer, 2006). Most mothers included their new partners and their children into their family configuration. On the contrary, the fathers rather tended to exclude their new partners, even when sharing a household. Interestingly, none of the mothers credited their former partner with the status of a family member,[3] while several fathers regarded their ex-wives as still being part of their family.

The children interviewed estimated the task to list up their family members as challenging and gave the impression that family structure after parental divorce can be complex and confusing, as illustrated by one girl: 'I don't know ... well, I couldn't write it down, I'd need a year to do so" (Valerie, ten years old). The children in this study were very much oriented towards their former nuclear family; usually all members of that family of origin still belonged to their family system: from their point of view, there had been no reduction of family members after parental separation. All children included their mothers, fathers and biological siblings. In most cases, grandparents or other kin were included as well. Only few children included their (resident or non-resident) step-parents and step-siblings. To summarize: biological relatedness was a very clear boundary and a salient aspect of children's representations of their families (see also Dunn et al., 2002). Residency, on the contrary, was not of primary importance with regard to inclusion and exclusion. The children's family configurations were not limited to the nuclear or binuclear family, and the children were rather inclusive in who they considered to be members of their post-divorce family, at least with regard to biological kin. The children placed a specific importance on the quality of relationships: their definitions of family comprised elements of care, support and commitment, and children frequently mentioned affective factors when talking about who was part of their family (Rigg and Pryor, 2007; Smart et al., 2001). In accordance with Carroll et al. (2007) we found children's views of family boundaries to be related to the post-divorce relationships with their parents (see also Ahrons, 2007; Hetherington, 2003; Smart, 2004; 2007a). Therefore, the following section will focus on children's relationships with their mothers and fathers.

Mother–child relationship

The relationship between children and their mothers is in many cases a factor of stability and constancy for children experiencing parental divorce (Wallerstein et al., 2000). Due to prevalent role models and custodial patterns, children usually spend more time with their mothers after a divorce than with their fathers, and only few children experience a reduction of contact with their mothers. This may be one reason why children often describe the relationships with their mothers as positive and warm (Moxnes, 2003). The majority of children in our study reported having a stable and secure relationship with their mothers and described them as being empathic, warm, supportive and responsive to their needs. The children interviewed reported a low level of conflict, as their mothers' parenting behaviour was consistent and reasonable. Nevertheless, a minority of children reported having an ambivalent or problematic relationship with their mother, characterized by feelings of insecurity and the impression that their wishes and needs were not taken seriously. Maternal time and availability was an important factor: most of these children wished their mothers could spend more time with them.

Mothers and fathers described the post-divorce mother–child relationship in most cases as being empathic, deep and trustful – the parents did not perceive ambivalent or problematic relationships, as one part of the interviewed children did. Almost all (custodial) mothers were satisfied with the relationship with their children and with the amount of time they could spend with them. Also the fathers judged the relationships between their children and their ex-partners as highly positive. Even fathers in a state of ongoing conflict with their former spouses conceded a high quality of parenting to them and appreciated their maternal abilities, 'I really have to tell you, she never was a bad mother, my ex-wife, really, and I know it's difficult' (Mr Weidinger). One father was no longer in direct contact with his former spouse due to ongoing conflict, but admitted nevertheless, 'She isn't that bad a mother' (Mr Baumann). To summarize, all groups of interviewees (children, mothers and fathers) regarded maternal involvement and inclusion in post-divorce families as one important factor for children's development and for establishing a positive climate in post-divorce families.

Father–child relationship

Relationships between children and fathers are one of the most important moderating variables in the course of the post-divorce reorganizational process. There is a broad consensus regarding the importance of continued contact between fathers and children for children's well-being (Amato and Gilbreth, 1999; Hetherington, 2003; Juby et al., 2007; Lamb, 2002). Accordingly, one of the key factors for children's perceptions of family boundaries following a divorce is their relationship with their fathers. In this respect, father–child relationships are of utmost importance for reassembling processes in post-divorce families. Fathers most frequently turn out to be the non-custodial parent after divorce. Traditional visiting patterns often foresee a relatively strict visiting plan, according to the schedule 'every other weekend for one or two overnight stays'. In order to maintain closeness between fathers and children, more differentiated parenting plans and shared custody models are up for discussion (Bauserman, 2002; Haugen, 2010; Kelly, 2007). The literature suggests that frequency and continuity of contact as well as schedule consistency are important for children's positive psychological and social adjustment and their long-term well-being (Amato et al., 2009; Pruett et al., 2004). Although new models of custody are on the rise, all children in our sample had non-custodial fathers. Children's, mothers' and fathers' opinions concerning custodial arrangements, contact frequency and emotional aspects attached to the father–child relationship differed considerably in our study.

Almost all interviewed mothers agreed that a positive father–child relationship is of utmost importance for their children's development. Therefore, they reported their own efforts to promote that relationship – or, at least, not to counteract paternal contacts with their child. Some mothers were critical that it was often the children's task to make appointments and to handle contact with their fathers. The interviewed mothers emphasized the relevance of transparent, though unrestrictive, contact patterns. The majority of mothers supposed their children to have empathic and warm relationships with their fathers. The quality of the co-parental relationship acted as a moderating variable: only mothers who had no severe conflicts with their ex-partners estimated the father–child relationship as positive. This is opposite to what we observed for fathers, as described above.

The fathers interviewed described the relationships with their children as rather positive, warm and empathic. All fathers were in contact with their children, and the contacts were – in the fathers' views – in most cases clearly arranged and regular (most often: every other weekend). Handling visiting arrangements was, in the fathers' perceptions, mainly influenced by two factors: priority was given to the children's wishes and needs regarding frameworks and organization of contact patterns. Several fathers, above all those still living in the vicinity of their children after divorce, were very positive about the fact that their children could always come and see them, as children didn't have to commute. In the fathers' views, this made arrangements needless, as the child could drop in 'whenever she wants' (Mr Baumann).

The second important factor was the role of their ex-partners who – even when being positive in terms of father–child contacts – were at times perceived as gatekeepers with a grave influence on the father–child relationship. If fathers had formed new unions, their new partners mainly stayed with them during the visiting weekends and spent that time together with the children. The interviewed fathers argued that their new spouses were now part of their lives and that their children were supposed to accept this as a matter of fact.

From the children's points of view, maintaining contact with their father was important for all family members. The children confirmed their parents' picture that they had contact with their fathers, mainly on weekends. But in contrast to the mothers' and fathers' statements, the children did not perceive these contacts as regular – more than half of the children reported irregular, sporadic and rather spontaneous contacts with their fathers. Some children had the impression that it was their role to take the initiative, as their father would not make a commitment. There were also remarkable discrepancies between fathers' and children's views regarding arrangements of visits. In the children's experience, it was the father's timetables and job requests that mainly structured their contacts – no child felt that his or her own wishes and needs had priority regarding custody arrangements, as the fathers had argued. Contact on a 'whenever you want' basis did not seem appropriate for the interviewed children: they did not consider this to be a positive, participatory option, but rather interpreted it as their fathers' lack of interest and responsibility. In general, children only had very limited possibilities to influence modes and frequency of contact. Although only a minority of children was satisfied with contact and visiting arrangements, they saw no possibilities for altering the situation.

Regarding qualitative aspects of the father-child relationship, the most important factor from the children's point of view was being certain that they were important to and loved by their fathers. This was manifest for children not only through emotional affection, but also through time spent together and the fathers' commitment regarding visiting contacts. Children with (perceived) frequent and regular contact with their father were mainly satisfied with the emotional aspects of the father–child relationship. In contrast, those children who were unsatisfied or unhappy with the relationship with their fathers often experienced a decline in contact without understanding why this had happened, had irregular contacts and/or did not experience their fathers' active involvement. The children themselves or their mothers were the ones to initiate contact. Those children wondered if they were no longer lovable since their father rejected their wish for contact:

> So I wrote him a letter, because I couldn't have said it to him, whether he didn't like me anymore or what. [...] So I wrote in the letter: and if you don't get in touch with me within ten days, then I'll be, then I won't talk to you for a year. Well, then he did call me on the phone. I would've been tough, even though it would've been hard, but I don't think I would've gone over to see him for a year. I wouldn't have talked.
>
> (Beate, 13 years old)

By contrast, Beate's father did not mention this letter in the interview, nor the withdrawal his daughter had referred to. He was convinced that contact with his daughter had improved since the divorce and said, 'I've always been in touch [with my daughter]. [...] If she needs anything or has a problem, she'll just come over. [...] If she wants to come, well, then she'll come. [...] Just as it happens" (Mr Baumann).

Beate's mother complained that her ex-partner had failed to treat their child in an adequate, responsible way ever since Beate was born. Mrs Berger accused her ex-partner of 'not having taken care of Beate' even during their partnership. This was the main reason for her to initiate separation. She also reproached her ex-partner with the fact that – in her perception – it was exclusively Beate who had to seek and initiate contact with her father, 'Everything was always up to Beate, always'. In contrast, Mr Baumann's complaint was that his ex-wife wanted to reduce his contacts with his daughter.

Our data showed, from the children's perspective, a remarkable coherence between father–child relationship quality and the exclusivity of father–child contacts. If the father had entered a new partnership, the children expressed a desire for exclusive contact with their father, which meant contacts without the presence of new partners or spouses, half- or step-siblings. Fathers mostly did not adhere, and children sometimes did not communicate that wish. Fathers argued that children had to get accustomed to their living circumstances, as was the case for Beate's father, 'This is my reality now. It includes that there is someone else in my life. I mean ... I mean, she [the daughter] really has to accept this as a matter of fact' (Mr Baumann).

Co-parental relationship

The co-parental relationship is a key category not only for children's adjustment but also for the ways in which post-divorce families interact and shape their boundaries of inclusion and exclusion. Adequate parental cooperation facilitates reassembling processes and reduces developmental risks for children (Emery, 1999; Flowerdew and Neale, 2003; Hetherington and Kelly, 2002; Moxnes, 2003; Sarrazin and Cyr, 2007). If parents co-parent effectively, 'the children continue to have relationships with both parents and maintain their sense of biological family' (Ahrons, 2007: 64). Therefore, one main task for parents after a divorce is to 'separate their former romantic roles from their ongoing parental roles and to develop at least minimally cooperative co-parental relationships' (Amato et al., 2009: 41). Nevertheless, although low parental conflict is a protective factor for children, this might also be the most challenging task for parents, as parental conflict is most frequently not a result of, but rather was typically one reason for divorce. Most divorced parents initially experience high levels of conflict for up to three years, after which couples tend to establish their separate lives and disengage from protracted conflict (DeGarmo et al., 2008). Kelly (2003) reports that 8 to 15 per cent of parents are involved in continuously high conflict; some 25 to 30 per cent of parents establish a cooperative co-parental relationship, characterized by joint planning for the children, frequent communication and coordination of activities and schedules. The majority of parents, however, engage in parallel parenting, in which low conflict, low communication and emotional disengagement between the ex-partners are the most typical features.

In our study, the children interviewed assessed the quality of parental relationships chiefly according to how their parents communicated with one another and the extent to which they could come to functional agreements. Several years post-divorce, they wanted more than close relationships with their fathers and mothers: they wished their parents would together remain to be parents in spite of their separation. For the children, this became manifest in common family life activities (such as birthday parties), as well as in terms of external representation on the occasion of family or school events (weddings, school parties, theatre performances and so on). Children were satisfied if their parents managed to re-establish former family boundaries on such exceptional occasions. The interviewed children, mothers and fathers evaluated the quality of parental relationships in relatively similar and mostly positive ways. We identified the two groups that Kelly (2003) had described, that is: (1) cooperative co-parental relationship and (2) parallel parenting.[4] Finally, satisfactory cooperation was no longer possible in a third group of interviewees. These three groups can be characterized as follows:

(1) Families showing a cooperative co-parental relationship represented the largest group: ex-partners were able to cooperate well and arrive at satisfactory solutions as to visiting arrangements, the frequency and extent of contacts, and cooperation in educational terms. The interviewed mothers were eager to reinforce their children's paternal relationships. Overall, there were no conflicts as to paying alimonies. The Wiener/Wolf family is presented as an ideal type for this group. The parents had been divorced for about six years, and although there was 'a fruitful skirmish and a struggle about the kids' (Mr Wolf), the parents were indeed able to establish a relationship at the parental level. Mr Wolf described his relationship with his ex-wife as 'excellent [...] It's become an absolutely wonderful relationship. It's alright'. His ex-wife's statement corresponds with this finding:

We've established a very good basis after those years. [...] I very much appreciate him and also consider him to be a good father and a wonderful being, and he's an important being for me, he's been important for my life, and he'll always be a part of my life.

(Mrs Wiener)

Both parents agreed that this cooperative co-parental relationship required clear rules, especially in the period immediately subsequent to divorce. Their children also appreciated their parents' relationship, said ten-year-old Valerie, 'They really get along with one another, and they don't quarrel. They almost get along like friends'. Her sister shared this perception:

They often get together, they talk and get along with one another really well, they're like best friends. I think that's really super, and I'm so happy about it because I've got some classmates who say their parents are separated and don't talk a single word with one another, and that's why I'm really happy that my parents do it so well.

(Veronika, 14)

(2) Organizational and financial cooperation worked well in families with parallel parenting: agreements were complied with, visiting

rules were kept and alimonies were paid regularly. In some cases, this functional cooperation was the result of a long process of negotiation which was strongly marked by emotional components, particularly shortly after divorce. These families took on their educational responsibilities on a strictly separated basis. Common external representation seemed complicated and practically did not occur.

(3)   In a small group in our study, the parents could not reach satisfactory cooperation, which is comparable with the 'angry associate' and 'fiery foe' types (Ahrons and Rogers, 1987; Kaslow, 2001). Conflict was continuous in various areas including visiting rules, alimonies or decisions concerning the child; the parents were hostile towards one another. The Berger/Baumann family was an example: the parents had been separated for five years and were no longer in touch, although they both lived in the same small rural community. Thirteen-year-old Beate characterized her parents' relationship, '*They* always talk to each other somehow like two complete strangers'. Beate's father, Mr Baumann, commented on the complete breakup with his ex-partner, 'For me, that person's dead and I wouldn't even take a look at her either''. The ex-partners avoid any direct contact when Beate's mother picks her up after visiting her father: 'She knows she can't drop in, and that's what I told her, too. Sometimes she brings Beate over or picks her up, then she'll drive over and honk' (Mr Baumann). Beate's mother, Mrs Berger, also described the relationship with her ex-partner as highly conflictual. She defined the father–daughter contacts as a most crucial issue: in her view, Beate was always the one to take the initiative, while her ex-partner showed no ambitions at all. Contact by telephone was established once when alimony payments were increased due to legal prescriptions, as Mr Baumann wanted to have those payments reduced, 'I thought he must be sick. That moment, I thought, because we hadn't talked for years, and then he gave me a call [...]. I thought he's sick, he has to die or something's wrong with him' (Mrs Berger).

Summing up, families who succeeded in establishing a cooperative co-parental relationship were most likely to meet children's expectations regarding familial boundaries of inclusion and exclusion. Children in those families reported satisfying relationships with both biological parents, and although boundaries were permeable enough to allow external influence on the post-divorce family, they were also stable enough to provide a strong sense of togetherness for children, mothers and fathers.

Conclusion

The data presented in this chapter illustrate that reassembling families after a divorce is a complicated process, as different views have to be integrated in order to form an adequate ensemble of living conditions for all persons involved. Divorce at times means something completely different to the children, women and men involved. In the perspectives of all family members, the issue of post-divorce family unity is closely linked to the quality of relationships (mother–child, father–child and co-parental relationships). What is crucial for children's well-being and for the 'making' of post-divorce families is to retain close relationships with other family members (primarily parents and siblings, but also grandparents and the extended family). Children's perceptions of family reassembling processes imply finding ways of 'maintaining' their family of origin at least for certain times and occasions. This provides them with certain continuity in spite of the changes of family structure. When relationships between biological parents and children are experienced as close, both children and parents seem to be better able to cope with the range of challenges and transitions they have to integrate into their biographies after a divorce. Key significance is attached to communication between all individuals involved. The serious differences in perception between family members are likely to be a rare issue in discussions – nevertheless, they should be made a topic of family communication, as this might contribute to avoiding negative effects, especially on children. Clearly, it is essential to listen to children, let them have their say and give them the possibility of participating in decisions concerning their living arrangements. Children must be viewed as competent social actors rather than '*voiceless victims*' (Smith et al., 2003) of parental divorce.

The differently shaped family boundaries described here are likely to have consequences for the post-divorce reorganizational process: everyday life could be more difficult due to unclear boundaries and role definitions, the development of a family identity might be more demanding and the certainty to belong to a family weakened. Different family members draw their lines of inclusion and exclusion in connection with qualitative aspects of the relationship. In this respect, children act as connective elements. They continue to integrate both parents in their family configuration and wish that joint parenthood would be established. It was shown that divorce does not break off former ties, but paves the way for the reorganization of family relationships and the reassembling of family members. Capturing the perspectives of several family members is a fruitful enterprise, and this process could inspire research in terms of further issues. One resulting question is whether and, if so, *how* families with highly inconsistent family configurations are able to perform the tasks assigned to them within modern society, for example, to provide security, reliability, identity and a sense of togetherness.

13
Families in a Globalized World

Elisabeth Beck-Gernsheim

We live in times of globalization and worldwide migration, and one of the results is a rapidly growing variety of transnational families, such as long-distance relationships, transnational couples, binational couples, marriage migrants, multi-racial families, immigrant families, transnational adoption, transnational divorce tourism, transnational forms of reproduction tourism, etc. However, this new reality of contemporary family demography has received only limited attention so far.

In this chapter I want to bring to mind this limitation, and argue against it. Put in a nutshell, my central idea is: it is high time that we recognize such trends – not only because they represent a growing sector of family life, but also because they represent a challenge to family research. By studying this part of the new demography, we may come to realize that some of the basic assumptions of family sociology have an implicit bias: they are built on a paradigm of methodological nationalism.

To present evidence for this claim, I shall take up the issue of 'family and equality', using it as both example and case study. In the many debates on family and family change, there is general agreement on one point. It is common knowledge that, in the course of history, the family has undergone a gradual move towards more equality: more individual autonomy, more rights for women and children. In the first part of my chapter, I will argue in favour of this position and refer to relevant evidence from social history.

In the next step I will make a turn-around and point to the limits of this position. By switching to a global perspective, the new interconnections (flows, pathways) between the 'West and the rest' come into focus. They reach right into the family and bring new hierarchies, new forms of social inequality. So when we look at both sides of the global divide, the question to be asked is: more equality – for whom?

The decline of old hierarchies: from patriarchal authority to the norm of gender equality

Patriarchal authority

I start with a brief look into history.

In most regions of preindustrial Europe, patriarchal authority was a basic principle of the social order and of everyday life. The man was the head of the house and its representative in all dealings with the outside world. He was privileged heir to the family property, family name and family line. He presided at table, had control of financial matters, settled contracts. He was the master, women and children subject to his rule; according to a German law of 1794, the man even had the right to decide how long the wife-and-mother should breastfeed the baby.

The norm of equality

But then, slowly and gradually, from the late nineteenth century onwards, the privileges of patriarchy became the subject of public debate and political controversy. A process of transformation began that is still going on. Today, throughout Western societies, the principle of equality is broadly accepted, from science and media to law and politics. This is not least in respect to the family: the uneven distribution of privileges is taken for granted no more. The rights of women and children have come into focus.

For the long and difficult road towards gender equality, take Germany for an example. In 1949, the principle of gender equality was made part of the German constitution. Yet family law continued to be embedded in the concept of polarized sex roles, with the male destined by nature to guide, protect and supervise the female. It took some more decades until in 1977 the big change finally came: a fundamental revision of family law.

Table 13.1 gives three paragraphs crucial for defining the power structure of the family. And for each paragraph first the earlier version, dated 1900; then the revised version, dated 1977. The differences stand out clearly.

Similar revisions of the law have taken place – some sooner, some later – in many Western countries, from Sweden to Spain to South Korea. The man is no more the master, women and children no more his subjects; they have gained more autonomy, rights and options. Or, to put it in a nutshell: patriarchy has lost. Democracy has finally reached the family.

On the legal level at least. For of course, the question to ask is: does everyday life match the norms of the law? Or is there a gap between the two?

Table 13.1 Three paragraphs crucial for defining the power structure of family

	Original version of the Civil Code, in force from 1900	Marital Law Reform Act of 1976, in force since 1977
§ 1354	The husband is entitled to decide on all matters concerning marital life; in particular, he decides residence and place of residence.	Revoked
§ 1355	The wife takes on the husband's name.	The spouses can choose either the birth name of the husband or the birth name of the wife as family name.
§ 1356	The wife . . . is entitled and obliged to run the family household.	The spouses decide by mutual agreement how the family household is managed.

From the range of possible issues relevant here, I will choose the sexual division of labour – a central topic in all debates on gender inequality. So in the next part of my chapter, I will look at the respective roles of men and women in household matters.

The unfinished social revolution

When we speak of the family, we mostly think of emotions, of love and longing and lust, of anger and hatred. Sometimes we romanticize the family as a 'haven in a heartless world' (Lasch, 1979). Sometimes we see it as a place filled with secrets and lies.

Yet quite some time ago, feminists brought into focus that the family is not only a site of emotions, but also a site of work. This work includes a broad range of activities, often summarized by the label 'Three Cs': caring, cooking, cleaning. And, of course, far into the twentieth century these tasks were considered to be women's tasks, so assigned by the will of God or of nature.

Claiming a new division of labour

Then in the 1960s, in many Western countries, a new role model for women began to make its way, slowly and accompanied by many controversial debates. No longer should women be confined to the home. Instead, they should take part in higher education, hold jobs, and earn their own money. Feminists, fiercely criticizing the polarized sexual division of labour, proclaimed a new gender order. Both men and women, so they claimed, should be active in the labour market *and* in the family household. In particular, men should do their share in regard to family work; for instance in respect to cleaning floors, sorting rubbish, changing nappies.

Not on the male menu

We know what has become of such claims. In recent years, the sexual division of labour has been the subject of many studies. From among the results, two trends stand out. First: yes, men have been changing. Men of the younger generation, when compared to their fathers or grandfathers, take much more part in the up-bringing of their offspring, from taking them to kindergarten to sports or playground activities. Second: apart from the Scandinavian countries, the changes are modest in scope. In most countries of the West, women still bear most responsibilities in regard to childrearing. And in the field of household activities, men's participation is even lower. Except for some rare heroic souls, routine activities such as changing sheets or doing the laundry are not on the male menu.

In past decades, women have been changing faster than men, so says the American sociologist Arlie Hochschild. While women have ventured beyond the confines of a 'woman's place', men's moves into family work lag behind. In short, a gender gap, or as Hochschild puts it: an 'unfinished social revolution' in gender matters.

With little support from their male partners, women who try to combine both motherhood and holding a job can do so only at high personal cost. For a survival strategy, many resort to delegating some of the family work to female helpers of all kinds, from grandmothers to neighbours to cousins. And in recent years, more and more often to another group: migrant women.

Here begins the third part of my chapter. Its topic: the outsourcing of family work to women from countries of the Second or Third world; or, put differently: the rise of a transnational shadow economy.

The rise of new hierarchies: The family household as a transnational shadow economy

When speaking of migrant domestic workers we speak of women from all over the globe: women from Mexico who work in California as nannies, women from the Philippines who care for the elderly in Italy, women from Poland who clean houses and do the laundry for German families.

Faced with high rates of unemployment in their home countries, these women have decided to look for work in the wealthier regions of the world, hereby following the millions of 'guest-workers' of earlier decades. Yet, meanwhile, most Western countries have severely restricted migration; in particular, options for legal labour migration have been cut down drastically.

But women in the poorer countries, desperately looking for ways to earn some money, are not put off easily. Rather, many try just harder to find some backdoor or side entry to the West. They make use of the communication networks that have come with globalization. Via such channels the news spreads that, in spite of official restrictions, in the domestic sector there are plenty of jobs to be found. Furthermore, because this sector is shut off from outside view, there is comparatively little risk of control. Here workers need no papers, no certificates and only little knowledge of the local language.

In this way, the needs of two different groups of women meet. Lacking help from their male partners, women of the First world resort to outsourcing: turning over some of the care for their children, elderly parents and homes to women from the Third World. And for the same reason, women of the Third World can find a way to earn money. While men's activity in household is modest at best, the work load has to be coped with, no matter what. Hence the market solution: job offers to fill the gap.

Seen like this it is a perfect fit. Supply and demand correspond closely. But a closer look shows that there is a massive flaw to this solution: a major imbalance of risks and profits for the parties involved. Obviously the migrant workers have to bear most of the risks. They are trapped in a semi-legal shadow economy. They often have no visa, no work permit, no residence rights; also, often no access to public health services, unemployment benefits or pension rights. They are vulnerable to exploitation. Last but not least, their political rights are severely restricted.

For Klaus J. Bade, historian and outstanding migration expert in Germany, it takes three words to characterize those working in the shadow economy. 'Fleißig, billig, illegal'; that is, hard-working, cheap, illegal.

By silent agreement

Of course this is why migrants are hired: because they are efficient and because they are cheap. At first sight it is the middle-class women of the First world who profit; but when looking closer we find that their male partners profit just as much, and probably even more. More than the women, the men are set free to follow their ambitions and pursue careers without being disturbed by tedious tasks. I suggest the following constellation.

In many middle-class families today, both men and women are well aware that gender is a sensitive issue, and that the 'unfinished revolution', if not handled carefully, might escalate into explosive conflicts. And many of these couples have come to a similar strategy of conflict management: they have reached a kind of silent treaty, an implicit agreement. If women see to it that the family household is functioning at a reasonable level, then men consent to their venturing out of the home and into the labour market, even to pursue some career of their own. And vice versa: if their men 'allow' them a career of their own, then the women consent to provide, as best they can, for the functioning of household and family affairs; and to do so by outsourcing the family work, not by constantly claiming male participation.

To illustrate this point, imagine just for a moment the following situation: what if out of a sudden, all migrant domestic workers would disappear; what if they did what politicians in Western countries officially expect them to do, namely return to their respective home countries – to Poland or Romania, to Mexico or Honduras? By all probabilities, then it would no more suffice that German men, or US men, talk highly of gender equality. In this emergency, women would no longer keep to their implicit agreement, but would demand that men do their share of family work. If this analysis holds true, here is a major area of hidden benefits – not for the migrants, but for their employers. By relieving Western families of some of their work load, migrant domestic workers stabilize – and contribute to – the precarious peace in the arena of gender.

At this point, we might come to ask: what about *their* families? What happens to the children, partners, parents of migrant domestic workers?

Global care chains: Who cares for the families of migrant domestic workers?

This is a question that we – natives of the West – mostly ignore. Yet it is no minor matter concerning but a few. Quite to the contrary: many of the women working abroad have families of their own, back in their home countries. These women have left partners, children and whoever else there is to go abroad and earn a living. In fact, it is often the children, or rather their responsibility towards them, that motivates the women to go abroad: the mothers want a better future for their sons and daughters, free from hunger and constant poverty. For this hope, they are willing to accept long separations and the lonely life in a far-away country.

Yet this behaviour means no less than a revolution of basic rules. In the old times it was proof of your love that you would stick together, no matter what. Yet now, in a globalized world, for many the opposite holds true. The new rule says: if you truly love your family, you must leave them. You must go to some distant part of the world, wherever there is money to be made, because this is the only way to lift your family out of the misery and desperation at home. Or to quote from a novel by Michelle Spring, *Z*: 'For migrant domestic workers all over the globe, love means, first of all: having to go away'.

But how does this work? How are the children of migrant mothers cared for? According to recent studies, the answer is: another division of labour is being established; starting in the respective homelands of female migrants and again involving women only. For instance, migrant women often rely on the help of other women in their home town (for instance grandmother, sister in-law, neighbour). By sending them money and other gifts from abroad, migrant mothers hope to grow a sense of responsibility among the recipients of such favours and make them willing to look after their children's well-being and care.

In this way, new patterns of motherhood are being created, named 'transnational motherhood' in recent studies. They result in so-called 'global care chains', based on elaborate networks and spanning countries and continents. To give a typical example: in some family of the Second or Third World, the eldest daughter is responsible for looking after her younger siblings; this sets her mother free to take care of some third woman's children and thus earn a little money, while the third woman has migrated to some Western country and is nanny to the baby boy of a family resident there. Transnational care chains are to be found for instance, when we look at the migration flows between Eastern Europe and Western Europe. Women from Poland go to Germany, cleaning the houses of middle-class families there; at the same time, women from the Ukraine go to Poland, managing the household and family tasks of the Polish migrant women at work in Germany.

A global hierarchy of care

While these care chains spread into many directions, crossing borders, mountains and oceans, they do so in no accidental way. On the contrary, they follow a distinct pattern, rooted in social inequality. As American sociologist *Arlie Hochschild* puts it Z: 'Motherhood is passed down the hierarchy of nation, ethnicity, race'. This sentence brings into focus that the age of globalization creates a new hierarchy, namely, a global hierarchy. For instance, a global hierarchy of delegation. The work implied by the three Cs – caring, cleaning, cooking – is cast off along the lines of nation, colour, ethnicity.

Naturally, those in need of care – children, old people, the disabled or ill people – will be the first to feel the consequences. With each step downward, the chances for receiving adequate help and good care are being diminished. If Polish women leave their homes to work for German families, and women from Ukraine leave their homes to work in Polish households; who then will do the caring, cleaning and cooking in Ukraine?

Empirical studies show that, indeed, those at the bottom of the hierarchy bear the costs of delegating. Take, for instance, the children of migrant mothers. Often their grandmothers, aunts, elder sisters are over-burdened by numerous responsibilities – or are too old, too tired, too sick – to master yet another task. Even if they try hard, the children left in their charge are more or less on their own, lack proper care and proper meals. At the same time there is little help to expect from the fathers. Some men disappeared years ago, taking leave from family bonds and family duties. And of those who stayed, many find it hard now to come to terms with the reversal of roles. The women working abroad and being the breadwinners: this turn of events threatens their male identity. Because many men are preoccupied with their own sense of crisis, they are hardly able to offer emotional support and protection. The effect is that many children lack a stable base, feel lonely and desperately long for their mother.[1]

In short, a care drain of major dimensions is taking place. The result is that families in poor countries will experience even more destabilization. Now they lack not only material resources, but also their most important 'human resources': women; women who care for the needs of everyday life, and for the special needs of children, old people and disabled people.

It remains to be seen how this care drain will affect the functioning of the societies concerned. Do they have the potential to compensate their losses? Or will they experience a new dimension of social problems, in addition to the political and economic problems that are burdening them today?

Conclusions

Now to the final part of my chapter, and to my conclusions. To sum up the main points:

(1) When we look at the family from a nation-state perspective, for instance in respect to the changes of national family law, we find that a move towards more equality has taken place.

(2) But the picture takes on a different colour when globalization comes into view. The forces that globalization sets into motion are not confined to economy or politics but reach deep into the family.

(3) On both sides of the global divide, among rich and among poor nations, families are being transformed. While in some ways they are drawn together, becoming mutually dependent, at the same time they grow further apart, moving in opposite directions. The former gain in vital resources and the latter lose. New hierarchies are building up, both within families (middle class families of the West hiring servants from the global 'rest'), and also among families (a care drain from poor to rich nations). On the global scale, the gap widens, and inequality increases.

(4) So we have got two contrasting pictures, one from the nation-state view, one from a global perspective. With this result, we can return to the beginnings of my presentation. Now we can see why the view from within the nation-state does not suffice: because it is misleading, one-sided and partial.

This is why family sociology has to move beyond methodological nationalism.

Part V

Family Relationships as Social Capital

14
Family Relations as Social Capital

Giovanna Rossi, Roberta Bonini and Sara Mazzucchelli

Today, as stated by Beck-Gernsheim in this book, the need for a comparative analysis of the family in Europe is rather compelling, both because of the drive towards globalization as a distinctive feature of contemporary society and the diversity of family forms. Such a diversity emerges for two reasons: first, because of the growing differentiation of the constituent elements of the family (relations between the sexes and between generations) and, second, because of the growing complexity of underlying relational interlacements (Rossi, 2009). Sociologically the development and dynamics of the family can be understood if seen as a reflection of the morphogenetic process of society (Archer, 2003); this enables us to understand the intense differentiation processes at work in our contemporary society. The relational approach conceives the family relationship as a social configuration (Widmer and Jallinoja, 2008) or, better, as a relationship of complete reciprocity among the sexes and generations.

In particular, 'the latent structure which confers social identity to the family consists of the intertwining of four interrelated elements or components: *gift, reciprocity, generativity* and *sexuality* seen as conjugal love' (Donati, 2006: 58). The etymology of the word 'relation' highlights a dual order of meanings inasmuch as it emphasizes the Latin *religo* ('a link between'), which refers to a bond between two or more subjects in a strict sense, to a connection, to inter-subjectivity and ultimately to interaction. This bond can, in turn, entail a dual meaning: it can be a *constraint* or an *asset*. In the latter case the relationship leads to *refero* ('refer to') which shows that the bonds never exist in isolation or only in the here-and-now but 'carry' with them a body of shared symbolic references, a 'memory'.

There is a structural aspect to the family relationship. There are mutual expectations deriving from the bond. There is an exchange between family members – and this is what the concept of *religo* expresses. However, there is something that goes beyond this: the subjects carry something with them. They are 'bearers' (*fero, latum, ferre*) of a cultural heritage, which is represented at the very heart of the bond. The family relationship, after all, cannot be reduced solely to *refero* or *religo*. It is for this reason that there is an interrelation of both which does not coincide with the sum of the properties of the individuals that make up a family. Whenever a bond is brought to life, the history of the family and the family tree – in which the individuals are embedded – is modified and something unusual, a surplus, is generated, which only becomes apparent when not only the individuals, but also the relationship is considered. Therefore it is advisable to observe the family relationship as a space defined by three dimensions or *semantics*: *referential, structural, generative* (Donati, 2006). The generative dimension, *specific to the family*, allows us to measure the relationship in depth and to see its capacity to generate something new and to crush individualisms. 'The family relationship is to be configured as a social modality of giving. It is formed according to three specific instances of this unique human phenomenon: *coming from* (a temporal perspective in the past), *coming with* (a temporal perspective in the present) and *coming to/becoming* (a temporal perspective in the future.) The *generative grammar* of the family is revealed through these three perspectives' (Prandini, 2006: 148). The distinctive trait of the family relationship will be observed through the lens of the social capital perspective.

Social capital: Main theoretical perspectives

The term social capital[1] refers to a multidimensional concept (Folgheraiter, 2004; Turner, 2000; Smith and Kulynych, 2002; Bagnasco et al., 2001). Though anticipated by the works of Hanifan (1920), Jacobs (1961), Loury (1977) and Granovetter (1973), the idea of 'other' capital – different from the traditional economic concept – has been mostly used metaphorically (Bankston and Zhou, 2002; Field, 2003). It has been seen as a 'utilitarian' aspect associated with the availability of social relations. Given its extreme complexity and its semantic ambivalence, a thorough analysis of the approaches to SC seems impossible. According to Donati (2007) we can observe two fundamental conceptions:

- Individualistic-instrumental-structuralist (Bourdieu, 1980, 1986; Coleman, 1988a, 1988b, 1990);
- Holistic-political-cultural (Putnam, 1993, 1995, 2000, 2002; Fukuyama, 1995).

The paradigms introduced above show significant criticalities, however. We can observe:

– A tendency to identify SC with those relationships which are useful to the individual to gain advantageous exchanges and favours;
– A lib/lab conception which mixes individual action (lib) with structural conditioning (lab);
– A lack of references and a reductive vision of the family.

According to an instrumental perspective, 'classical' scholars seem to have failed to consider SC as a product of interactions; they see SC 'inside' networks, mainly focusing on structural connections.

Social capital in the relational perspective

The relational perspective allows us to see SC as the *quality of social relations* at a *meso* level, as an attribute of individuals or of social structures or a combination of both. According to this theoretical approach, SC is the very social relation, if and when it is seen as resource for the individual and/or society.[2]

Its primary function, as a *sui generis* bond, is not instrumental, yet is something which favours social relationality. It is an exchange that produces a common good, from which subsequently particular resources derive. Within the relational perspective SC is not only a competitive advantage for the individual who 'uses and consumes it', and/or for the society that has to rely on it to regenerate itself. It is a good that can be seen (a) from the perspective of an individual, as a resource that individuals use for their actions and (b) from the perspective of our society, as a network of relationships which constitute the world (Donati, 2003; Donati and Prandini, 2007).

In this sense, the relational perspective allows us not to lose sight of the subject and, at the same time, not to reduce SC to an economic perspective. It is rather something that is generated or degenerates within a relational dimension which is made up of fiduciary, mutual and cooperation-oriented elements.

SC is thus a relation in which the good or service is inextricably and undeniably incorporated with three qualities: relational networks always generate trust, cooperation and reciprocity. If the relation fails, so does the good or service. 'The good/service always implies a debt that is a relation characterized by the availability to exchange' (Donati, 2007: 20–1). In this sense, SC is the specific relation of relational goods.

The dimensions of the social capital in the relational perspective

In this approach it is evident that the concept of SC can be understood following four main dimensions (Mazzucchelli, 2007):

- *Network*, namely the structural dimension that refers to the relational networks with their different levels of consistency, size and density (Widmer, 2007);
- *Trust*, as the expectation of a social actor that others will carry out beneficial or harmless actions to him/her, made under conditions of uncertainty (interpersonal trust);
- *Reciprocity*, the actor knows that giving something he/she will get something in return not only at an instrumental level but also at a symbolic and relational level;
- *Cooperation*, as a way of interacting together that can establish itself also without external control mechanisms.

We can thus refer to SC when we are dealing with relations that are simultaneously based on networks, reciprocity, trust and cooperation. The adverb 'simultaneously' shows that these four dimensions are necessary to discuss SC in a relational perspective even when variably present (the *quantum* should be verified). There are various forms of SC – even if it is not for the moment possible to state that their differentiation is based on different degrees of network relationships, reciprocity, solidarity and orientation towards cooperation. It seems that such a differentiation takes place in relation to the social spheres in which SC is located: private market spheres, public spheres of political-administrative institutions, civil spheres of non-profit associations, spheres of family and informal networks.

Although we can see an instrumental use of SC in all these spheres, this is particularly true with the financial market and institutional fields, whereby SC is solely produced to be consumed. On the contrary, in the civil spheres of non-profit associations and in those of family and informal networks, social relation is produced to be used and such consumption does not ruin SC but regenerates and values SC as if it were a relation that allows the very existence of the goods. Thanks to SC's widespread relationality, these two spheres, more and better than others, favour the generation of SC, in that they are networks which are able to produce relationships based on trust that can lead to cooperation in terms of reciprocity and regeneration of the very same social relations. The privileged fields that create SC are those of family and primary relation networks and the third sector (when it enhances family relations) (Donati, 2007).

Social capital and relational goods

In our perspective SC is a specific relation which values and promotes relational goods. This allows us to analyze SC in specific dimensions, in its analogical relation with typical relational goods. We consider a relational good as an indivisible good, produced by human relations, which can be produced and consumed solely by those who take part in it. Relational goods satisfy primary and secondary relational needs. They are produced and used inside primary relational contexts (family, networks of friends and neighbours) and are defined as primary relational goods. However, they can also be produced inside secondary relational networks (relational contexts of social privacy or third sector) and are consequently defined as secondary relational goods.

Taking into account these two forms of relational goods it is thus possible to distinguish two types of relational contexts:

– Primary SC: relations which value primary relational goods following an informality code. This type of capital is typical of social relations characterized by primary trust, interpersonal reciprocity as symbolic exchange (gift) and represents a civilization factor.
– Secondary SC: relations which promote secondary relational goods, with higher structural informality. It belongs to the sphere of the associations of civil society, and is characterized by secondary trust, social reciprocity and constitutes a *civicness* factor.

Each type of SC may be subdivided into two further subtypes (Tronca, 2008): family SC (family and kinship relationships) and extended community SC (networks of friends and neighbours). These two subtypes can be considered subtypes of primary SC, whereas associative SC (typical of voluntary associations of the third sector) and generalized SC (relations with the others in general) can be considered subtypes of secondary SC.

The specificity of family social capital

In spite of extensive studies conducted on SC, the correlation between family and SC needs further research. Most studies do not sufficiently clarify if and how the family contributes to SC. The reality of the family also appears in a stereotypical and marginal way.

The family is defined as SC for society provided that it complies with the conditions of the economic market and that of political democracy. The idea that the family can be a source of SC for society has been discussed in an abstract way. Today this discussion seems obsolete.

One does not seem to notice that 'the existence of SC in the public sphere depends on the existence of worlds of every-day life. SC is generated in these worlds' (Donati, 2003: 21).

The family is a relation that can offer individuals the necessary opportunities to experiment and create reliable social relations based on trust and reciprocity. The family is a primary SC and contributes to secondary SC in that it is a social form which is able to value mutual help. 'The family is the only place where people stay, create bonds, and interact by sharing not only some aspects of themselves but their entire selves. This is the extraordinary force, but at the same time the true manifestation of the family, which is for human beings the only access to the construction and the development of their own identities' (Cigoli and Scabini, 2006).

Which features does family social capital assume?

Family social capital (FSC) is a quality of the social relations which derives, even if not intentionally, from the ties among family members and assumes the character of living memory of those relations, conferring them a distinguishing subjectivity (Prandini, 2007). It is a mutual orientation among family members, based on gift and expectation and becomes a real family *modus vivendi*. Thus, relational reciprocity is seen as the fundamental and distinguishing element of FSC. However, it is not possible to sustain that the family, as a relation, is a FSC for all its members.[3] As stated by De Carlo and Widmer in this volume, FSC is not a common good to all family members, it is contingent and depends on the interaction of complex factors which cannot be predicted and must be carefully evaluated. It is a quality of family relations.

It certainly refers to complex webs of emotional interdependencies, but in particular to the dimension of mutual orientation. It is responsible for the creation of reliable bonds, based on gift and reciprocity, which in turn are able to produce cooperation-oriented behaviour. Nonetheless FSC strongly depends on the real orientation and the nature of the relationships among family members: an instrumental or violent relation does not create FSC, but a relational evil. Thus, family relations do not automatically generate FSC, which is related to the quality of family relations.

Sociological research on family social capital carried out in Italy

Researches on SC carried out in Italy help us better understand the nature and the spreading of FSC and its link to other types of SC. The project was carried out by a research team at the University of Bologna (Donati and Colozzi, 2007; Donati and Tronca, 2008) on a representative sample of Italians.[4] The project analyzes the different types of SC in Italian society and the relationship between the different SCs.

Methodologically speaking the items related to the measurement of SC indicators are made up of fixed reference scales (ranging from 0 to 10). The interviewees are inserted into these indicators according to what they express: how much they trust others when their relationships is reciprocal; how much they can rely on the support that primary and secondary networks offer. The set of questions used tries to identify the structures of the networks of the interviewees.

This survey distinguishes the previously mentioned types of primary and secondary SC. Primary SC could be differentiated into: family SC, kinship SC, community or extended SC. Secondary social capital implies associative and generalized SC. These types of SC are seen as different expressions of relationality. In particular:

- *FSC* is typical of the family in terms of reciprocal trust, received and help offered, and intensity of contacts;
- *Kinship SC* refers to the reciprocal support between a person and his/her family or extended family;
- Community or extended SC is specific to friendship and neighbourhood networks;
- *Associative SC* identifies SC related to the participation in associations;
- *Generalized SC* is related to trust and reciprocity in general and towards society as a whole.

There have been attempts to distinguish the bridging/bonding functions of SC. The most widespread SC among Italians is FSC and, specifically, the intranuclear SC (average = 7.42) in terms of trust (9.34) and concrete support (8.45). Kinship SC is also relevant (6.48), yet it is more significant according to the trust to which it is correlated (7.08) than to real help in case of need (5.67). Associative SC has the same trend (6.06). It is the most widespread SC after FSC and kinship SC. Generalized SC is poorly distributed among Italians (4.47). Extended community SC follows the same trend. However, this cannot be sustained for the networks of neighbours and those typical of the workplace, probably due to their different natures (they are instrumental and aim at achieving a specific goal).

Family-based community and social capital

A survey,[5] recently carried out on a sample of families engaged in fostering minors and adults in need, allows us to study the dimensions of FSC in depth (Rossi, 2006; Bramanti, 2007; Rossi and Bramanti, 2007; Bonini and Mazzucchelli, 2007). This research aims at identifying family communities in Italy, with 498 interviewees – 244 couples from a variety of communities. The survey used structured interviews and three types of questionnaires.[6] Other types of existing SC have been studied along with the set of questions aimed at identifying the nature of family communities (type of association, ways of regulating internal and external relationships, levels of sharing of resources, the number and type of people in the family, and reference cultures). Levels of reliability in relationships, the composition and the density of networks, reciprocity in relationships, received and offered support have also been analyzed within the types of SC examined.

This survey focuses on the centrality of the conjugal bond of the couple. The related SC was analyzed according to three main dimensions: the reliability of the conjugal bond, the mutual support offered and received between partners, and the frequency of the moments spent by the whole family together in a day.

A synthetic index of the couple's SC was created on the basis of these different variables and distributed as follows: 13.3 per cent low SC, 53.3 per cent medium SC and 33.3 per cent high SC. The analyzed SC is fundamentally 'bonding' SC, that is essentially within a couple, and represents yet another 'indicator' of internal cohesion. SC varies with the passing of time. It diminishes among the strongest couples and is present among the youngest couples. It is probably linked to the cycle of family life.

SC is a fundamental element to understanding the relational goods produced by the couple. SC is a good which paradoxically is not consumed, provided that it is used, and it is regenerated in its use. A relation, in other words, gets stronger because it is constantly used and regenerated. The generativity of the couple can be explained through the observation of the couple's SC. Generativity also becomes social generativity, whereby the opening out to others means hospitality both towards the couple's own children and towards strangers. If we link conjugal SC to the type of family it is evident that couples with a higher SC are families that take care of their own children and adults in need. Taking care of adults in need requires relational resources which are very complex and strong. SC, while reaffirming its vocation to generativity, is tightly linked to the average number of the people fostered by families. Couples with low SC (31 per cent) foster an average of 1–2 people like the families with medium SC (35 per cent), whereas 30.8 per cent of the couples with a high SC foster six or more people. A reliable and mutual conjugal bond allows the couple to open up towards social generativity, which is enhanced by foster care.

Family associations and social capital

Secondary SC has relative autonomy. It exists because the family creates its best premises. Secondary SC is an external positive effect of primary FSC, as shown in the case of family associations.

The surveys carried out show how family associations are organizations built around a specific need of the family, supported by families. Their actions involve the family. They are a manifestation of the family generative code that carries out a pro-social orientation. In particular the first national survey was conducted in 1993 (Donati and Rossi, 1995). It highlighted the extension of the phenomenon and its features. Among the various kinds of ways of associating, it highlighted those of the family (accomplished by the family and addressed to the family). Other qualitative analyses have followed (Carrà, 1998; Rossi and Maccarini, 1999; Di Nicola and Landuzzi, 2004). These analyses have examined the nature and the outcome of the action of the associations. More recently a research has been carried out on all family associations in Lombardy (Carrà Mittini, 2003). This research has identified areas of intervention, services and the ways in which these associations take action. The most interesting area of family associations is that of the initiatives that organize services aimed at everyday life, both in normal situations as well as in 'pathological' ones. In this area we can find all the 'caring' tasks carried out by families through experiences of solidarity that follow a strictly oriented family-oriented code. In particular, the area in which family associations distinguish themselves is that of training/education, which corresponds to the increasing need for 'pedagogical guidance' in all the phases of a person's life. More than a third of these organizations safeguard the rights of the family.

These associations aim at making the State aware of issues related to the family and families aware of their role in society. These associations create and promote the network of associations with different objectives and features.

Family associations thus *produce* family through a pro-social behaviour and represent a form of socialization of family needs. Families that bond with other families reinforce community bonds that represent an intermediate position (meso) between the family (micro) and society (macro) (Figure 14.1). Family associations are generative in a broad sense: the action of the associations that are formed by families who satisfy family needs produces the family (addressee of the action) and consequently reproduces the family (actor of the action) (Rossi, 2003). *Familiarity* lies in the capacity for triggering pro-active family reactions, reinforcing the family (allocating resources) so that it can find solutions to its needs on its own (Carrà, 2006). In this way, family associations strengthen the competence of family relations whereby the interdependence between individual and inter-subjective rights is constantly

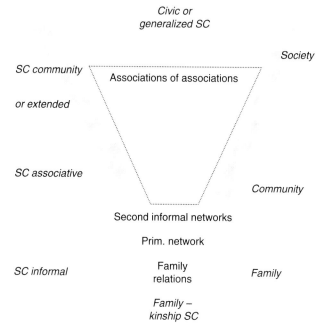

Figure 14.1   From primary FSC to civic or generalized SC

proposed and renovated. Family associations create networks, trust among people, solidarity, relations cooperation-oriented and aim at a common good rather than an individual interest (Rossi, 2007).

To summarize, we can state that family relations, characterized by trust, open to generativity and able to produce a relational well-being, constitute *primary SC* (or *informal, family kinship SC*). When these features become catalysts of a chain reaction that pushes families towards open and greater solidarity, *secondary SC* (or *associative SC*) is created. The value of secondary SC increases with bonds that are not linked to a personal action code. They become a resource for the community and leave a mark on the well-being of society (*civic or generalized* SC) (Figure 14.1).

If we put the 'private' perspective aside, families interact as 'protagonists' in their socio-territorial context. The SC that has been generated is not only used by the community but it also becomes a common resource for society as a whole and goes back to the families. In this way, families can reinforce their primary SC acquiring the right to true social citizenship.

The relation between FSC and other types of SC

SC is originated from family contexts and extended in terms of forms and contents which are different from those of other relational contexts. How can we explain the interpretative hypothesis of '*Amoral Familism*' (Banfield, 1967; Putnam, 1993; Cartocci, 2007)? Or, rather, how can we explain that in certain countries, such as Italy, there is an overall high presence of FSC, and weak community, associative and generalized SC in some regions, and vice versa: in areas where the generalized SC is high, there is no corresponding high FSC?

The answer may be easily found in the analysis of the data of the first research presented above, whereby the function of SC emerges as substantial. Bonding FSC seems strictly linked to bonding kinship SC and weakly to bonding extended community SC: families who have this type of bonding SC are likely to generate a SC for their own members but not for the more extended society.

The connective path of bridging FSC implies not only bridging kinship SC but also all the other types of bridging SC. This highlights both the action of a conservative process of form and function[7] of SC and the power of the family as a broker who is able to turn the bonds between people and realities beyond the family into ties based on trust and reciprocity. Family contexts, endowed with bridging SC, have a real *nursery* function in the creation and reproduction of SC in other contexts.

Thus FSC is not only the first form of SC to be generated, as many psychological studies have shown,[8] but it is also within the family that a certain type of SC (either bonding or bridging) lays its foundations. In this sense research on the pro-social behaviours between generations is paradigmatic.

Family and pro-social behaviour: Family as SC broker

Both psycho-social (Marta and Pozzi, 2007; Boccacin and Marta, 2003) and sociological (Bonini, 2005) surveys have shown how an altruistic behaviour typically expressed in a voluntary action is transmitted from one generation onto the next. The project involved 492 young volunteers between 24 and 32 years old and highlighted the relationship between young adults and their families as well as examining scales and levels of individual pro-sociality and how young people were involved in volunteer associations. The origin of caring /altruistic behaviour within the family has been identified by reconstructing the nature and the quality of the bonds between parents and children, and the intergenerational transmission of values.

The results have shown that a good bonding FSC – groups made up of strong trust cooperative-oriented bonds – may be linked to a good bridging SC that would lead families and their members to create many friendly and associative bonds which extend beyond the family. This opening towards society 'goes' back' as an emerging effect to family bonds, regenerating them. In this case the family is a broker for its own members: by joining different social spheres family members allow their children to have access to multiple relational resources and to be closer to the world of associations and that of voluntary work than other children.

Conclusions

In the light of the present chapter, we will now focus our attention on various challenges that have been raised by the theorizations of SC. First, we must observe that the difficulty in using such concept is strictly linked to the type of measurement adopted. This is evident in the case of FSC. There is an initial epistemological process that has to be undertaken with regards to the nature and the identity of the family. FSC can be measured in various ways. Nonetheless our reflections enable us to highlight how a measurement is effective and how parameters and indicators must refer to certain factors which are influenced by the quality of family relations: the number of its members (which determines a higher/lower density of relations), the amount of time spent in family activities (the more the time spent together the greater the strength of the family bond), the types of family activities (which may influence the quality and the outcome of family interactions), the atmosphere within the family, and mutual trust between family members. These factors are significant in that they interact simultaneously: FSC is the emerging effect of family interactions – FSC cannot be explained starting from single parameters or from their mere sum (Donati, 2003: 78). In spite of this positive effort, we must improve research indicators to overcome a certain rigidity that is indicative of the use of the metaphor 'family'.

Secondly and subsequently, we need to understand better the relationship between primary and secondary SC and distinguish predictive and effective variables methodologically. Finally, we should better understand *the role of policies in valuing FSC*. With reference to what has been stated in this chapter, the type of recognition given to the family influences the type of legislative initiatives and concrete intervention policies which give precise contents (social functions, assignments, values) to the family, considering it as a 'social subject'. People who accept an individualistic vision of the family and consider it as an empty box, where individuals can express their preferences as much as they like without their choices having a social impact or a public relevance, end up supporting welfare and the passivity of families. What can we do to increase FSC? Which strategies can we adopt? The choice or rather the challenge is that of reorienting and redefining social policies so that they can attribute a more accomplished citizenship to the family and, in this way, endlessly create and regenerate FSC and civic SC.

15

The Fabric of Trust in Families: Inherited or Achieved?

Ivan De Carlo and Eric D. Widmer

Families are often considered an example of thick and cohesive social capital. Scholars intuitively compare strong ties inside the family to weak ties outside the family. In this perspective, social capital benefits are supposed to be equally shared among family members. Because the family is defined as a cohesive and homogeneous group, a series of issues were raised concerning its contribution to social integration in late modern societies. In particular, individualization theorists believe families to be dead as instances of social integration.[1] Others have strong doubts about their ability to maintain their function of socialization of children and adolescents, as well as to resist economic hardship when facing divorce. The complexity of contemporary families questions this set of assumptions and suggests that social capital is an individualized resource in families of late modernity.

Various conditions, we propose, stimulate the development of social capital in families. Social capital can be seen as a by-product of specific roles and status. It may also derive from a history of dyadic relations, both positive and negative. Finally, as the configurational perspective states, social capital develops in a large network of inter-dependent individuals. This chapter stresses the importance of family interdependencies for understanding the development of social capital in families. Based on exploratory empirical research, it first explains why trust should be considered a central dimension of social capital in late modernity societies. It goes on to underline the importance of specific family statuses and roles for the development of social capital. The influence of such roles on trust is not, however, without ambiguity: are they important for social capital by their own merit or because they are linked with supportive, multiplex, and reciprocal interactions between two role incumbents? Is reciprocity of support between role holders enough to predict where trust in families arises, or may other explanations also be relevant? By using a configurational perspective on families, the chapter shows that a larger set of dimensions of family interactions should be taken into account for the understanding of social capital in families of late modernity.

Trust as social capital

Simmel (1908) considered trust to be one of the most important integrative forces of society. As such, it was considered as a key element of social capital (Coleman, 1988a). Trust is defined as a hypothesis on others' future behaviour, grounding practices and actions, and as a midpoint between total knowledge and absence of knowledge of others. Möllering defines trust as

> a reflexive process of building on reason, routine and reflexivity. Suspending irreducible social vulnerability and uncertainty *as if* they were favourably resolved, and maintaining a state of favourable expectation toward the actions and intentions of more or less specific others.
>
> (2006: 356, emphasis in original)

Individuals' trust creates ties and relational history. The importance of trust has been underlined by several scholars in recent decades. Fukuyama (1995) asserts that a high level of trust in society ensures a healthy and competitive economy. Putnam (1993, 2000) invokes the essential role of interpersonal trust for the survival of democracy.

The pace of change of societies in late modernity has transformed social relations and foundations of actions and identities. Individuals are now embedded in networks of relationships that cross over multiple contexts such as friendships, family, occupation, etc. Trust allows individuals to be active in a variety of situations while having only a limited knowledge and little control over the interactions and people embedded in those fields. It makes actions and relations possible in situations where face-to-face interactions are not possible (Giddens, 1990). Therefore, trust is a resource for individual actions as well as for collective purposes in highly complex societies. It is possible for individuals to take risks while accepting the possible state of disappointment when a decision is made that is contrary to their expectations. Trust helps people get over the complexities of everyday life (Luhmann, 1968). It is indeed a central dimension of social capital (Coleman, 1988a; Paxton, 1999) which allows the achievement of personal and collective goals that could not be achieved by an isolated individual.

Families were supposed to provide social capital based on thick ties fostering an emotional component and undifferentiated strong trust among all their members. This, however, does not correspond to the many contemporary families stemming from non-marital cohabitation, divorce, remarriage, lack of fertility and other non- or only weakly-institutionalized organizations of the family (Cherlin, 2004; Cherlin and Furstenberg, 1994). We have stressed elsewhere the importance of weak ties and bridging social capital in families (Widmer, 2006). The study of trust between family members reveals the importance of complex associations between people in late modernity (Cook, 2005). Therefore, the functionalist interpretation of the family as a monolithic unit, producing trust for all family members, seems inadequate.

Family statuses and doing family

Roles and statuses have great importance in the understanding of trust as they often relate to a normative basis defined by society as a whole. In a functionalist perspective, family statuses such as parent, child and partner are normatively trustworthy. Unless the family is on the verge of collapse, one should trust the incumbents of such statuses. The mother is normatively defined as the main provider of love, and the father as the main breadwinner. In this perspective both are, therefore, trusted as they fill a clear functional role in the family structure. They are trusted because they are the incumbents of family statuses to which trust is normally ascribed.

The normative dimension of family statuses may, however, have less importance than expected, in late modern societies, because family statuses and roles are associated with less clearly defined normative expectations. The role of a stepfather, for instance, was acknowledged as normatively undefined (Cherlin and Furstenberg, 1994); expectations towards step-parents are not provided by the societal context and are induced by a constant work of 'doing' family (Schneider, 1980). This is the case of a variety of family roles related with the kinship network, including siblings. In a time of deinstitutionalization of marriage itself (Cherlin, 2004), it may well be that the level of trust in roles of the nuclear family varies to a significant extent.

In this perspective, each family member is trusted according to that person's involvement in family practices. A long acquaintance, shared experiences and actualized interdependencies in reciprocal supportive relationships are likely to influence the ways in which family statuses relate to trust. Therefore, the relational history of family members should be considered when explaining the development of trust. Acquaintance length, contact frequency, the ways in which loyalty issues among family members are resolved, and the development of reciprocal supportive relationships towards specific family members may explain the extent to which incumbents of specific statuses are or are not trusted in families.[2]

Ambivalence

Trust may develop as an outcome of cooperation and reciprocity. The focus on positive interactions, however, presents a limitation for family research. One major criticism of the functionalist perspective concerns its understanding of family as a normative institution wherein adults find the emotional support necessary to cope with the stresses of modern life. Instead, empirical research shows that families are embedded in conflicts, power relationships and interpersonal stress (Widmer, 1999). Strong emotional interdependencies often bring about conflict relationships. The concept of ambivalence enables researchers to overcome the opposition between the family as a cooperative group (Bengtson, 2001) and the family as a group characterized by conflict (Sprey, 1969). This makes it possible to take a middle stance between the family as a support unit and the family as an antagonistic group (Lüscher, 2002; Lüscher and Pillemer, 1998; Merton, 1976).

Individuals are in ambivalent situations when support is tied with conflict. This contradiction emerges in various family situations. For instance, this is seen in the case when normative expectations linked to a family role do not correspond to individuals' expectations. Individuals experience ambivalence when two or more relations have contradicting demands. For example, a mother breadwinner may be easily torn between the expectations of her boss and colleagues, and the expectations of her partner and children. No easy solution may be found in that situation. Multiple participations in various social fields can create antagonistic forces, which pressure individuals to make ambivalent choices.

In that regard, Lüscher and Pillemer (1998) apply ambivalence to the understanding of intergenerational relations. They show that many family relationships between parents and adult children are characterized by feelings of ambivalence. The norm of autonomy competes with the norm of solidarity when parents become physically dependent on care from adult children. Similar ambivalences are found in conjugal relations, when individualistic needs compete with marriage obligations, which presuppose a shared life with a partner. When dealing with the development of trust in families one should, therefore, take into account conflict in family relations that are not always supportive and cooperative. A range of possible relations structure trust, ranging from unilateral support or conflict to fully reciprocal relationships. We hypothesize that trust is explained by the development of positive, negative and ambivalent interdependencies between family members.

Trust beyond the nuclear family

In expanding on what occurs in the dyads of the nuclear family several sound reasons support a configurational perspective on trust. Elias defined configurations as 'structures of mutually oriented and dependent people' (1994: 214). Individuals are interdependent in a configuration because each one fulfils some of the others' needs for social recognition, power, emotional proximity, financial and practical resources, or other socially defined needs (Quintaneiro, 2004). As such, configurations have to deal with power issues: resources are scarce and individuals, while cooperating, also compete for them within groups. This competition creates tensions and conflicts that are beyond individual control. The patterns of interdependencies that characterize any configuration are therefore largely unintended (Newton, 1999). They, in turn, shape the cooperation strategies and the conflicts that occur in each dyad belonging to it (Widmer and Jallinoja, 2008; Widmer et al., 2009).

Like 'Gestalts' (Köhler, 1992), a family configuration is not equal to the sum of its dyads. Any dyad belonging to a configuration is influenced by the shape of the configuration. At the same time, all dyads participate in the shaping of the family configuration. Ties within a configuration are not randomly organized but, instead, follow informal rules such as reciprocity and transitivity. Moreno and Jennings (1938) and Moreno (1953) also underline that configurations concern actual relationships rather than official groupings, as defined by organizational charts, administrations or census offices. On the basis of this theoretical stance, the configurational perspective on families posits that trust developed in dyads of the nuclear family must be referred to their relational context (Widmer and Jallinoja, 2008). The configurational perspective stresses the complex patterns of interdependencies, both positive and negative, which link respondent with relatives, friends and others. On one hand, these patterns of interdependencies depend to some extent on the distribution of conflict and support in the dyads, namely respondent-family member relations. On the other hand, it is stressed that trust is shaped by the larger network of interdependencies with relatives, friends and others in which individuals are embedded.

Summary

Family statuses, because they combine long-lasting relations, interactions and feelings of shared membership, may at first sight explain trust in families. Dyadic interdependencies, such as support and conflict are, however, expected to explain the propensity to trust between family members with various statuses. Reciprocal support is expected to consolidate temporary social exchanges by establishing long-lasting relationships (Gouldner, 1960). When more support is present in a dyad, trust is expected to be stronger. Support, however, does not come without a cost. Ambivalence and conflict may take their toll on trust. This might be true not only for specific dyads of the nuclear family but for the family configuration as a whole.

Data and measures

Under which conditions do respondents trust their family members? To answer this general question, an innovative data collection about family configurations was carried out with a sample of middle-aged women. The survey was based on the *Family Network Method* instrument (Widmer, 1999; Widmer and La Farga, 2000). A standardized questionnaire was submitted to 100 women in the Geneva Lake region during the winter of 2008. Two criteria were used in the sampling design: respondents had to be in a couple and mothers of at least one child between 3 and 16 years old and living at home.

We collected valid information on 94 family configurations, almost a third of which involved a divorce and a remarriage. For each of them, detailed information was available about all significant family members included ($N = 1020$) and about conflict and support relationships among all of them, as according to the respondent. Respondents first included significant family members (the mean of cited terms is nine). They could cite additionally up to five significant friends (the mean of cited friends is three). Observations are nested in two levels: the first level identifies the significant family members cited by each respondent and the second corresponds to the characteristics of the respondents and the respondents' family characteristics. This particular data structure has required a multilevel analysis to overcome problems due to non-independent observations (Gelman and Hill, 2008). We measured trust relationships by asking how much respondents trust or consider loyal each of their family members.[3] A similar measure applied to loyalty.[4] The impact of the overall processes of family configurations was measured by density of support and conflict (Wasserman and Faust, 2006). Density was expressed in percentage the number of dyadic relationships actualized on the number of dyadic relationships possible in the whole network. The higher the ratio, the more family members are tied by support or conflict relationships.

A case study

Before turning to the statistical analyses and a formal approach of the problem, we first wish to present a case study which exemplifies some of the processes underpinning the development of trust in families. Lea is a 35-year-old woman, holding a rather unskilled job as an office clerk and living in a small rural town. She has a son, Theo, ten years of age, from her previous marriage, which lasted only two years. Since then, after some years spent single, she met Laurent, with whom she currently lives. Laurent has two sons from two distinct partnerships, one not yet ten and the other one a young adult who does not live with him. Lea's parents divorced and her father remarried. She has one sister. Her paternal grandfather is the only grandparent still alive. Her family configuration is a mix between her current husband and her previous husband, who is the father of her son. She first included her son in her list of significant family members, followed by her current husband, his ten-year-old son, her previous husband, her mother, the second son of her current husband, the mother of her previous husband, her father, her sister, two female friends and a male friend. The composition of the family configuration is, therefore, very heterogeneous; it expresses her relational history (as her parents and sibling are included), as well as her former husband and his mother. Long-time friends are also part of the family configuration. The order of inclusion is mixed, with the ex-husband having an unusually high ranking in it, demonstrating his importance in the family configuration.

If we look at trust relations between Lea and her family members, we see that her trust is quite differentiated. She does not trust her mother much (two to three points on trust scale), nor does she particularly trust her current husband's son, her previous husband, her previous husband's mother and a friend. She has intermediate levels of trust (four points) in her current husband, her father and other friends. Lea absolutely trusts (five points on the trust scale) only two family members: her sister and her son.

Considering the statuses of Lea's family members gives a first insight on the processes of trust development. In this case, Lea's current husband, her son, her sibling and her father are clearly the first trusted persons. Trust is then less developed outside this family core. Lea's trust levels in her step-family are mixed as is, counter-intuitively, trust in her mother. Development of Lea's trust follows the timing of her relationships: more recent family relationships and elective ones are more trusted. Blood links between Lea and her family members appear also to be a structuring factor of trust, with the noteworthy exception of the Lea's mother.

We now look at her emotional support and conflict networks. In the support network (Figure 15.1) there is a clearly visible denser part, which includes Lea, her son, her current husband, her sister, her mother and her husband's son. The most trusted family members are included in this subgroup. Interestingly, the trusted family members are embedded in a dense part of the conflict network as well. Therefore, trust has developed in this family configuration in a subgroup of individuals connected by support and conflict ties.

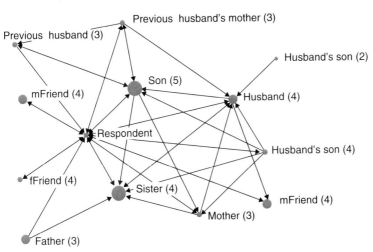

Figure 15.1 Respondent-family member trust embedded in *Emotional Support Network*

Notes: Point size corresponds to trust relation strength; arrows point to support persons; respondent-family member loyalty in parenthesis

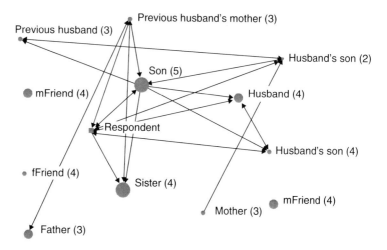

Figure 15.2 Respondent–family member trust relation embedded in *Conflict Network*

Notes: Point size corresponds to trust relation strength; arrows point to support persons; respondent-family member loyalty in parenthesis

Although there is not a perfect correlation between loyalty and trust, strong loyalty feelings correspond to high levels of trust. Actually a friend outside the subgroup has high loyalty score; the husband's son has priority but a little trust level, the mother obtains very little trust while she is the object of middle-low level of loyalty. Ambivalent relationships are present in the core of the family configuration: the respondent, the son, the husband and the sister are all embedded in both conflict and support relationships.

Overall, a complex pattern of relationships among family members' statuses influences Lea's trust. This example suggests that a varied set of explanatory factors is at work, such as lengths of duration of relationship, frequency of contacts, availability of reciprocal support and conflict. Therefore, a statistical analysis is necessary to disentangle the various explanations that relate to the development of trust.

Statuses or doing family?

Let us now turn to statistical analyses. A bivariate analysis of the effect of family statuses on trust is shown in Figure 15.3. A ranking obtained by trust mean for each family status shows that husbands, daughters and sons are the most trusted people. Parents and sisters are the second most

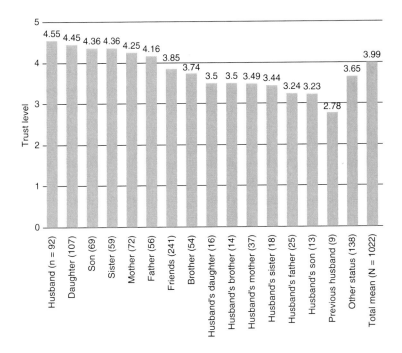

Figure 15.3 Trust mean by respondent–family member

trusted statuses, with brothers having more mixed results. All these statuses, except for brothers, are considered more trustworthy than other family members.

In a series of additional bivariate analyses, we found that loyalty, contact frequency, support and conflict relationships, as well as length of acquaintance, vary according to family statuses. Loyalty is primarily granted to sons, daughters, husbands, mothers, sisters and fathers. Along with tendencies found for these members, parents and siblings are viewed as the second most loyal. In turn, respondents felt a low level of loyalty towards stepsons and -daughters; loyalty towards brothers was mixed. A strong association is present between family statuses, dyadic support, and dyadic conflict. Most dyads link respondents with their husband (83 per cent), their mother (57 per cent), their sisters (46 per cent) and their friends (40 per cent) in terms of support. Relationships with daughters and sons more often are non-reciprocal, with respondents providing support. Most other family statuses do not develop supportive relationships. For conflict, 40 per cent of respondent-husband and 32 per cent of respondent-son dyads are reciprocal. Interestingly, the respondent-previous husband relationships are more conflict-loaded (50 per cent of reciprocal conflicts). Because family statuses are associated with uneven levels of loyalty, contacts and support, they may have an impact on trust. Indeed, a high contact frequency reinforces trust significantly. The length of the acquaintance influences trust as well. Figure 15.4 shows how loyalty, support and conflict relate with trust.

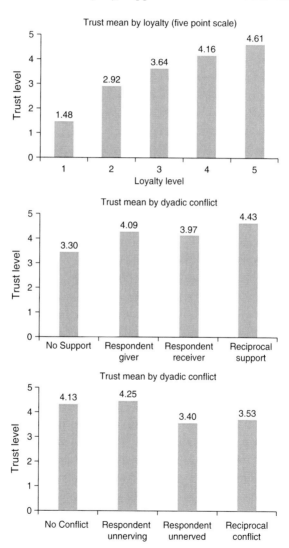

Figure 15.4 Trust mean (five point scale) by explanatory variables

Loyalty correlated strongly with trust. Presence of support enhances trust and presence of conflict weakens trust. Associations between dyadic processes of support and conflict, contact frequency and acquaintance length are present as well; there is a positive association between dyadic support, contact frequency and trust, and a negative association between conflict and acquaintance length.

To sum up, family statuses have an impact on trust because they are associated with unequal length of acquaintance and everyday contacts. Parents, siblings, husband and children are those family members with whom the most frequent interactions occur and the longest acquaintances exist. Trust also closely corresponds with loyalty issues and dyadic relationships. The effect of family statuses might well be related to the fact they are associated with such processes. Those factors are interrelated. Multivariate analyses are therefore needed to confirm which factors are the most important.

Multivariate analyses

The following multilevel regression analysis considers trust of family members by respondents as the dependent variable (Table 15.1). Going from model 1 to model 3 of Table 15.1, we introduce additional explanatory factors. The configurational perspective leads us to ask which kinds of interdependencies, both at the dyadic and network levels, account for interpersonal trust. The configurational perspective on families stresses the importance of reciprocity as founding relational processes of trust. In the first model we deal with the effects of family statuses. In the second model we test the impact of the frequency of contacts, respondent–family member acquaintance length and respondent loyalty feelings towards family members, while controlling for the educational level of each family member. We add variables measuring reciprocity relations in emotional support and conflict as well. Finally, in the third model we introduce variables characterizing the family configuration as a whole, such as the density of emotional support and conflict. We control for second-level variables, such as the respondent's age, her educational level and her family structure (step-family versus first family structure).[5]

Model 1 provides a confirmation of the bivariate analysis. Partners, children, parents and siblings are more likely to be trusted. Partners come first, followed by daughters and sisters. Mothers and fathers come afterwards. Respondents trust their daughters more than their sons. The same gendered trend exists for trust in siblings; the 94 interviewed

Table 15.1   Multilevel logistic regression analysis of trust in significant family members (N = 1020)

Predictor	Model 1 e^B	Model 2 e^B	Model 3 e^B
Family member status (ref.: other statuses)			
Friend	1.57	0.75	0.79
Daughter	8.98***	5.37	0.56
Husband	13.01***	7.10	1.32
Son	6.15***	6.23	0.51
Mother	5.56***	2.83	1.02
Sister	8.44***	5.05	2.86
Father	5.01***	5.16	1.91
Brother	1.20	1.25	0.60
Husband's mother	1.50	1.39	1.41
Husband's father	0.61	0.90	0.88
Husband's sister	1.38	2.53	2.64
Husband's daughter	1.02	1.48	0.90
Husband's brother	0.40	0.66	0.49
Husband's son	1.22	1.36	0.76
Previous husband	0.00	0.00	0.00
Contact Frequency		1.22	1.24
Acquaintance length		1.02	1.02
Respondent–family member loyalty		17.10***	16.42***
Educational Level: University		1.30	1.38
Emotional Support Respondent-family member (ref.: no support)			
Respondent giver		2.69**	2.50**
Respondent receiver		5.36**	4.87**
Reciprocal support		6.99***	6.22***
Conflict Respondent–family member (ref.: no conflict)			
Respondent unnerving		1.28	1.34
Respondent unnerved		0.16***	0.17***
Reciprocal conflict		0.19***	0.19***
Support Network Density*10			1.88**
Conflict Network Density*10			0.65
Respondent Age: more than 36			1.00
Respondent Educational Level: University			1.00
Recomposed Family Structure			1.00
Intercept	0.15***	0.03***	0.02***
Random intercept variance (Families, N=94)	2.80	3.67	3.17
Standard Error	*1.67*	*1.92*	*1.78*

Notes: Entries are exponentiated B. *p≤0.1; **p≤0.05; ***p≤0.01. Network densities variables vary between 0 and 1.

mothers declare a statistically significant stronger trust in their sisters than in their brothers.

In model 2, we introduce contact frequency, acquaintance length and loyalty, as well as dyadic processes such as reciprocal support and conflict. The explanatory power of family statuses drops to insignificance in all cases. An impressive boosting effect of loyalty on trust is present; to grant loyalty to a cited significant family member increases the chance of trusting her by a factor of 17. Dyadic processes exert an important effect on trust as well. Support between respondents and their family members strengthens trust. If respondents are the support givers, the chance to enhance trust is multiplied by 2.7 when compared with an absence of supportive ties. If respondents are the support receivers, the chance is multiplied by 5.3. If support is reciprocal, the chance is multiplied by seven.

Interestingly, the direction of support influences trust: individuals are more trusted when they are support givers than when they are support recipients. Conflict presents an opposite pattern of results. When respondents upset a family member, their trust in the upset person does not change when compared with an absence of conflict relationships. In turn, the case in which respondents are upset significantly reduces trust in family members. Reciprocal conflict also weakens trust, but to a lesser extent.

In model 3 we introduce support and conflict densities, controlled for respondents' age, educational level and family structure. An increase of support density is associated with a rise in trust by a factor of 1.8. The density of conflict does not have a direct impact on trust, although it is correlated with conflict in each specific dyad, which, in turn, has a negative effect on trust. In other words, individuals embedded in dense negative networks have a higher likelihood of developing a conflict relationship with their closest family members, a situation that disrupts the development of trust towards them. Interestingly, a positive and strong correlation is found between conflict network and support network densities, confirming that conflict and support are not antithetical but that they often come hand in hand, as research on ambivalences shows. Family configuration properties such as densities are valid explanatory factors for interpersonal trust.[6]

Conclusion

Parents, siblings, partners and children (either resident or not) are the main persons that adults trust. Therefore, trust in family members goes beyond the nuclear family, as it concerns not only spouses or resident children but also individuals from the family of orientation. Social capital is not limited to the immediate household but crosses generational lines to link individuals who have a history of shared intimacy.

Family statuses, however, cover a variety of processes that, to a large extent, explain their effect on trust. The development of trust as a central dimension of social capital in late modernity is structured by a set of clearly defined and related family processes at the dyadic and configurational levels. Indeed, trust is explained by dyadic processes such as the development of reciprocal supportive interactions and loyalty feelings between individuals and their family members. Family statuses are likely to be activated in a variety of relational interdependencies between specific persons. In other words, individuals trust in their father, mother or siblings in adulthood because positive and reciprocal interactions and feelings of loyalty have developed throughout their lives. Individuals give a high priority to a particular family member not because of their social status, the results show, but because there is a history of supportive relationships with that person that gives them a high level of priority in one's life. Doing the family work in daily interactions provides the basis for trust to develop. The highest levels of trust are found in cases in which both respondents and family members provide and receive support. Interestingly, being a receiver of support without providing support is associated with higher trust than being a support giver only. Therefore, being in debt to somebody for support creates a large share of trust. Individuals trust others who help them; they do not necessarily trust those that they help.

A main factor of trust holds in the extent to which family members achieve a high level of priority in one's life, a situation we referred to as loyalty. Various practices and rituals help this level of loyalty to be developed and maintained in family assemblages (Jallinoja, this volume): weddings, birthdays and other transitional events are occasions in which the loyalty towards family members can be expressed publicly by gifts and other material means (Finch, 1989). Attendance (or non-attendance) at such events is also interpreted by individuals as signs of the meaningfulness of relationships. The level of loyalty towards family members is also expressed in the occurrence of non-normative events such as divorce, health problems or death of a family member. The extent to which individuals care for each other going through those hardships provides clear indications to all about the level of priority given to each relationship.

Trust as social capital does not only depend, however, on the reciprocity of positive interactions such as support, but also on negative or ambivalent dyadic interactions. Dyadic conflicts, indeed, have a negative impact on trust. Some interdependencies create frustration and tensions in families, and such effects make the level of trust towards specific family members decline. In other words, the level of social capital individuals develop from their family ties is a function not only of supportive ties, but also of the extent to which conflict is present. Interestingly, conflict and support are not two opposite processes. In the sample considered in this chapter, the correlation between conflict and support is positive, not negative. Family configurations in which a higher density of support exists are also those in which a higher density of conflict is present. Therefore, a significant number of family dyads in late modernity are characterized by ambivalence.

Overall, the development of trust relates to specific dyads, such as the parent–child, the sibling or the conjugal dyads. Those dyads, however, belong to larger family configurations, by which they are shaped to a significant extent. Individuals embedded in dense and supportive family configurations have a much greater likelihood of benefiting from a high level of trust and social capital. In other words, the level of individual trust in family members not only depends on one's relationships with others, but also on the patterns of connections (or disconnections) that exist overall in family configurations. These results confirm that in order to understand processes occurring in any family dyad, its relational context should be taken into account. Indeed, density of support and density of conflicts within family configurations have a strong impact on the likelihood that parent–child, sibling or conjugal dyads develop reciprocal supportive ties and conflict. Families in which there are a greater number of interactions among members provide a higher level of trust. Confirming the hypothesis of Coleman (1988a) that bonding social capital is associated with greater trust, our results stress that trust does not only depend on the ability of respondents to develop active relationships with family members, but also on the general collective processes occurring in their family configurations. Although respondents participate in the shaping of their family configuration, they are not fully in control of it, as their ability to influence relationships among others is limited. Indeed, the extent to which family configurations develop dense sets of ties depends on their composition. As shown in Widmer (2006), beanpole family configurations, which are made up of individuals of multiple generations linked by blood, develop a higher level of connectivity. The inclusion of parents, grandparents, uncles and aunts in one's family configuration makes the likelihood of benefiting from bonding social capital and trust higher because many family members have a long history of interactions and support that link them. In other words, dyadic relationships in beanpole family configurations last longer and, therefore, are more interconnected than in other family configurations, such as post-divorce family configurations.

The impact of density of family configurations on trust is also indirect, as it influences the development of reciprocal relationships between respondents and their family members. In that latter case, density of support makes the development of trust in specific family dyads more likely. For instance, individuals tend to develop a supportive relationship with their parents, spouse or siblings when they are embedded in densely connected family configurations. The more reciprocal and supportive dyadic relationships they develop has a positive impact on trust. Family configurations are, therefore, the turf on which key family dyads (such as the conjugal or the parent–child dyads) develop. Respondents are often not aware of this indirect influence of the overall organization of their family configurations, as they focus on their relationships with their closest family members. It has been shown in several studies, however, that conjugal and parent–child relationships do respond to the overall pattern of interdependencies of families (Widmer et al., 2006).

Finally, the development of trust in families is certainly not homogeneously distributed across individuals. Respondents without a spouse or parents as members of their family configurations develop lower amounts of social capital. For a variety of reasons they have not developed strong and long-lasting relationships with individuals of such status. They lack prominent sources of trust in families of late modernity and, therefore, miss one important dimension of social capital. Therefore, access to family social capital is unequally shared. Of course, individual agency is not the main factor explaining the absence of parents, spouse or siblings in one's family configuration. A whole set of life trajectories come into play in the shaping of family configurations: fertility decisions of parents, grandparents, uncles and aunts have an impact on the number of cousins and siblings available; divorce of parents and grandparents, as well as their life expectancy and the migration patterns of various family members, are also influential. Social mobility is also a dimension of family configurations as it increases the social distance among family members if only some have experienced it. Overall, family configurations are the results of a mix of structural constraints imposed by a variety of individual life courses that come to interact, as well as the ability of individuals to develop meaningful and long-lasting interdependencies with others.

Social capital is an individualized resource in families of late modernity, which depends to a large extent on the set of reciprocal supportive relationships that have been built in childhood, adolescence and early adulthood. These sets of dyadic interdependencies are not fully personal, however, as they are embedded in larger configurations of family relationships and their overall relational logic. Rather than focusing on divorce or problems supposedly raised by a mother's employment to estimate social capital made available by families, one should consider how interpersonal trust develops in the complex network of interdependent individuals who are included in one's family configuration.

16
Afterthoughts

Riitta Jallinoja and Eric D. Widmer

'Sometimes the population is broken up into little groups who wander about independently of one another, in their various occupations; each family lives by itself . . . trying to procure its indispensable food by all the means in its power. Sometimes, on the contrary, the population concentrates and gathers at determined points for a length of time . . . This concentration takes place when a clan or a part of the tribe is summoned to the gathering, and on this occasion they celebrate a religious ceremony' (Durkeim, 2008: 214–15). This is how Durkheim depicts the dual existence of families among the Australian tribes long ago, but this duality is also very relevant in late modernity, as manifested in the divide between everyday life and family assemblages. Both of them contribute to the making of families, each in a different way. This is what we have described and analyzed in this volume; in Part II, the focus was on family assemblages, in Parts III and IV on the analysis of daily life practices, as they manifest themselves in encapsulated episodes of family making in different life stages. In Part V, the analysis was focused on social capital, a perspective that enabled us to see that the bonds between family members and kin are an individualized resource for the members. However, these bonds do not necessarily presuppose warmness and supportiveness only, but also ambivalent and negative dyadic interaction.

First, we take family gatherings, which form a specific body of events referring to population concentrations, under further analysis. Durkheim analyzed these in length in *The Elementary Forms of the Religious Life*. In all cultures special occasions are marked family gatherings, although the occasions may be named differently and the specific rites and ceremonies may vary from one culture to another. In Western cultures, many family assemblages are linked to annual Christian festivals, but the connection

234

should be seen as cultural rather than spiritual (Forbes, 2007: 17–32; Nissenbaum, 1997). Their significance is also affirmed by laws that dictate a suspension of general business activity in order to commemorate or to celebrate particular events (Etzioni, 2004: 6; Nissenbaum, 1997: 308–9). Christmas is perhaps the most popular and most significant holiday of this kind, but Easter has nearly the same status, particularly in societies where the Orthodox Church is the dominant denomination. The Soviet Union provides an illustrative example of Christmas as a cultural idea, common to a wide range of cultures. Under the Soviet regime, New Year festivities substituted for Christmas with the adoption of rituals and symbols similar to those associated with the Christmas holiday. In the United States, Thanksgiving Day parallels Christmas in significance for family gatherings (Muir, 2004). Common to all these holidays is that they give a compelling reason for families to gather together annually, at the same time each year. In doing so, they mark the boundaries of their family configurations.

Another body of family gatherings consists of those which take place occasionally, when 'great events of a lifetime' or rites of passage are solemnized (Martin-Fugier, 1990; cf. Bourdieu, 1990; 19; Pleck, 2000: 162–83). The most typical include weddings, christenings, first communions or confirmations, and funerals. In addition, families may gather together to celebrate, for example, the birthdays and graduations of family members. Whether annual or occasional, these festivities share common features in that they are not only largely stylized in a similar manner but also experienced as personal occasions. In other words, they are practised and shared by virtually everyone in society, but at the same time they are family-wise celebrations, with a perception that the celebration is 'our own' performance and in this respect unique. This dualism, the co-existence of the *general* and the *personal* is characteristic of family gatherings in particular, and this is examined in the following.

The four different family assemblages analyzed in this volume: weddings, Christmas celebrations, obituaries and family photos, reveal that it is *rules* that exercise a constitutive impetus for these family gatherings to incline towards similarity, and rules that guide the selection of guests to these gatherings. This is in fact an extraordinarily important factor in explaining the formation logic of family configurations. The *rule of genealogical proximity* has a decisive influence in this respect: the closer persons are genealogically to each other the more surely are they invited to weddings and to celebrate Christmas together. The closest relatives most surely appear in obituaries, too, and their photos – if any, are put on display. Obituaries in particular underline the logic of this rule because the mourners are ranked openly for public view, although this most probably happens at weddings as well, though more privately – when making seating arrangements for wedding guests, for instance.

Another rule that we recognized from our data sets was the *rule of bilaterality*. It is influential when inviting guests to weddings and Christmas celebrations, as well as in the assembly of family photos on display, although it tends to be irrelevant in the drawing-up of obituaries. Bilaterality requires that the kin of both spouses are regarded genealogically as equal. This provides couples with a duty to bear: kin from both lineages must be invited to weddings and other family festivities, such as christenings and confirmations. Bilaterality is in force when two groups of relatives unite, for example, at weddings; although nowadays it is largely symbolical, as interaction between the relatives of the two spouses is otherwise virtually minimal. More important than this aspect is the idea of descent, or our perception that we are rooted in our parents' ancestry. This is confirmed first at christenings and then again at confirmations, when grandparents from both sides are invited. Death functions differently, particularly in the case of the elderly deceased: losing a family member is the concern of one lineage only, that of the deceased. The special character of death as a cause for family assembling also manifests itself in an overall intensification of interaction when a family member is dying. Its symbol is 'good death' or 'proper death' (Pleck, 2000: 197; Howart, 2008: 132–53; Metcalf and Huntington, 2008: 207–8), indicating that those who form or once formed a family of procreation gather together once again, not only in the formal expression of funerals and obituaries, but also in informal memorialization of the common history.

The third rule, the *rule of equality*, may be a newcomer among the rules that guide family gatherings. We observed two different ways this rule functions. First, it complements the rule of bilaterality, by providing a balancing principle for those occasions where the principle of bilaterality causes unbalance in the sizes of the two kin guest groups. In the strictest sense, the rule of bilaterality is in force even when the numbers of guests from both sides does not match. However, the principle of equality has gained more ground and now people perceive bilaterality also as a question of equality, requiring an approximately equal number of guests to be represented from both sides. As a consequence, more distant relatives are invited from the less-populated side. The second application of the rule of equality is apparent in obituaries where, as mentioned, the principle of bilaterality is irrelevant. In the case of obituaries, the rule of equality requires that all representatives of each kin category are treated equally: all of them must be either present in the obituary or omitted. This rule is particularly influential for the closest kin.

In Durkheim's citation extracted earlier there is a noteworthy observation that helps to understand the workings of the rules described here. Durkheim maintains that the concentration of the population gathering together is not confined to the members of a small family unit, but extends to a wider range of people, a clan. The family gatherings we have discussed here show that they indeed gather together kin beyond the nuclear family, but clans have been nowadays reduced to smaller entities. Nevertheless, family gatherings still remind us of the idea of the clan: families are associated with larger wholes, grounded in genealogy. They associate kin with each other but, in most cases, without the symbol of the totem; or maybe it is the case that these gatherings have become the last clan totems: signs by which each kin distinguishes itself from the others (cf. Durkheim 2008: 206). In assemblages each family tacitly determines its scope, under the guidance of the rules but differently in different gatherings. Christmas celebrations tend to be limited to the intimate groupings of family and kin, as are family photos on display, while at weddings and in obituaries the scope often extends far beyond this small circle.

When looking at the compositions of different family gatherings we easily notice that the closest relatives present at all family gatherings belong to the family of origin. These persons are the parents and their grown-up children who once belonged to the same family but who have since dispersed or, as Durkheim (2008: 214) puts it, each family is living by itself. This leads us to specify the workings of the rule of genealogical proximity: the closest relatives who are prioritized in family gatherings are not chosen randomly but regularly and systematically from the same family of origin. Family gatherings thus signify the strong bond tie between the family of origin and the subsequent families of procreation, in effect between three subsequent generations. Together they form the most notable family configuration, and they can be seen as today's clans.

Rules as the generators of the general have been delineated by several scholars. For example, Metcalf and Huntington (2008: 53–4) in their research on death rituals ask: 'Why it is that the normal emotional response of people at a funeral is never random, but falls within an obligatory pattern, [for example,] to wear black and be solemn at an English funeral'. Patterns take shape only if perceptions are shared in the community as a whole, or in a group. At this level, the display of families brings to light 'the fundamentally social nature of family practices, where the meaning of one's actions has to be both conveyed to and understood by relevant others', as Finch (2007: 66–7) remarks. This means, as Finch notes, that the actions 'need to be linked in a sufficiently clear way with the wider systems of meaning to enable them to be fully understood as such'. Although Bourdieu (1989: 72–3) opts for the concept of '*habitus*', he outlines the same principle of patterning as Metcalf and Huntington. Habitus pieces together durable 'principles of the generation and structuring of practices and representations, which can be objectively "regulated" and "regular" without in any way being the product of obedience to rules. These principles are collectively orchestrated without being the product of the orchestrating action of a conductor, without being the product of a genuine strategic intention'. All these references speak for the existence of influential rules that compellingly direct people's attitudes and behaviour towards common patterns.

Bourdieu admits that the term rule is problematic; it has particularly puzzled those scholars who ground their interpretations on the individualization theory. Bourdieu's (ibid: 27) concept analysis is very useful for us in the specification of the term. According to him, 'the only way to escape the crudest naiveties of the legalism which sees practices as the product of obedience to the rules is to play on the polysemous nature of the word *rule*: most often used in the sense of a social *norm* expressly stated and explicitly recognized, like moral or juridical law, sometimes in the sense of a *theoretical model*, a construct derived by science in order to account for practices, the word is also, more rarely, used in the sense of a *scheme* (or principle) immanent in practice, which should be called implicit rather than unconscious, simply to indicate that it exists in a practical state in agent's practice and not in their consciousness, or rather, their discourse'. On the basis of our research results, we can conclude that rules may, indeed, turn into norms, but this is not the meaning we have in mind. Rather, rules are like principles, meaning an implicit or tacit knowledge about proper behaviour, which is fairly seldom pronounced but learnt in practice when certain ways of conduct are recurrently repeated. Rules are also general or abstract, therefore applicable in different situations, for example, at weddings, funerals and Christmas festivities. In his research on collective remembering, James Wertsch (2007: 60–1) distinguishes 'schematic narrative templates' from 'specific narratives'. This is the distinction that also functions in our family gatherings: the rules generate not only more generalized, abstract patterns that underlie a range of specific family gatherings, such as weddings, Christmas festivities, obituaries and family photos, but also all variation arising from the applications of the rules, which always implies the personal as a constitutive component.

Thus, the rules must not be considered to lead to uniform behaviour. First, the constellations of family ensembles in family gatherings may differ because of circumstances which are often outside the reach of personal authority. The kindred may be very limited, for example, both spouses may be from single-child families or their parents may have passed away; or the kindred may be very populous, with living parents and several siblings from both sides, all of them with several children. Family members may live close or far away from each other. However, when discussing variation in family formation, references to these kinds of differences are not made; instead, recent interest in variation arises from the assumption that variation is inherently grounded upon individualization. In this assumption, the composition of family gatherings results from personal aspirations, lifestyles and tastes, which make individual family configurations vary from small ensembles, merely the nuclear family, to extended families with grandparents and other relatives, as the 'typology' of Christmas celebration in this volume shows. The data sets prove that this kind of variation is true, but let us take a glance at such situations which perhaps most often cause variation and change in family gatherings and which also provide us with valuable information about the interplay between the rules and their individual applications.

The causes concerned can be condensed into a phrase, 'family rupture', which is often a result of divorce and/or the breaking off of family and kin relationships because of severe misbehaviour. In these families, the rules of genealogical proximity, bilaterality and equality lose some of their power as the organizing principles of family gatherings. For example, ex-spouses and blood-relatives with whom relationships have been severed can be left out of guest lists of weddings and funerals, and mourner lists in obituaries. Divorce also gives permission for individuals to remove family photos of ex-spouses from tables or book shelves and replace them with photos of new spouses. Personal manoeuvres are manifold in the situations of family rupture, and they cause variation because people's attitudes towards the parties of divorce and family conflicts vary. These situations also put the power of the rules to the test: in each individual case, the result is dependent on how much weight is given to personal feelings and interests, instead of yielding to the dominance of the rules. In all cases, however, the rules keep haunting, serving as a kind of background to one's considerations. If the three rules discussed are broken, it reveals that in their considerations people are inclined to react to the breaking of the rules, whether negatively or positively, understandingly or mournfully. Regardless of what stand is taken, the various reactions from people reveal the existence of the rules.

When families are made and remade on a daily basis, in everyday practices, the rules discussed here do not play as strong a role as in family assemblages. This is also true for the processes examined in this volume: those processes that stand out from the daily flow of family life as discernable processes with a logic of all their own. We also suppose that because they are more culturally patterned, they are more expressly constitutive of the formation of family configurations than the daily flow of family life. Our consideration dealt with the setting up of a family and the events and conditions that are specifically inclined to generating the remaking of families. In the same way as before, we are looking at how family members and kin and sometimes friends, too, are involved in these processes, what kind of common regularities can be recognized, and how they are interwoven with individualization tendencies.

In the first phase of an individual's transition to steady couplehood, friends and often siblings, too, play the most important role as confidants, whereas the parents get involved in the next phase, when the couple relationship has been stabilized. This phase is important to family configurations: the parents of both sides show great interest in their children's partner choices, assess them and, if having accepted them, integrate them into their family configurations, on both sides, for example, by inviting a potential new family member to family gatherings. Our research findings clearly indicate that this is the phase where the foundation for future family configurations is laid. The way the integration takes place also bears witness to the cultural strength of the rule of bilaterality, even though introduction formalities have toned down considerably of late.

The analysis of social networks affords some additional knowledge about the integration of young partners into other family configurations. For some young adults, the relationships with friends continue to be important, while for others the family of origin and kin remain more important. This divide coincides directly with their immediate intentions to remain childless or to have children. The former group holds an individualized family conception, while the latter a family-centred conception. This anticipates the typologies of family configurations apparent in later life: some people restrict their emotional commitment to their families, be it the nuclear family or beyond, while others include friends (Jallinoja, 2008). But a decision to have children tends to change the individualized orientations: contacts with kin intensify, often resulting in a change of family configurations, most probably also adding willingness to participate in family gatherings. Social networks function as notable mediators of orientations, particularly if the networks are dense, personal orientations that are apt to conform, both at the levels of attitudes and behaviour. This reminds us of the remarks by Finch (2007: 66–7) on the fundamentally *social nature of family practices*, where the meaning of one's actions has to be conveyed to and understood by relevant others. Social networks mediate and strengthen these meanings, but social networks also change according to life cycles. Even then they have the same function: to support one's choice in the framework of the wider systems of meaning.

Having a child through adoption brings to light a more complicated situation: instead of just two parents, adopted children have in fact four parents, particularly in transnational adoption. The two birth parents are not incorporated into the family configurations of the adoptee parents; on the contrary, they are totally excluded from these circles, even if the birth mothers would like to maintain their relationships with their children, in compliance with the system of meaning prevalent in their culture. This family conception collides with the system of meaning that prevails in the adoptee parents' societies, that is, the exclusive family system. Family configurations tend to take shape according to the pattern that is culturally most powerful, particularly if affirmed by the law. In the case of transnational adoption, therefore, the rules of genealogical proximity, bilaterality and equality are relevant for only the adoptee parents.

When moving on to look at the making of families later in life, we eventually come to a point where the term 'remaking' becomes highly relevant. It illustrates well the logic of family formation as an ongoing process: families are remade again and again, often in new constellations due to the changes contemporary people confront in their lives. Families must then be re-considered. In these re-considerations, *negotiations* play a decisive role, aiming at the re-formation of configurations so that they fit the new circumstances. To set up a stable couple relationship partners must integrate into each other's family configurations, as discussed earlier, but another concern lurks in the shadows. If they seek continuity in the relationship, the couple's inevitable fate is to make their individual biographies match. Our research indicates that there is, within the family, a dyadic relationship that is crucial to the formation of families. The rule of equality seems to guide the workings of this relationship, meaning a balance in sharing rights and duties between the partners. Negotiations play a central role in the search for balance but, as the presence of divorce indicates, negotiations do not necessarily guarantee the continuity of the relationship. Thus, they are also framed by other structures of meaning, most probably by individualized understandings of the partnership. Giddens (1991, 1992) was not off the mark when he suggested that 'pure relationship' will more and more frame the perception of partnership. The partnership in particular has been co-opted by individualism, even though the partners say they are making every effort to guarantee the continuity of the relationship.

The importance of negotiations is also apparent between elderly parents and their grown-up children, as well as between the siblings when their parents are in need of care. The process evolves into a remaking of the family that rearranges the relationships between the members of the family of origin and the subsequent families of procreation, whose interaction intensifies when the elderly parents need care. When living apart, the members of the family of origin feel relatively independent; interaction between them is intermittent and the relationships are quite distinct. This changes after elderly parents fall ill or become disabled. This situation actualizes *ambivalence* about the relationships, both among the parents and the grown-up children. Ambivalence is born from considerations of each party's *autonomy* and *solidarity* towards one another, appearing as a struggle between mutual distance and closeness.

Ambivalence between autonomy and solidarity is solved in negotiations, which are not always actual negotiations expressed verbally; instead, they may be negotiations based on a tacit knowledge of each party's rights (autonomy) and duties (solidarity), which are repeatedly monitored. This often leads to the rectification of interaction to make it more compliant with each party's wishes. This is characteristic of the relationships between parents and their children; in this respect they differ from relationships among siblings, where negotiations are not always as discreet as between the parents and the children. Many studies in this book verify the peculiarity of the relationship between the parents and their children: they have a central place in family gatherings and other interaction that is repeated, even though the participants live apart. Negotiations, implicit or explicit, aim at this continuity. Thus, negotiations should not be seen as totally individual measures, carried out for the sake of one's own interest only, or as struggles between two autonomous individuals, but they are also governed by yearnings for belongingness and the maintenance of the relationship, as was seen earlier when discussing the continuity of partnership.

Divorce represents another situation in which the views of different parties are at variance. After every divorce family members are required to establish new patterns of contact between themselves. This is a demanding task. The place of the ex-spouses in new family configurations needs to be negotiated, as well as the position of the former family configuration and the children circulating between these configurations. In all these respects, mothers', fathers' and children's views differ. Mothers and fathers are apt to dismiss their ex-spouses from their current families, whereas children willingly continue to regard both parents as members of their families. How the dyadic relationships after divorce are described vary extensively, depending on the person whose attitudes are in question. The mother–child relationship is mostly characterized as warm and supportive by all parties, but the views differ remarkably when looking at the father–child relationship. The mothers' opinion is dependent on the quality of her existing relationship with the ex-spouse, while fathers characterize their relationship with their children very positively. There are remarkable discrepancies between fathers' and children's views regarding visit arrangements: fathers announce that they act in accord with their children's wishes, whereas children regret their fathers' passivity in this respect. What really matters in the reassembling of one's new family is the quality of the co-parental relationship, which in turn means the establishing of new rules for co-parenting in new family structures. Besides ordinary interaction, this also concerns family gatherings like Christmas, weddings, and confirmations: children want both parents present there, which in turn often leads to negotiations with new spouses and their relatives.

Negotiations are generally seen as a symptom of individuality that has profoundly transformed family life. From this perspective, it seems sound to assume that, in tandem with the increased significance of negotiations, the power of the rules discussed in this book has eroded. Our research results verify that this is not the case, rather the current situation should be perceived as a *dynamic interplay between negotiations and rules*, which also affect each other: negotiations modify rules and, vice versa, rules persistently provide a background for negotiations. To specify this interplay we can state that the rules examined in this book adhere to certain points of family-making processes, like a bur, marking them as significant, that is, as part of the systems of meaning, where shared attitudes are located. There the rules crystallize the idea of the family, in its nuclear and extended forms, an idea that is implemented in different forms, as we have described in this volume.

Let one example illustrate the point. The rule of equality should lurk behind arrangements for disabled parents' care, requiring the grown-up children to share the care equally between the siblings. In practice, however, it often happens that one sibling takes the main responsibility for the care. Taking merely this outcome into account, it looks like the rule of equality would be entirely irrelevant in this context. If we instead take a look at the whole process, from the first signs of the parents' failing health up to the stabilized care practices, we can see that the process is full of negotiations. There would be no negotiations if the rule of equality were the only effective principle; negotiations are needed, because the siblings' individual conditions and dispositions are different. In negotiations, they are adjusted to the rules of equality so that each sibling can be satisfied, at least to some extent.

Social capital introduces an interesting perspective to family configurations by providing another kind of individualized aspect regarding family interdependencies. In this perspective, relationships between family members and kin are considered individual resources. We found that trust, as a basic resource of social capital, is above all expected from partners, children, parents and siblings, that is, in the members of the family of origin and the family of procreation. Thus, trust crosses the same generational lines as family gatherings and those family-making processes examined here. In this respect, we can talk about 'family social capital', which is constituted because positive and reciprocal interaction and feelings of loyalty have developed since childhood. However, social capital does not only depend on the reciprocity of mere positive interaction such as support, but also on negative or ambivalent dyadic interaction. Dyadic conflicts, indeed, have a negative impact on trust, but there is no reason to see conflict and support as two opposite processes, as our data sets show. Family configurations in which a higher density of support exists are also those in which a higher density of conflict is present (see also Haavio-Mannila et al., 2009: 48, 115). Families seem to tolerate conflicts more than other relationships, as shown in this volume: dyadic family conflicts may sometimes escalate into family rows leading to the breaking off of the relationships. In these cases, trust has eroded, most probably, over a long period of time, when reciprocal support, a necessary precondition for trust, has become severely unbalanced. Partnership is especially vulnerable in this respect, as instances of divorce indicate.

In this book, we have concentrated on the analysis of social ensembles called family configurations. The focus is on their *formation logics*, apparent in family gatherings and long-term distinct processes, which together lay a firm foundation for the making of relatedness through families and kinship. This kind of scholarly work is necessary if we want to avoid a one-sided individualistic perspective that easily prevents us from seeing how strongly people are bound to their families and kin, even in late modernity, which has been characterized as the era of individuality. Yet, this turn should not lead to the opposite extreme: to overemphasizing the significance of family relationships. Instead it is better to search for a balanced delineation of actual family relationships, which in practice *vacillate between individualistic dispositions and family solidarity*. There are moments defined by free choice, for example, the decision to embark upon a partnership or to have a child, but after the choices have been made, people are bound to the partner and the child, nowadays less to the partner than to the child, but nevertheless they cannot avoid this binding effect. However, the maintenance of relationships cannot be taken for granted; instead, many kinds of transactions are needed between family members and relatives, not only practical transactions, but also such ones that symbolize togetherness and belonging to the same family and kin.

Relatedness does not as such guarantee the elimination of the upper hand of individualism, because relationships can also be seen as individually chosen and maintained as, for example, Giddens's (1991, 1992) 'pure relationship' proves. His analysis centres round relationships as he perceives them in late modernity, lasting as long as the parties wish. In this ideal-typology he constructs a totally individualistic perspective concerning the formation logic of relationships, leaving out the patterning principles which direct the making of family relationships towards processes shared by a vast number of people. In this respect, informal rules are of remarkable significance. They structure practices like an unseen hand, but they also leave room for personal orientations. This duality, the interplay between structuring rules or the general and the personal, is ultimately an empirical question; their mutual relation must be verified in empirical research to see where the weight is at a given time, in rules or personal aspirations. It also seems to be so that it is impossible to assess the significance of individualization in a convincing way, if its symptoms are not examined against the workings of the rules. Many of these rules have a long history; despite the fact that they have been transformed, their elementary core has remained the same, witnessed here by the rules of genealogical proximity, monogamy and bilaterality. The application of the rules is likely to generate further changes in the rules, an inspiring challenge for future family sociology.

The next challenge could be the issues of same-sex relationships, ethnicity, class and religion that are missing from this volume. They most obviously modify the rules and practices we have examined here; to get a glimpse of this we briefly draft the way the future analysis might look like, particularly in regard to same-sex relationships.

In his book on the transformation of intimacy Giddens (1992: 134–56) takes lesbian couples as an instrument to trace the 'pure relationship', which he sees as an emergent pattern becoming more and more commonplace for heterosexual couples, too. As evidence of lesbian love relationships as pure relationships Giddens cites Hite's report (1978) on women's sexuality as experienced by women themselves. Some three quarters of the sample dwell upon their insecurities in respect of love, which Giddens identifies as characteristic of the pure relationship. It can be terminated, more or less at will, by either partner at any particular time, which makes relationships episodic. In his characterization, Giddens contrasts love relationships stripped of all external referents with institutionalized marriage relationships, short-term more or less free-floating relationships with conjugal relationships that are burdened with the principles of monogamy and patriarchy. In this light, homosexual relationships appear different from heterosexual relationships, a distinction that was generally made, particularly at the time when homosexuality became openly and widely a political issue in the 1970s. In the 1980s, a new category, 'families we choose', was launched; Weston's (1991) book on this family pattern gained enormous currency; 'families of choice' provided an apt concept to discern a post-modern family pattern (cf. Stacey, 1990) that was seen to model families more and more. 'Families we choose' is parallel to Giddens's 'pure relationship' and methodologically constructed in the same way; in both cases the individual is the central agent of relatedness. Weston identifies a remarkable difference between families of homosexuals and heterosexuals, a difference that is drawn from the interviews with lesbians and gays in the US. In the case of lesbians and gays, families are expressly constituted at will and motivated by love only, for which reason the members are mostly selected from among the closest friends. The modelling of the family of heterosexuals is not grounded in similar interview data but is constructed on the basis of literature. Thus, their families are constituted according to institutionalized practices, that is, through marriage or marriage-like partnership between a man and a woman and their biological offspring. This family pattern is characterised as exclusive, while chosen families are seen as inclusive.

Although this kind of distinction is correct, it only partly holds, as in fact Weston (1991) also herself demonstrates when bringing up the variety of couple and family patterns among lesbians and gays. This view has, however, surfaced more explicitly in recent studies only

(Smart, 2007c: 672). Smart suggests 'a different dimension to be added to this existing debate; one that draws from the views and feelings of gay and lesbian couples who have been through a commitment ceremony or have registered their partnerships'. Her study shows that family ties still matter among gays and lesbians, although maybe not to the extent Verhaeghe (1999: 1–2) depicts when describing the drastic change family life has faced. He maintains that 'the couple of yesterday has almost vanished and paradoxically (at least in most Western European countries) the main defenders of marriage are to be found in the gay community'.

When looking at Smart's study, as well as other similar studies in the frame of reference adopted in this book, we can notice that, among lesbian and gay couples, the rule of genealogical proximity is influential in the maintenance of familial and kin relationships. This is most apparently manifested in the will to maintain relationships with the members of the family of origin and with one's own children from previous heterosexual companionships, in particular, or to reconcile these kin relationships if broken (Weston, 1991; Smart, 2007c; Suoranta, 2005; Jämsä, 2003). Weston's short review on obituaries published in a local weekly newspaper verifies this, too: blood relatives, along with friends, former lovers and 'community members' present at the death or assisting during an illness are mentioned among the mourners (Weston, 1991: 110). As Jallinoja shows (see Jallinoja, in this volume) these are also present in the obituaries of the deceased who lived in a heterosexual relationship. Also if married (or cohabited) twice, the first partner sometimes appears on the list of mourners but most often at the end of the list. The accounts of obituaries in turn prove that lesbian and gay couples are presented together in the obituaries, in the same line, if the relationship has been approved by the closest relatives. The respondents appreciated this very much in their accounts and interviews. Interestingly, such expressions of gratitude were not found in the accounts and interviews of heterosexual couples. Their co-presence was seemingly seen as natural, therefore no comments were needed. The rule of bilaterality functions among lesbian and gay couples as willingness to maintain relationships with family members from both sides, and also at weddings (Smart, 2007c), typically in the same way as at the weddings of heterosexual partners (see Maillochon and Castrén, this volume). How effective this rule is depends on approval: if the relationship is approved by relatives on both sides, the rule of bilaterality is operative. If approved on one side only, the rule of bilaterity may be even totally ignored.

The most consequential difference between same-sex couples and heterosexual couples seems to be that not all parents, siblings and other relatives of same-sex couples accept their sexual orientation or the decision to register their partnership. Interestingly again, heterosexual orientation has not been recorded as a reason for disapproval. However, the denunciation of a partner is not totally non-existent in the case of heterosexual couples but in their cases, disapproval stems from other mismatches than those of sexual orientations, for example, from 'wrong' choices in terms of ethnicity, class or status, and religion (Sayer, 2005; Watanabe, 2005; Ketokivi, 2008). These social determinants of family formation processes have mostly been investigated separately; however, in putting together the results of these separate studies we find that each social determinant has its own working logic, but common to all of them is that doing 'otherwise' or being 'different' is hierarchically structured, that is, those who behave 'differently' are seen as being inferior to what is considered 'normal' or 'better off'. This divide is not only made of personal choices, depending on individual views and feelings, but is a deeply social and cultural matter meaning that the milieu where people live has an impact on their perceptions. Belonging to the same intimate ensemble unavoidably exerts pressure on the members of the ensemble to yield to each others' wishes, desires and demands. In G. H. Mead's framework this is the notion of 'taking the role or the attitude of the other' (Carreira da Silva, 2007: 30). The extent to which the feeling of sameness presupposes similarity is a question that must be studied empirically. The question itself is, nevertheless, relevant in family formation processes, in all phases.

The rule of equality that more and more influentially directs the formation and maintenance of couple and parental relationships has eroded the power of conventional social and cultural distinctions. In this kind of situation it is not reasonable to characterize differences between families exclusively according to social determinants examined ahead. Instead of labelling families categorically as of a certain type merely on the basis of one single social determinant it is better to look at how families, in spite of some specific characteristics, resemble each other in other respects. For example, in which way are same-sex partnerships similar to matrimonial heterosexual partnerships and in which respects do they differ from each other, that is, in which ways do the demarcation lines cross the boundaries between sexual orientations? The same questions are relevant to families in different classes and ethnic groups. Endogamy still affects the choice of partner, even though contemporary people mostly deny wealth and social status as criteria for choosing a partner. Ethnicity is also a characteristic that tends to favour those who are similar to 'us'. When asking to what extent people would take an immigrant as a friend and a spouse, much greater part of Finns would take an immigrant as their friend than as their spouse (Jaakkola, 1999: 78). The same study shows that white immigrants and particularly those nationalities that are culturally seen as close to Finns (for example, Swedes, Americans) are favoured much more as spouses than non-white (for example, Somalis) and non-Christian (for example, Muslim) immigrants. However, it is important to remember that partnerships and families are formed across ethnic boundaries, both against the will of the parents and with their support, in the same way as class and educational boundaries are transgressed in the name of love.

Irrespective of the ways family making is determined by social barriers, be it along the lines of these barriers or crossing dividing lines, the social determinants tend to build, the question of exclusiveness and inclusiveness arises, sooner or later. Family configurations take shape in the continuous vacillation of exclusive and inclusive forces, which widen and reduce the scope of ensembles where family members, kin and friends form the nucleus.

Notes

2 Relationality and Socio-Cultural Theories of Family Life

1. These photographs were taken as part of an ESRC project on Family Resemblances led by Jennifer Mason with Katherine Davies which in turn is part of the ESRC's Centre for Research Methods called (for short) Real Life Methods (http://www.reallifemethods.ac.uk) at the University of Manchester. The photographs were taken professionally by Ed Swinden and each member of the family has given their permission for us to use their photographs for educational purposes and for scholarly publications.

3 Making Family at a Wedding: Bilateral Kinship and Equality

1. The birth of the new unit is often marked by a change of name, for example.
2. We do not intend to deny that brides are often more active in the wedding arrangements and more passionately involved in finding information, choosing decorations, clothing etc. than their grooms (see Boden, 2003; Sniezek, 2005; Maillochon, 2009b).
3. People are getting married at older ages (28 for women and 30.5 for men in both countries; Eurostat 2008) and cohabitation has become very common (Kiernan, 2004).
4. The age of the brides varied from 23 to 33 (mean: 27.7) and of the grooms from 24 to 36 (mean: 28.5).
5. The French cases are a part of a larger dataset comprising 25 couples (see Maillochon, 2002, 2008). The 12 cases were chosen to match the Finnish cases.
6. The French data were collected and studied by F. Maillochon. The Finnish data were collected by A.-M. Castrén and a group of sociology students.

7 Couple Formation as a Transition between Families

1. In this tradition, the couple's life course has specific timing, turning points and stages in which the dyad experiences changes in attitudes and values related to their union (Lewis, 1972). However, little is said on the social and relational dimensions of such changes.
2. The interviews were collected within the frame of a larger research project (ELFI: Explaining Low Fertility in Italy) supported by grants from the National Institute of Child Health and Human Development (R01 HD048715) and the National Science Foundation (BCS 0418443).

8 Social Networks and Family Formation

1. They can be differentiated in expressing different types of fertility intentions: some are uncertain (and feel unable to decide when to have a child), others feel that parenthood is far and they will start thinking about the issue at a later point in time, few are ambivalent and feel unable to decide whether to have a child.
2. This traditional structure could imply a persistency of the self-evidence of traditional bonds. However, friends and neighbours do not automatically constitute traditional ties (that is ties that are 'naturally' given via kin relations or place of living and taken as self-evident); they may also be chosen as friends based on individual interests and affection. We shall take a closer look at selection effects in the following section.
3. There is one instructive exception: three persons are, despite their individualized family conception, embedded in networks that structurally resemble the family centered networks. However, these networks show a structural peculiarity: they consist of two dense cliques which hold opposite ideas on family formation. One clique favours the traditional family conception, while the other clique opts for postponing or forgoing childbirth. The respondents embedded in these networks feel highly ambivalent about whether to have a child.
4. Note that childcare facilities in western Germany (especially for children below age three) that would allow mothers to work full-time or even half-time are limited and/or expensive, so that most mothers either limit their working hours (or do not work at all), invest a large share of their earnings into private childcare (which only makes sense for women with a considerable income) or rely on parental support.
5. Among our respondents a dual earner model with two full-time working parents is largely valued negatively, arguing that children would suffer from the absence of the parents. This argument is also brought forward by those who intend to remain childless. Hence, those performing the most individualistic behaviour by intending to remain voluntarily childless are able to conform with those displaying the most traditional behavior, a gendered division of tasks in the family: it is better to remain childless than to be bad parents neglecting their child over personal interests and career aspirations.

10 Money and the Dynamics of Intimate Relationships

1. The wording 'individual-in-couple' is used for referring to our relational perspective on intimate relationships as 'realities *sui generis*': the couple is more than the sum of its parts and moreover the individual as subject is defined and constituted as being part of a couple or intimate relationship.
2. Research Project B6 'Living Together with Separate Budgets: Intimate Relationships and the Limits to Individualization' is a part of the Research Centre 536 'Reflexive Modernization'.
3. Instead of using the term 'marriage' according to Berger and Kellner (1970), the notion 'intimate relationship' is preferred, to refer to a dyadic relationship whether the two 'significant others' are married or not.
4. Or, in Thomas' words, 'If men define situations as real, they are real in their consequences' (Thomas and Thomas, 1928: 572).

5. These ideas also imply different (normative) modes of proceeding and maintaining a relationship (Hirseland et al., 2005). In this paper the notion 'relationship concept' is used as a 'sensitizing concept' (Blumer, 1954) to reconstruct the actors' interactive construction of their private world and the definitions of intimate relationships from the perspectives of the spouses (see also Allmendinger and Schneider, 2005; Schneider et al., 2005).
6. See, for example, Levinger (1983), Blumstein and Kollock (1988), Scanzoni et al. (1989).
7. The original wording in German is 'Aufbauphase', 'Bestandsphase', 'Krisenphase' and 'Auflösungsphase'.
8. Earlier the transition between the phases was determined by marriage (Lenz, 2006: 78ff.). Nowadays the transition is indefinite and can be for example signaled by the purchase of a washing machine (Kaufmann, 1994).
9. Stability is the continuance of the relationship and its foundations.
10. Continuity is conceived as a smooth development, the constant and steady flow of the intimate relationship.
11. By interviewing partners in joint interviews they have to interact and to negotiate what they present to the interviewers, as well as who presents it, etc. Already Allan (1980) points out: 'interviewing spouses together may lead data being generated that could not be obtained from interviews with individuals' (ibid.: 205).
12. With respect to intimate relationships as 'realities *sui generis*', the couple is more than the sum of its parts.
13. The analysis is based on a hermeneutic reconstructive interpretation (Hitzler et al., 1999) of key sequences, which were identified with the help of an 'open coding' (Strauss, 1987).
14. The reconstructions only portray selected portions of the cases with a summarized interpretation.
15. What seems to be a phenomenon of gender inequality is presented as an economic rationale: the firm (and not the partner) requires such a control structure (see also Wimbauer, 2003: 185ff.).
16. Instead of using the word 'saving'.
17. The original wording in German is 'Seinsqualität'.
18. Mr B is particularly fond of art objects, on which he spends a lot of his 'own' money.

11 Making Families at an Old Age

1. The research was realized with the support from the Czech Science Foundation (No. 403/02/1182, Sýkorová, 2006, 2007). In this project the stress was laid on the inductive strategy in correspondence with the adopted constructivist-interpretative perspective.

12 Reassembling Families after Divorce

1. The study was financed by the Austrian Federal Ministry for Social Security and Generations and was conducted at the European Centre for Social Welfare Policy and Research, Vienna. The presentation of a former version of

this paper at the ESA interim meeting in Helsinki (September 2008) was supported by the Austrian Research Association (ÖFG).
2. The following sections will refer exclusively to the term 'divorce'; disunions of non-marital cohabitations have been included with a clear understanding that there are many differences and that this equation bears some problems.
3. This result is in contrast to Rosenberg and Guttman (2001) who report that 43 per cent of the mothers included their ex-husbands into their subjective family configuration.
4. In this connection, the typologies of Ahrons and Rogers (1987) and Kaslow (2001) refer to 'perfect pals' or 'cooperative colleagues'.

13 Families in a Globalized World

1. Enriques Journey.

14 Family Relations as Social Capital

The chapter is the result of a common project of the authors: Rossi wrote paragraphs 1, 2, 3, 10; Mazzucchelli paragraphs 4, 8, 9; Bonini 5, 6, 7.
1. From now social capital will be abbreviated 'SC'.
2. In relational sociology SC consists in 'those features which are inherent in the structure of social relations and facilitate the cooperation among individuals, families, social groups and organizations in general [...] a certain type of social relations and precisely those relations in which individuals show and practise mutual trust and follow norms of cooperation, solidarity and reciprocity' (Donati, 2003: 33).
3. In the survey researchers ask the interviewees to specify how much they trust their relatives in general or how much they trust each single family member. In both cases the consequent measure of FSC is an average.
4. The results of the project refer to Italy as a whole, within the limits of sociological surveys.
5. The research *Di generazione in generazione. Le comunità familiari e la generazione delle famiglie* (2005–2006) (Rossi, 2006; Bramanti, 2007; Rossi and Bramanti, 2007; Bonini and Mazzucchelli, 2007) – was carried out at a national level first.
6. One for the wife, one for the husband (to be filled in separately) and one for the person, who was in charge of the community.
7. This hypothesis was advanced after carrying out a research on two samples of parents who had at least one child attending a state/private school. The survey was carried out in 2004 through structured interviews. The collected data shows that, extended community SC has the same tendency to be present either bonding or bridging from a community context that is closer to the individual (for example a group of friends) to a context that is somewhat distant (network of people with strong bonds of trust within the services offered to their children) (Donati and Colozzi, 2006a; 2006b).
8. Erikson (1982); McAdams et al. (2004).

15   The Fabric of Trust in Families: Inherited or Achieved?

1. Beck (1992) describes individualization as a structural transformation of the social institutions and the relationship of the individual to the society. In the field of family and intimate life, these developments allow new and democratic forms of living, freeing men and women from their traditional roles (Beck and Beck-Gernsheim, 1999).

2. We agree here with Elias about the ways in which groups set up their boundaries and establish a distinction between their members and the outsiders (Elias and Scotson, 1965). During this process, individuals stock memories, develop attachments and share aversions that narrow the group boundaries and qualify individuals with insider or outsider status.

3. The question reads: for all persons included in your list, can you tell me how much you trust her? The possible responses were: absolute trust, a large trust, some trust, low trust, no trust at all. The answers were initially coded on a five point scale. The scale was then dichotomized to perform logistic regressions. The active modality in further analysis corresponds to higher scores on the scale.

4. The question reads: 'In your relationships, what level of priority do you give to this family member?'. The answer items were: full priority, a large priority, some priority, a low priority, no priority at all.

5. Models one and two include first-level variables; model three includes both first- and second-level variables.

6. The diminution of the random intercept variance in model 3 explains a significant share of the interindividual variance of trust.

Bibliography

Adam, B. (1996) 'Detraditionalization and the Certainty of Uncertain Futures' in
P. Heelas, S. Lasch and P. Morris (eds) *Detraditionalization: Critical Reflections on
Authority and Identity* (Cambridge, MA and Oxford, UK: Blackwell Publishers).

Africa's Orphaned Generations (2003), Unicef, Unaids, New York, November
2003.

Ahrons, C. (2007) 'Family Ties after Divorce: Long-Term Implications for Children',
Family Process, Special Issue 'Divorce and Its Aftermath', 46(1), 53–65.

Ahrons, C. R. and Rogers, R. H. (1987) *Divorced Families: A Multi-Disciplinary
Developmental View* (New York: Norton).

Albertini, M., Kohli, M. and Vogel, C. (2007) 'Intergenerational Transfers of Time
and Money in European Families: Common Patterns Different Regimes?',
Journal of European Social Policy, 17, 319–34.

Aldous, J. (1996) *Rethinking the Developmental Perspective* (Thousand Oaks: Sage).

Allan, G. (1980) 'A Note on Interviewing Spouses Together', *Journal of Marriage
and the Family*, 42, 205–10.

Allegra, S. F. (2002) Il rapporto tra genitori e figli in Osservatorio Nazionale sulle
famiglie e le politiche locali di sostegno alle responsabilità familiari (50–65).

Allen, A. L. (2005) 'Open Adoption is Not for Everyone' in S. Haslanger and
C. Witt (eds) *Adoption Matters: Philosophical and Feminist Essays* (Ithaca and
London: Cornell University Press).

Allmendinger, J. and Schneider, W. (2005) *Projekt B6, Gemeinsam leben, getrennt
wirtschaften? Chancen und Grenzen der Individualisierung in Paarbeziehungen.
Fortsetzungsantrag an die DFG. SFB 536* (Munich).

Amato, P. R. (2000) 'The Consequences of Divorce for Adults and Children',
Journal of Marriage and the Family, 62(4), 1269–87.

Amato, P. and Booth, A. (1997) *A Generation at Risks: Growing up in an Era of
Family Upheaval* (Cambridge: Harvard University Press).

Amato, P. and Gilbreth, J. (1999) 'Nonresident Fathers and Children's Well-Being:
A Meta-analysis', *Journal of Marriage and Family*, 61(3), 557–73.

Amato, P., Meyers, C. and Emery, R. (2009) 'Changes in Nonresident Father–
Child Contact From 1976 to 2002', *Family Relations*, 58(1), 41–53.

Antonucci, T. (1986) 'Hierarchical Mapping Technique', *Generations: Journal of the
American Society on Aging*, 10(4), 10–12.

Antúnez, R. (2008) Fotografias inmediatas, Available at: http://www.
henciclopedia.org.uy/autores/Antunez/fotografiainmediata.htm (Accessed 22
October 2009).

Aquilino, W. S. (2005) 'Impact of Family Structure on Parental Attitudes Toward
the Economic Support of Adult Children Over the Transition to Adulthood',
Journal of Family Issues, 26(2), 143–67.

Arai, L. (2007) 'Peer and Neighbourhood Influences on Teenage Pregnancy and
Fertility: Qualitative Findings from Research in English Communities', *Health &
Place*, 13, 87–98.

Archer, M. (2003) *Structure, Agency and the Internal Conversation* (Cambridge: Cambridge University Press).

Audehm, K. and Zirfas, J. (2001) 'Familie als ritueller Lebensraum' in C. Wulf, B. Althans, K. Audehm, C. Bausch, M. Göhlich, S. Sting, A. Tervooren, M. Wagner-Willi, and J. Zirfas, *Das Soziale als Ritual. Zur performativen Bildung von Gemeinschaften* (Opladen: Leske + Budrich).

Axinn, W. G., Clarkberg, M. E. and Thornton, A. (1994) 'Family Influences on Family Size Preferences', *Demography*, 31(1), 65–79.

Back, L. (2007) *The Art of Listening* (Oxford: Berg).

Bagnasco, A., Piselli, F., Pizzorno, A. and Trigilia, C. (2001) *Il Capitale sociale. Istruzioni per l'uso* (Bologna: Il Mulino).

Banca d'Italia, Eurosistema, La ricchezza delle famiglie italiane 1995–2005, supplementi al Bollettino statistico, nuova serie, anno XVII, n. 75–19 dicembre 2007.

Banfield, E. (1958/1967) *The Moral Basis of a Backward Society* (New York/London: The Free Press Collier-Macmillan).

Bankston, C. L. and Zhou, M. (2002) 'Social Capital as a Process: The Meaning and the Problems of a Theory Metaphor', *Sociological Inquiry*, 72(2), 123–34.

Barbagli, M., Castiglioni, M. and Dalla Zuanna, G. (2003) *Fare famiglia in Italia. Un secolo di cambiamenti* (Bologna: il Mulino).

Bauman, Z. (2003), *Liquid Love: On the Frailty of Human Bonds* (Cambridge: Polity).

Bauserman, R. (2002) 'Child Adjustment in Joint-Custody versus Sole-Custody Arrangements: A Meta-Analytic Review', *Journal of Family Psychology*, 16(1), 91–102.

Beck, U. (1986) *Risikogesellschaft. Auf dem Weg in eine andere Moderne* (Frankfurt a. M.: Suhrkamp).

Beck, U. (1992, German orig. 1986) *Risk Society: Towards a New Modernity* (London: Sage Publications).

Beck, U. and Beck-Gernsheim, E. (1995/1999, German orig. 1990) *The Normal Chaos of Love* (Cambridge: Polity Press).

Beck, U. and Beck-Gernsheim, E. (2002, German orig. 2001) *Individualization, Institutionalized Individualism and Its Social and Political Consequences* (London, Thousand Oaks & New Delhi: Sage Publications).

Beck-Gernsheim, E. (2002, German orig. 1998) *Reinventing the Family: In Search of New Lifestyles* (Cambridge: Polity Press).

Belleau, H. (1996) Les réprésentations de l'enfant dans les albums de photographies de famille. Thèse doctorale (Dept. Sociologie, University de Montréal).

Bengtson, V. L. (2001) 'The Burgess Award Lecture: Beyond the Nuclear Family: The Increasing Importance of Multigenerational Bonds', *Journal of Marriage and Family*, 63(1), 1–16.

Bengtson, V. L., Olander, E. B. and Haddad, A. A. (1976) 'The Generation Gap and Aging Family Members: Toward a Conceptual Model' in J. Gubrium (ed.) *Time, Roles and Self in Old Age* (New York: Human Science Press).

Bengtson, V. L. and Schrader, S. S. (1982) 'Parent-Child Relations' in D. Mangen and W. Peterson (eds) *Research Instruments in Social Gerontology, Vol. 2: Social Roles and Social Participation* (Minneapolis: University of Minnesota Press).

Bengtson, V. L., Giarusso, R., Mabry, J. B. and Silverstein, M. (2002) 'Solidarity, Conflict, and Ambivalence: Complementary or Competing Perspectives on Intergenerational Relationships?', *Journal of Marriage and the Family*, 64, 568–76.

Bengtson, V., Biblarz T. and Roberts, R. (2002) *How Families Still Matter: A Longitudinal Study of Youth in Two Generations* (Cambridge: Cambridge University Press).

Bennett, L., Wolin, S. and McAvity, K. (1988) 'Family Identity, Ritual, and Myth: A Cultural Perspective on Life Cycle Transitions' in Celia J. Falicov (ed.) *Family Transitions. Continuity and Change over the Life Cycle* (New York: Guilford Press).

Berger, J. (1972) *Ways of Seeing* (Harmondsworth: Penguin).

Berger, P. (1963) *Invitation to Sociology: A Humanistic Perspective* (New York: Doubleday & Co., Inc.).

Berger, B. and Berger, P. (1984) *The War over the Family: Capturing the Middle Ground* (Harmondsworth: Penguin Books).

Berger, P. and Kellner, H. (1970) 'Marriage and the Construction of Reality: An Exercise in the Microsociology of Knowledge' in H. P. Dreitzel (ed.) *Recent Sociology 2: Patterns of Communicative Behaviour* (London: Macmillan).

Berger, P. and Kellner, H. (1988) 'Le mariage et la construction de la réalité', *Dialogue*, 4e trimestre.

Berger, P. and Luckmann, T. (1981, orig. 1966) *The Social Construction of Reality: A Treatise in the Sociology of Knowledge* (Harmondsworth: Penguin Books).

Berger, R. (1998) *Stepfamilies: A Multi-Dimensional Perspective* (New York: Haworth).

Bernard, J. (1972) *The Future of Marriage* (New York: Times Mirror).

Bernardi, L. (2003) 'Channels of Social Influence on Reproduction', *Population Research and Policy Review*, 22(5–6), 527–55.

Bernardi, L., Keim, S. and von der Lippe, H. (2006) 'Freunde, Familie und das eigene Leben. Zum Einfluss sozialer Netzwerke auf die Lebens- und Familienplanung junger Erwachsener in Lübeck und Rostock' in B. Hollstein and F. Straus (eds) *Qualitative Netzwerkanalyse: Konzepte, Methoden, Anwendungen* (Wiesbaden: VS Verlag).

Bernardi, L., Keim, S. and von der Lippe, H. (2007) 'Social Influences on Fertility: A Comparative Mixed Methods Study in Eastern and Western Germany', *Journal of Mixed Methods Research*, 1(1), 23–47.

Billy, J. and Udry, J. (1985) 'Patterns of Adolescent Friendship and Effects on Sexual Behavior', *Social Psychology Quarterly*, 48(1), 27–41.

Bison I. and Esping-Andersen, G. (2000) 'Unemployment, Welfare Regime and in Packaging' in D. Gallie and S. Paugam (eds) *Welfare Regime and the Experience of Unemployment in Europe* (Oxford: Oxford University Press).

Bloklan, T. (2005) 'Memory Magic: How a Working-Class Neighbourhood Became an Imagined Community and Class Started to Matter when It Lost Its Base' in F. Devine, M. Savage, J. Scott and R. Crompton (eds) *Rethinking Class* (Basingstoke: Palgrave Macmillan).

Blossfeld, H-P. and Drobnič, S. (eds) (2002) *Careers of Couples in Contemporary Society: From Male Breadwinner to Dual-Earner Families* (New York: Oxford University Press).

Blumer, H. (1954) 'What is Wrong with Social Theory?', *American Sociological Review*, 18, 3–10.

Blumer, H. (1969) *Symbolic Interactionism: Perspective and Method* (Englewood Cliffs, NJ: Prentice Hall).

Blumstein, P. and Kollock, P. (1988) 'Personal Relationships', *Annual Review of Sociology*, 14, 467–90.

Boccacin, L. and Marta, E. (2003) *Giovani-adulti, famiglia e volontariato. Itinerari di costruzione dell'identità personale e sociale* (Milano: Unicopli).

Boden, Sharon (2003) *Consumerism, Romance and the Wedding Experience* (Houndmills: Palgrave Macmillan).

Bongaarts, J. and Watkins, S. (1996) 'Social Interactions and Contemporary Fertility Transitions', *Population & Development Review*, 22(4), 639–82.

Bonini, R. (2005) *Una transizione generativa* (Milano: Led).

Bonini, R. and Mazzucchelli, S. (2007) 'La cura del legame coniugale nelle comunità familiari' in E. Scabini and G. Rossi (eds) *Promuovere famiglia nella comunità* (Milano: Vita e Pensiero).

Boss, P. G. (1980) 'Normative Family Stress: Family Boundary Changes across the Lifespan', *Family Relations*, 29, 445–50.

Boss, P. G. and Greenberg, J. R. (1984) 'Family Boundary Ambiguity: A New Variable in Family Stress Theory', *Family Process*, 23, 535–46.

Bourdieu, P. (1976, French orig. 1972) 'Marriage Strategies as Strategies of Social Reporduction' in R. Forster and O. Ranum (eds) *Family and Society: Selection from the Annales, Economies, Sociétés, Civilations* (Baltimore and London: The Johns Hopkins University Press).

Bourdieu, P. (1977/1989, French orig. 1972) *Outline of a Theory of Practice* (Cambridge: Cambridge University Press).

Bourdieu, P. (1979) *La fotografia: un arte intermedio* (México: Nueva Imagen).

Bourdieu, P. (1980) 'Le Capital Social: Notes Provisoires', *Actes de la recherche en sciences sociales*, (31), 2–3.

Bourdieu, P. (1986) 'The Forms of Capital' in J. Richardson (ed.) *Handbook of Theory and Research for the Sociology of Education* (New York: Greenwood Press).

Bourdieu, P. (1990, French orig. 1965) *Photography: A Middle-Brow Art* (Stanford: Stanford University Press).

Bourdieu, P. (1998) *Teorie jednání* (Praha: Karolinum).

Bowie, F. (2004) 'Adoption and the Circulation of Children' in F. Bowie (ed.) *Cross-Cultural Approaches to Adoption* (London and New York: Routledge).

Bramanti, D. (2007) 'Come si declina la generativita' sociale nelle comunità familiari: accoglienza e capitale sociale' in E. Scabini and G. Rossi (eds) *Promuovere famiglia nella comunità* (Milano: Vita e Pensiero).

Brannen, J., Moss, P. and Mooney, A. (2004) *Working and Caring over the Twentieth Century* (Basingstoke: Palgrave Macmillan).

Bruno, G. (1990) 'Ramble City: Postmodernism and Blade Runner' in A. Kuhn (ed.) *Alien Zone* (New York: Verso Books).

Bühler, C. and Fratczak, E. (2007) 'Learning from Others and Receiving Support: The Impact of Personal Networks on Fertility Intentions in Poland', *European Societies*, 9(3), 359–82.

Burgess, E. and Locke, H. (1945) *The Family: From Institution to Companionship* (New York: American Book Company).

Burkitt, I (2008) *Social Selves: Theories of Self and Society*, 2nd edn (London: Sage).

Burt, R. S. (1983) *Applied Network Analysis* (Beverly Hills: Sage Publications).

Buzzi C., Cavalli A. and de Lillo A. (2002) *Giovani del nuovo secolo*. Quinto rapporto IARD sulla condizione giovanile in Italia (Bologna: Il Mulino).

Carrà, E. (1998) 'I molti "volti" dell'associazionismo familiare: due studi di caso', *Sociologia e politiche sociali*, 1(3), 153–79.

Carrà Mittini, E. (2003) *Dentro le politiche familiari. Storia di una ricerca relazionale sulla l.r. 23/99 'Politiche regionali per la famiglia' della Regione Lombardia* (Milano: Led).

Carrà, E. (2006) 'L'associazionismo familiare', in E. Scabini and G. Rossi (eds) *Le parole della famiglia* (Milano: Vita e Pensiero).

Carreira da Silva, Filipe (2007) *G. H. Mead. A Critical Introduction* (Cambridge: Polity).

Carroll, J., Olson, C. and Buckmiller, N. (2007) 'Family Boundary Ambiguity: A 30-Year Review of Theory, Research, and Measurement', *Family Relations*, 56 (2), 210–30.

Carsten, J. (2000a) '"Knowing Where You've Come From": Ruptures and Continuities of Time and Kinship in Narratives of Adoption', *Journal of the Royal Anthropological Institute*, 6, 687–703.

Carsten, J. (2000b) 'Introduction: Cultures of Relatedness' in J. Carsten (ed.) *Cultures of Relatedness: New Approaches to the Study of Kinship* (Cambridge: Cambridge University Press).

Carsten, J. (2004/2005) *After Kinship* (Cambridge: Cambridge University Press).

Cartocci, R. (2007) *Mappe del tesoro. Atlante del capitale sociale in Italia* (Bologna: Il Mulino).

Castel, Robert (1995) *Métamorphoses de la question sociale* (Paris: Fayard).

Castells, M., Fernández-Ardèvol, M., Linchuan Qiu, J. and Sey, A. (2006) *Comunicación móvil y sociedad. Una perspectiva global* (Barcelona: Ariel).

Castrén, A-M. (2008) 'Post-Divorce Family Configurations' in E. D. Widmer and R. Jallinoja (eds) *Beyond the Nuclear Family: Families in a Configurational Perspective* (Bern: Peter Lang).

Castrén, A-M. (2009a) 'Onko perhettä eron jälkeen' in R. Jallinoja (ed.) *Vieras perheessä* (Helsinki: Gaudeamus).

Castrén, A-M. (2009b) *Onko perhettä eron jälkeen? Eroperhe, etäperhe, uusperhe* (Helsinki: Gaudeamus).

Castrén, A-M. and Maillochon, F. (2009) 'Who Chooses the Wedding Guests, the Couple or the Family? Individual Preferences and Relational Constraints in France and Finland', *European Societies*, 11(3), 369–89.

Chalfen, R. (1987) *Snapshot Versions of Life* (Bowling Green, Ohio: Bowling Green State University Popular Press).

Chambers, D. (2001) *Representing the Family* (London, Thousand Oaks and New Delhi: Sage Publications).

Chapman, T. and Hockey, J. (1999) *Ideal Homes? Social Change and Domestic Life* (London: Routledge).

Cherlin, A. J. (2004) 'The Deinstitutionalization of American Marriage', *Journal of Marriage and Family*, 66(4), 848–61.

Cherlin, A. and Furstenberg, F. (1994) 'Stepfamilies in the United States: A Reconsideration', *Annual Review of Sociology*, *20*(1), 359–81.

Cigoli, V. and Scabini, E. (2006) *Family Identity: Ties, Symbols, and Transitions* (London: Routledge).

Coleman, J. S. (1988a) 'Social Capital in the Creation of Human Capital', *American Journal of Sociology*, (94), 95–120.

Coleman, J. S. (1988b) 'The Creation and Destruction of Social Capital: Implications for the Law', *Notre Dame Journal of Law, Ethics and Public Policy*, (3), 375–404.

Coleman, J. S. (1990) *Foundations of Social Theory* (Cambridge, MA: Harvard University Press).

Connidis, I. A. and McMullin, J. A. (2002) 'Ambivalence, Family Ties, and Doing Sociology', *Journal of Marriage and Family*, 64, 594–601.

Cook, K. S. (2005) 'Networks, Norms, and Trust: The Social Psychology of Social Capital 2004 Cooley Mead Award Address', *Social Psychology Quarterly*, 68(1), 4–14.

Cooper, D. (1971) *The Death of the Family* (New York: Vintage Books, Random House).

Corijn, M., Klijzing, E. and Baizan, P. (2001) *Transition to Adulthood in Europe* (Amsterdam: Kluwer).

Cott, N. F. (2002) *Public Vows: A History of Marriage and the Nation* (Cambridge, MA and London: Harvard University Press).

Cowan, P. A. and Hetherington, E. M. (1991) (eds) *Family Transitions: Advances in Family Research* (Hillsdale: Erlbaum).

Currie, Dawn H. (1993) '"Here Comes the Bride": The Making of a "Modern Traditional" Wedding in Western Culture', *Journal of Comparative Family Studies*, XXIV(3), 403–21.

Dalla Zuanna, G. (2001) 'The Aeoulus' Banquet', *Demographic Research*, 4, 133–62.

Dalla Zuanna, G. and Micheli, G. (2004) (eds) *Strong Family and Low Fertility: A Paradox?* (Kluwer, Dordrecht: Springer).

De Rose, A., Racioppi, F. and Zanatta, A. (2008) 'Italy: Delayed Adaptation of Social Institutions to Changes in Family Behaviour', *Demographic Research*, 19, 665–704.

Déchaux, Jean-Hugues (2002) 'Paradoxes of Affiliation in the Contemporary Family', *Current Sociology*, 50(2), 229–42.

Déchaux, Jean-Hugues (2003) 'La parenté dans les sociétés modernes: un éclairage structural', *Recherches et Prévisions*, 72, 53–63.

DeGarmo, D., Patras, J. and Eap, S. (2008) 'Social Support for Divorced Fathers' Parenting: Testing a Stress-Buffering Model', *Family Relations*, 57(1), 35–48.

Del Boca, D. (1997) 'I trasferimenti di reddito nelle famiglie' in M. Barbagli, and C. Saraceno (eds) *Lo stato delle famiglie in Italia* (Bologna: Il Mulino).

Di Nicola, P. and Landuzzi, G. (2004) 'Le Associazioni familiari' in P. Donati (ed.) *Il terzo settore in Italia: culture e pratiche* (Milano: FrancoAngeli).

Dindia, K. (2000) 'Relational Maintenance' in C. Hendrick and S. Hendrick (eds) *Close Relationships. A Sourcebook* (Thousand Oaks: Sage Publications).

Donati, P. (2003) (ed.) *Famiglia e capitale sociale nella società italiana* (Cinisello Balsamo: Edizioni San Paolo).

Donati, P. (2006) 'Relazione familiare: la prospettiva sociologica' in E. Scabini and G. Rossi (eds) *Le parole della famiglia* (Milano: Vita e Pensiero).

Donati, P. (2007) (ed.) 'Il capitale sociale nella prospettiva relazionale' in *Sociologia e Politiche Sociali* (Milano: FrancoAngeli).

Donati, P. and Colozzi, I. (2006a) (eds) *Terzo settore e valorizzazione del capitale sociale in Italia, luoghi e attori* (Milano: FrancoAngeli).

Donati, P. and Colozzi, I. (2006b) (eds) *Capitale sociale delle famiglie e processi di socializzazione* (Milano: FrancoAngeli).

Donati, P. and Colozzi, I. (2007) *Terzo settore, mondi vitali e capitale sociale* (Milano: FrancoAngeli).

Donati, P. and Prandini, R. (2007) 'The Family in the Light of a New Relational Theory of Primary, Secondary and Generalized Social Capital', *International Review of Sociology*, 17(2), 209–23.

Donati, P. and Rossi, G. (1995) (eds) *Le associazioni familiari in Italia* (Milano: FrancoAngeli).

Donati, P. and Tronca, L. (2008) *Il capitale sociale degli italiani. Le radici familiari, comunitarie ed associative del civismo* (Milano: FrancoAngeli).

Duck, S. (1994) 'Steady as (S)he Goes: Relational Maintenance as a Shared Meaning System' in D. Canary, and L. Stafford (eds) *Communication and Relationship Maintenance* (New York: Academic Press).

Dunn, J., O'Connor, T. and Levy, I. (2002) 'Out of the Picture: A Study of Family Drawings by Children from Step-, Single-Parent and Non-Step Families', *Journal of Clinical Child and Adolescent Psychology*, 31(4), 505–12.

Durkheim, É. (2001, French orig. 1912) *The Elementary Forms of Religious Life* (Oxford: Oxford University Press).

Durkheim, È. (2008, French orig. 1912) *The Elementary Forms of the Religious Life* (Mineola, New York: Dover Publications, Inc.).

Elder, G., Johnson, M. K. and Crosnoe, R. (2003) 'The Emergence and Development of Life Course Theory' in J. Mortimer and M. Shannan (eds) *Handbook of the Life Course* (New York: Kluwer Academics).

Elias, N. (1978, German orig. 1970) *What is Sociology?* (London: Hutchinson of London).

Elias, N. (1987, German orig. 1983) *Involvement and Detachment* (Oxford: Basil Blackwell).

Elias, N. (1994) *The Civilizing Process* (Oxford: Blackwell).

Elias, N. and Scotson, J. (1965) *The Established and the Outsiders: A Sociological Enquiry into Community Problems* (London: Frank Cass & Co).

Elzinga, G. and Liefbroer, A. (2007) 'Destandardization of Life Trajectories of Young Adults: A Cross-National Comparison Using Sequence Analysis', *European Journal of Population*, 23, 225–50.

Emery, R. (1999) *Marriage, Divorce, and Children's Adjustment* (Thousand Oaks: Sage Publications).

Eriksen, Thomas (2001) *Small Places, Large Issues* (London: Pluto Press).

Erikson, E. H. (1982) *The Life Cycle Completed* (New York: Norton).

Esping-Andersen, G. (1995) 'Il welfare state senza il lavoro. L'ascesa del familismo nelle politiche sociali dell'Europa continentale', *Stato e Mercato*, XLV, 3, 347–80.

Esping-Andersen, G. (1999) *Why We Need a New Welfare State* (New York: Oxford University Press).

Etzioni, A. (1996) *The New Golden Rule: Community and Morality in a Democratic Society* (New York: Basic Books).

Etzioni, A. (2004) 'Holidays and Rituals: Neglected Seedbeds of Virtue' in A. Etzioni and J. Bloom (eds) *We are What We Celebrate: Understanding Holidays and Rituals* (New York and London: New York University Press).

Facchini, C. (2002) 'La permanenza dei giovani nella famiglia di origine' in C. Buzzi, A. Cavalli and A. De Lillo (eds) *Giovani del nuovo secolo. Quinto rapporto IARD sulla condizione giovanile in Italia* (Bologna: Il Mulino).

Feldhaus, M. and Huinink, J. (2006) Panel Analysis of Intimate Relationships and Family Dynamics (PAIRFAM). Working Paper 6. Available at: http://www.pairfam.uni-bremen.de/uploads/tx_sibibtex/arbeitspapier_6.pdf. Accessed 20 May 2010.

Ferrera, M. (1996) 'The Southern Model of Welfare in Social Europe', *Journal of European Social Policy*, 6, 179–89.

Field, J. (2003) *Social Capital* (London: Routledge).

Fiese, B. and Kline, C. (1993) 'Development of the Family Ritual Questionnaire: Initial Reliability and Validation Studies', *Journal of Family Psychology*, 6, 290–9.

Finch, J. (1989) *Family Obligations and Social Change* (Cambridge: Polity Press).

Finch, J. (2007) 'Displaying Families', *Sociology*, 41(1), 65–81.

Finch, J. and Mason, J. (1993) *Negotiating Family Responsibilities* (London and New York: Tavistock/Routledge).

Finch, J. and Mason, J. (2000a) *Passing On: Kinship and Inheritance in England* (London: Routledge).

Finch, J. and Mason, J. (2000b) 'Family Relationships and Responsibilities' in N. Abercrombie and A. Warde (eds) *The Contemporary British Society Reader* (Cambridge: Polity).

Finlex (1985) Laki lapseksiottamisesta. Laki 153/1985. (Finnish adoption law). Available at: www.finlex.fi/fi/laki/alkup/1985/19850153. Accessed 5 May 2010.

Finnish Board of Inter-Country Adoption Affairs (2008). Annual Report 2007. Ministry of Social Affairs and Health.

Flowerdew, J. and Neale, B. (2003) 'Trying to Stay Apace: Children with Multiple Challenges in their Post-Divorce Family Lives', *Childhood*, 10(2), 147–62.

Folgheraiter, F. (2004) 'Capitale sociale', *Lavoro Sociale*, 4(1), 133–40.

Fonseca, C. (2003) 'Patterns of Shared Parenthood among the Brazilian Poor', *Social Text 74*, 21 (1), 111–27.

Forbes, B. (2007) *Christmas: A Candid History* (Berkeley, Los Angeles and London: University of California Press).

Forster, M. (1996) *Hidden Lives: A Family Memoir* (London: Penguin Books).

Foss (2004) 'Framing the Study of Visual Rhetoric: Toward a Transformation of Rhetorical Theory' in C. Hill and M. Helmets (eds) *Defining Visual Rhetorics* (Mahwah, NJ: Erlbaum).

Freeman, J. D. (1961) 'On the Concept of the Kindred', *Journal of the Royal Anthropological Institute*, 91, 192–220.

Froschauer, U. and Lueger, M. (2003) *Das qualitative Interview. Zur Praxis interpretativer Analyse sozialer Systeme* (Wien: WUV, UTB).

Fthenakis, W. E. (1995) 'Ehescheidung als Übergangsprozess im Familienentwicklungsprozess' in M. Perrez, J. L. Lambert, C. Ermert and B. Plancherel (eds) *Familie im Wandel. Freiburger Beiträge zur Familienforschung* (Bern: Hans Huber).

Fukuyama, F. (1995) *Trust: The Social Virtues and the Creation of Prosperity* (London: Hamish Hamilton).

Gager, C. and Sanchez, L. (2003) 'Two as One? Couples' Perceptions of Time Spent Together, Marital Quality, and the Risk of Divorce', *Journal of Family Issues*, 24, 21–50.

Ganong, L. H. and Coleman, M. (2004) *Stepfamily Relationships: Development, Dynamics, and Interventions* (New York: Kluwer Academic/Plenum Publishers).

Geertz, C. (1973) *The Interpretation of Cultures: Selected Essays* (New York: Basic Books).

Gelman, A. and Hill, J. (2008) *Data Analysis Using Regression and Multilevel/ Hierarchical Models* (New York: Cambridge University Press).

Gerhardt, U. (2002) *Talcott Parsons: An Intellectual Biography* (Cambridge: Cambridge University Press).

Giddens, A. (1990) *The Consequences of Modernity* (Stanford: Stanford University Press).

Giddens, A. (1991) *Modernity and Self-Identity. Self and Society in the Late Modern Age* (Stanford: Stanford University Press).

Giddens, A. (1992) *Transformation of Intimacy: Sexuality, Love and Eroticism in Modern Societies* (Cambridge: Polity Press).

Gillis, J. R. (1997) *A World of Their Own Making: Myth, Ritual, and the Quest for Family Values* (Cambridge, MA: Harvard University Press).

Gillis, J. (2004) 'Gathering Together' in A. Etzioni and J. Bloom (eds) *We are What We Celebrate* (New York: New York University Press).

Glaser B. and Strauss, A. (1956) 'Temporal Aspects of Dying as a Non-Scheduled Status Passage', *American Journal of Sociology*, 71(1), 48–59.

Glaser, B. and Strauss, A. (1999) *The Discovery of Grounded Theory: Strategies for Qualitative Research* (Hawthorne, NY: Aldine De Gruyter).

Goffman, E. (1967) *Interaction Ritual: Essays on Face-to-Face Behavior* (New York: The Anchor Books).

Goffman, E. (1982, orig. 1959) *The Presentation of Self in Everyday Life* (Harmondsworth: Penguin Books).

Goldscheider, F. and Davanzo, J. (1989) 'Pathways to Independent Living in Early Adulthood: Marriage, Semi-Autonomy, and Premarital Residential Independence', *Demography*, 26(4), 597–614.

Goody, E. (1982) *Parenthood and Social Reproduction* (Cambridge: Cambridge University Press).

Goody, Jack (1983) *The Development of the Family and Marriage in Europe* (Cambridge: Cambridge University Press).

Gordon, A. (2008) *Ghostly Matters: Haunting and the Sociological Imagination*, 2nd edn (London: University of Minnesota Press).

Gouldner, A. W. (1960) 'The Norm of Reciprocity: A Preliminary Statement', *American Sociological Review*, 25(2), 161–78.

Granovetter, M. (1973) 'The Strength of Weak Ties', *American Journal of Sociology*, 78(5), 1360–80.

Gribaudi, Maurizio (1998) 'Réseaux egocentrés et inscriptions sociales: Continuités et discontinuités dans les formes de structuration de l'espace parisien' in M. Gribaudi (ed.) *Espaces, temporalités, stratifications. Exercices sur les réseaux sociaux* (Paris: Editions de l'EHESS).

Griffiths, M. (1995) *Feminisms and the Self: The Web of Identity* (London: Routledge).

Gye, L. (2007) 'Picture This. The Impact of Mobile Camera Phones on Personal Photographic Practices', *Journal of Media and Cultural Studies*, 221(2), 279–88.

Haavio-Mannila, E., Majamaa, K., Tanskanen, A., Hämäläinen, H., Karisto, A., Rotkirch, A. and Roos, J.P. (2009) *Sukupolvien ketju. Suuret ikäluokat ja sukupolvien välinen vuorovaikutus Suomessa*, Sosiaali- ja terveysturvan tutkimuksia 107 (Helsinki: Kela).

Hagestadt, G. (1991) 'Trends and Dilemmas in Life-Course Research: An International Approach' in W. Heinz (ed.) *Theoretical Advances in Life-Course Research* (Weinheim: Deutscher Studienverlag).

Hall, D. (2002) 'Risk Society and the Second Demographic Transition', *Canadian Studies in Population*, 29(2): 173–93.

Halle, D. (1991) 'Displaying the Dream: The Visual Presentation of Family and Self in the Modern American Household', *Journal of Comparative Family Studies*, 22, 217–29.

Hamm, B. and Jałowiecki, B. (1990) 'Introduction' in B. Hamm and B. Jałowiecki (eds) *The Social Nature of Space* (Warszawa: Państwowe wydawnictwo naukowe), pp. 7–15. http://21st.century.phil-inst.hu/Passagen_engl4_Strassoldo.pdf. Downloaded 23.6.2006.

Hanifan, L. J. (1920) *The Community Center* (Boston: Silver, Burdette and Co.).

Haskey, J. (2005) 'Living Arrangements in Contemporary Britain: Having a Partner Who Usually Lives Elsewhere and Living Apart Together (LAT)', *Population Trends*, 34–45.

Haugen, G. M. (2010) 'Children's Perspectives on Everyday Experiences of Shared Residence: Time, Emotions and Agency Dilemmas', *Children & Society*, 24(1), 112–22.

HCCH (1993) *Hague Convention on Protection of Children and Co-Operation in respect of Intercountry Adoption*. Available at: www.hcch.net/index_en.php?act= conventions.statusprint&cid=69. Accessed 5 May 2010.

Hecht, A. (2001) 'Home Sweet Home: Tangible Memories of an Uprooted Childhood' in D. Miller (ed.) *Home Possessions* (Oxford: Berg).

Heikinmäki, M-L. (1981) *Suomalaiset häätavat. Talonpoikaiset avioliiton solmintaperinteet* (Helsinki: Otava).

Held, V. (1993) *Feminist Morality* (London and Chicago: University of Chicago Press).

Hetherington, E. M. and Kelly, J. B. (2002) *For Better or For Worse: Divorce Reconsidered* (New York: Norton).

Hetherington, E. M. (2003) 'Social Support and the Adjustment of Children in Divorced and Remarried Families', *Childhood*, 10(2), 217–36.

Hetherington, E. (1999) 'Should We Stay Together for the Sake of the Children?' in E. Hetherington (ed.) *Coping with Divorce, Single Parenting, and Remarriage: A Risk and Resiliency Perspective* (Mahwah: Erlbaum).

Hill, R. (1949) *Families under Stress* (New York: Harper & Row) [Reprinted Westport, CN: Greenwood Press, 1971].

Hirseland, A., Herma, H. and Schneider, W. (2005) 'Geld und Karriere. Biographische Synchronisation und Ungleichheit bei karriereorientierten Paaren' in H. Solga and C. Wimbauer (eds) *Wenn zwei das Gleiche tun . . . Ideal und Realität sozialer (Un-) Gleichheit in Dual Career Couples* (Opladen: Leske + Budeich Verlag).

Hirvonen, H. (2007) 'Biologinen sosiaalisen mallina', *Sosiologia*, 44(4), 279–96.

Hite, Shere (1978) *Hite Report: A Nationwide Study of Female Sexuality* (New York: Dell).

Hitzler, R., Reichertz, J. and Schröer, N. (1999) (eds) *Hermeneutische Wissenssoziologie. Standpunkte zur Theorie der Interpretation* (Konstanz).

Hoelgaard, S. (1998) 'Cultural Determinants of Adoption Policy: A Colombian Case Study', *International Journal of Law, Policy and the Family*, 12, 202–41.

Högbacka, R. (2008) 'The Quest for a Child of One's Own. Parents, Markets and Transnational Adoption', *Journal of Comparative Family Studies*, 39(3), 311–30.

Högbacka, R. (2009) 'Ikioma lapsi vieraasta maasta. Yhteisyys ja erot kansainvälisissä adoptioperheissä' in R. Jallinoja (ed.) *Vieras perheessä* (Helsinki: Gaudeamus).

Hollenstein, T., Leve, L., Scaramella, L., Milfort, R. and Neiderhiser, J. (2003) 'Openness in Adoption, Knowledge of Birthparent Information, and Adoptive Family Adjustment', *Adoption Quarterly*, 7(1), 43–52.

Howart, G. (2008). *Death and Dying: A Sociological Introduction* (Cambridge: Polity).

Howell, S. (2006a) *The Kinning of Foreigners: Transnational Adoption in a Global Perspective* (New York and Oxford: Berghahn Books).

Howell, S. (2006b) 'Changes in Moral Values about the Family. Adoption Legislation in Norway and the US', *Social Analysis*, 50(3), 146–63.

ISTAT (2006) *La vita di coppia, Indagine multiscopo sulle famiglie. Famiglie e soggetti sociali* (Roma: Istat).

ISTAT (2003) *Parentela e reti di solidarietà. Indagine multiscopo sulle famiglie. Famiglie e soggetti sociali* (Roma: Istat).

Jaakkola, Magdalena (1999) *Maahanmuutto ja etniset asenteet*. Työpoliittinen tutkimus 213. (Helsinki: Edita).

Jacobs, J. (1961) *Life and Death of Great American Cities* (New York: Random House).

Jallinoja, R. (2008) 'Genealogical Proximity as a Constitutive Rule of Family Configuration', paper presented at the ESA Research Network of Sociology of Family and Intimate Lives conference *Family in the Making: Theorizing Family in the Contemporary European Context*, Helsinki University, 27–29 August 2008.

Jallinoja, R. (2008) 'Togetherness and Being Together: Family Configurations in the Making' in E. D. Widmer and R. Jallinoja (eds) *Beyond the Nuclear Family: Families in a Configurational Perspective* (Bern: Peter Lang).

Jamieson, L. (2005) 'Boundaries of Intimacy' in L. McKie and S. Cunningham-Burley (eds) *Families in Society: Boundaries and Relationships* (Bristol: Polity Press).

Jämsä, J. (2003) ' "Isä joka on homo" – homomiehen perhe ja vanhemmuus'. Unpublished MA thesis (Department of Sociology, Helsinki University).

Jonas, N. and Le Pape, M-C. (2008) 'My Own Relatives or My Partner's Relatives? A Configurational Approach of Kinship Prioritization' in E. D. Widmer and R. Jallinoja (eds) *Beyond the Nuclear Family: Families in the Configurational Perspective* (Bern: Peter Lang).

Jones, G. (1995) *Leaving Home* (Buckingam IRP/CNR – Institute for Population Research/National Research Council: Open University Press).

Jones, M. (2007) *Feast: Why Humans Share Food* (Oxford/NY: Oxford University Press).

Juby, H., Billett, J.-M., Laplante, B. and Le Bourdais, C. (2007) 'Nonresident Fathers and Children. Parents' New Unions and Frequency of Contact', *Journal of Family Issues*, 28(9), 1220–45.

Kahn, R. and Antonucci, T. (1980) 'Convoys over the Life Course: Attachment, Roles and Social Support' in P. Baltes and G. Brim (eds) *Life-Span Development and Behavior*, 3 (New York: Academic Press).

Kaslow, F. (2001) 'Spaltung: Familie in der Scheidung' in S. Walper, and R. Perkun (ed.) *Familie und Entwicklung. Aktuelle Perspektiven der Familienpsychologie* (Göttingen: Hogrefe).

Kaufmann, J-C. (1994) *Schmutzige Wäsche. Zur ehelichen Konstruktion von Alltag* (Konstanz).

Keim, S., Klärner, A. and Bernardi, L. (2009) 'Qualifying Social Influence on Fertility Intentions: Composition, Structure and Meaning of Fertility-Relevant Social Networks in Western Germany', *Current Sociology*, 57, 888–907.

Kelly, J. (2003) 'Changing Perspectives on Children's Adjustment Following Divorce: A View from the United States', *Childhood*, 10(2), 237–54.

Kelly, J. (2007) 'Children's Living Arrangements Following Separation and Divorce: Insights from Empirical and Clinical Research', *Family Process*, Special Issue 'Divorce and Its Aftermath', 46(1), 35–52.

Kemppainen, I. (2006) *Isänmaan uhrit. Sankarikuolema Suomessa toisen maailmansodan aikana*, Bibliotheca Historica 102 (Helsinki: SKS).

Ketokivi, K. (2009) 'Torjuttu autonomia: Lapsuudenperheen vieraantuneet siteet ja aikuisten lasten vaihtoehtoiset elämänpolut' in R. Jallinoja (ed.) *Vieras perheessä* (Helsinki: Gaudeamus).

Kiernan, K. (2004) 'Redrawing the Boundaries of Marriage', *Journal of Marriage and Family*, 66, 980–7.

Kohler, H-P. (1997) 'Learning in Social Networks and Contraceptive Choice', *Demography*, 34, 369–83.

Kohler, H-P. (2000) 'Social Interaction and Fluctuations in Birth Rates', *Population Studies*, 54, 223–37.

Kohler, H-P. and Bühler, C. (2001) 'Social Networks and Fertility' in N. J. Smelser and P. B. Baltes (eds) *International Encyclopedia of the Social & Behavioral Sciences* (Oxford: Pergamon/Elsevier Sciences).

Köhler, W. (1992) *Gestalt Psychology: An Introduction to New Concepts in Modern Psychology* (Reissued) (New York: Liveright).

Kuhn, A. (1991) 'Behind the Painted Smile' in P. Holland and J. Spence (eds) *Family Snaps: The Meanings of Domestic Photography* (London: Virago Press).

Kuhn, A. (1995) *Family Secrets: Acts of Memory and Imagination* (London: Verso).

Lamb, M. (2002) 'Nonresidential Fathers and Their Children' in C. S. Tamis-LeMonda and N. Cabrera (eds) *Handbook of Father Involvement* (Mahwah, NJ: Erlbaum).

Lasch, C. (1979) *Haven in a Heartless World: The Family Besieged* (New York: Basic Books).

Laslett, P., Oosterveen, K. and Smith, R. (1980) (eds) *Bastardy and Its Comparative History* (London: Edward Arnold).

Latour, B. (2005/2007) *Reassembling the Social: An Introduction to Actor-Network-Theory* (Oxford/NY: Oxford University Press).

Leeds-Hurwitz, Wendy (2002) *Wedding as Text: Communicating Cultural Identities Through Ritual* (Mahwah, NJ: Lawrence Erlbaum Associates, Publishers).

Lenz, K. (2006) *Soziologie der Zweierbeziehung: Eine Einführung* (Wiesbaden: VS Verlag).

Levin, I. (2004) 'Living apart together: A New Family Form', *Current Sociology*, 52(2), 223–40.

Levinger, G. (1983) 'Development and Change' in H. Kelley (ed.) *Close Relationships* (New York: Freeman Press).

Lévi-Strauss, C. (1969, French orig. 1949) *The Elementary Structures of Kinship* (Boston: Beacon Press).

Lewis, R. A. (1972) 'A Developmental Framework for the Analysis of Premarital Dyadic Formation', *Family Proceedings*, 11, 17–48.

Loury, G. (1977) 'A Dynamic Theory of Racial Income Differences' in P. Wallace and A. Mund (eds) *Women, Minorities, and Employment Discrimination* (Lexington: Lexington Books).

Luhmann, N. (1968) *Vertrauen: Ein Mechanismus Der Reduktion Sozialer Komplexität* (Stuttgart: F. Enke).

Lüscher, K. (1999) 'A Heuristic Model for the Study of Intergenerational Ambivalence'. Available at: http://w3.ub.uni-konstanz.de/v13/volltexte/1999/277//pdf/277_1.pdf. Accessed 11 September 2006.

Lüscher, K. (2002) 'Intergenerational Ambivalence: Further Steps in Theory and Research', *Journal of Marriage and Family*, 64(3), 585–93.

Lüscher, K. and Pillemer, K. (1998) 'Intergenerational Ambivalence: A New Approach to the Study of Parent–Child Relations in Later Life', *Journal of Marriage and Family*, 60(2), 413–25.

Macmillan, R. and Copher, R. (2005) 'Families in the Life Course: Interdependency of Roles, Role Configurations, and Pathways', *Journal of Marriage and Family*, 67, 858–79.

Madden-Derdich, D. and Arditti, J. A. (1999) 'The Ties that Bind: Attachment between Former Spouses', *Family Relations*, 48, 243–49.

Madden-Derdich, D., Leonard, S. and Christopher, F. (1999) 'Boundary Ambiguity and Co-Parental Conflict after Divorce: An Empirical Test of a Family Systems Model of the Divorce Process', *Journal of Marriage and Family*, 61, 588–98.

Maillochon, F. (2002) 'Le coût relationnel de la robe blanche', *Réseaux*, 115, 52–90.

Maillochon, F. (2008) 'Le mariage est mort, vive le mariage! Quand le rituel du mariage vient au secours de l'institution', *Enfances, Familles, Générations*, no 9, Faculté de droit, Université de Montréal. Available at: http://id.erudit.org/iderudit/029630ar. Accessed 18 November 2010.

Maillochon, F. (2009a) 'L'invitation au mariage. Une approche des réseaux de sociabilité du couple', *Redes*, no 16. Available at: http://revista-redes.rediris.es/html-vol16/vol16_5e.htm. Accessed 18 November 2010.

Maillochon, F. (2009b) 'La femme du ménage. La préparation du mariage au principe du 'partage inégal' du travail domestique', *Temporalités*, 9. Available at: http://temporalites.revues.org/index1047.html. Accessed 18 November 2010.

Makiwane, M. (2003) 'Response to Paper 2' in *Fertility. Current South African Issues of Poverty, HIV/AIDS & Youth. Seminar proceedings*. Human Sciences Research Council and Department of Social Development (Cape Town).

Mandemakers, J. and Dykstra, P. (2008) 'Discrepancies in Parent's and Adult Child's Reports of Support and Contact', *Journal of Marriage and Family*, 70(2), 495–506.

Mannheim, Karl (1982) *Structures of Thinking* (London: Routledge).

Marsden, P. (1987) 'Core Discussion Networks of Americans', *American Sociological Review*, 52(1), 122–31.

Marta, E. and Pozzi, M. (2007) *Psicologia del volontariato* (Roma: Carocci).

Martin-Fugier, A. (1990, French orig. 1987) 'Bourgeois Rituals' in M. Perrot (ed.) *A History of Private Life: From the Fires of Revolution to the Great War* (Cambridge, MA and London: The Belknap Press of Harvard University Press).

Mason, J. (2002) *Qualitative Researching*, 2nd Edition (London: Sage).

Mason, J. (2004) 'Personal Narratives, Relational Selves: Residential Histories in the Living and Telling', *Sociological Review*, 52(2): 162–79.

Mason, J. (2008) 'Tangible Affinities and the Real Life Fascination of Kinship', *Sociology*, 42(1), 29–45.

Matsuda, M. (2007) 'Mobile Media and the Transformation of Family', Keynote speech for Mobile Media 2007. University of Sydney, 4 July 2007.

Matthews, S. (1979) *The Social World of Old Women: Management of Self-Identity* (Beverly Hills, CA: Sage Publications).

Mazzucchelli, S. (2007) *Formazione alla genitorialità e capitale sociale. Il contributo sociologico alla valutazione* (Milano: Unicopli).

Mc Adams, D., De St. Aubin, E. and Kim, T. (2004) *The Generative Society: Caring for Future Generations* (Washington, DC: America Psychological Association).

Mead, G. H. (1934) *Mind, Self and Society* (Chicago: University of Chicago Press).

Mead, G. H. (1997) *Mind, Self, and Society* (ed. by Morris, CH. W.) (Chicago: University of Chicago Press).

Menniti, A., Misiti, A. and Savioli, M. (2000) 'Italian "Stay at Home" Children: Attitudes and Constraints', paper presented at the Workshop on 'Leaving home – A European focus' Max Planck Institute for Demographic Research, 6–8 September.

Merton, R. K. (1976) *Sociological Ambivalence; and Other Essays* (New York: Free Press).

Metcalf, P. and Huntington, R. (2008, orig. 1991) *Celebrations of Death: The Anthropology of Mortuary Ritual* (New York: Cambridge University Press).

Meyers, D. (1997) (ed.) *Feminists Rethink the Self* (Colorado: Westview Press).

Mieneke, W. and Midden, C. (1991) 'Communication Network Influences on Information Diffusion and Persuasion', *Journal of Personality and Social Psychology*, 61(5), 734–42.

Miettinen, S. (2006) *Eron aika. Tyttärien kertomuksia ikääntyneen vanhemman kuolemasta.* Yhteiskuntapolitiikan laitoksen tutkimuksia 4/2006 (Helsinki: Yliopistopaino).

Milardo, R. (2008) 'Configurations of Family Relationships: Aunts and Nieces, Uncles and Nephews' in E. D. Widmer and R. Jallinoja (eds) *Beyond the Nuclear Family: Families in a Configurational Perspective* (Bern: Peter Lang).

Miller, D. (1993) 'A Theory of Christmas' in D. Miller (ed.) *Unwrapping Christmas* (Oxford: Clarendon Press).

Miller, D. (1998) (ed.) *Material Cultures: Why Some Things Matter* (London: UCL Press).

Miller, D. (2001) (ed.) *Home Possessions* (Oxford: Berg).

Mills, C. Wright (1967, orig. 1959) *The Sociological Imagination* (Oxford: Oxford University Press).

Mitchell, W. E. (1963) 'Theoretical Problems in the Concept of Kindred', *American Anthropologist*, 65(2).

Misztal, B. (2003) *Theories of Social Remembering* (Milton Keynes: Open University Press).

Modell, J. (1994) *Kinship with Strangers* (Berkeley, Los Angeles and London: University of California Press).

Modell, J. (1999) 'Freely Given: Open Adoption and the Rhetoric of the Gift' in L. Layne (ed.) *Transformative Motherhood* (New York and London: New York University Press).

Modell, J. (2002) *A Sealed and Secret Kinship* (New York and Oxford: Berghahn Books).

Mollberg, E. (2008) *Molle, isäni* (Helsinki: Otava).

Möllering, G. (2006) 'Trust, Institutions, Agency: Towards a Neoinstitutional Theory of Trust' in R. Bachmann and A. Zaheer (eds) *Handbook of Trust Research* (Cheltenham, UK and Northampton, MA: Edward Elgar).

Montgomery, M. R. and Casterline, J. B. (1996) 'Social Learning, Social Influence and New Models of Fertility', *Population and Development Review, 22 (Supplement: Fertility in the United States: New Patterns, New Theories)*, 151–75.

Moreno, J. L. (1953) *Who Shall Survive? Foundations of Sociometry, Group Psychotherapy and Sociodrama* (Beacon: Beacon House).

Moreno, J. and Jennings, H. (1938) 'Statistics of Social Configurations', *Sociometry*, 1(3/4), 342–74.

Morgan, D. H. J. (1996) *Family Connections: An Introduction to Family Studies* (Cambridge: Polity Press).

Morris, P. (1996) 'Community Beyond Tradition' in P. Heelas, S. Lasch and P. Morris (eds) *Detraditionalization: Critical Reflections on Authority and Identity* (Cambridge, MA and London, UK: Blackwell Publishers).

Moxnes, K. (2003) 'Risk Factors in Divorce: Perceptions by the Children Involved', *Childhood*, 10(2), 131–46.

Muir, D. (1996) 'Proclaiming Thanksgiving throughout the Land: From Local to National Holiday' in A. Etzioni and J. Bloom (eds) *We are What We Celebrate: Understanding Holidays and Rituals* (Mineola, NY: New York University Press).

Muir, D. (2004) 'Proclaiming Thanksgiving throughout the Land: From Local to National Holiday' in A. Etzioni and J. Bloom (eds) *We Are What We Celebrate. Understanding Holidays and Rituals* (New York and London: New York University Press).

Murphy, M., and Wang, D. (2001) 'Family-Level Continuities in Childbearing in Low-Fertility Societies', *European Journal of Population*, 17(1), 75–96.

Neil, E. (2006) 'Coming to Terms with the Loss of a Child: The Feelings of Birth Parents and Grandparents about Adoption and Post-Adoption Contact', *Adoption Quarterly*, 10(1), 1–23.

Newton, T. (1999) 'Power, Subjectivity and British Industrial and Organisational Sociology: The Relevance of the Work of Norbert Elias', *Sociology*, 33(2), 411–40.

Nissenbaum, S. (1997) *The Battle for Christmas* (New York: Vintage Books. A Division of Random House, Inc.).

Oppo, A. and Ferrari, M. (2005) 'Genitori e figli: immagini e pratiche di solidarietà a Cagliari' in C. Facchini (ed.) *Diventare adulti* (Milano: Edizioni Angelo Guerrini).

Parsons, T. and Bales, R. (1955) *Family, Socialization and Interaction Process* (Glencoe: The Free Press).

Paxton, P. (1999) 'Is Social Capital Declining in the United States? A Multiple Indicator Assessment', *American Journal of Sociology*, 105(1), 88–127.

Peterson, D. and Christensen, D. (2002) 'Factors Predictive of Boundary Ambiguity after Divorce', *Journal of Divorce and Remarriage*, 37(3–4), 19–40.

Pink, S. (2004) *Home Truths: Gender, Domestic Objects and Everyday Life* (Oxford: Berg Publishers).

Pleck, E. (2000) *Celebrating the Family: Ethnicity, Consumer Culture, and Family Rituals* (Cambridge, MA and London, UK: Harvard University Press).

Poggio, T. (2005) 'La casa come area di welfare', *Polis*, XIX, 279–305.

Popenoe, D. (1988) *Disturbing the Nest: Family Change and Decline in Modern Societies* (New York: Aldine de Gruyter).

Prandini, R. (2006) 'La famiglia italiana tra processi di in-distinzione e ri-distinzione relazionale. Perché osservare la famiglia come relazione sociale "fa la differenza"' in P. Donati and I. Colozzi (eds) *Il paradigma relazionale nelle scienze sociali: le prospettive sociologiche* (Bologna: Il Mulino).

Prandini, R. (2007) 'Il capitale sociale familiare in prospettiva relazionale: come definirlo, misurarlo e sussidiarlo' in P. Donati (ed.) 'Il capitale sociale nella prospettiva relazionale', *Sociologia e Politiche Sociali* (3).

Pruett, M. K., Ebling, R. and Insabella, G. (2004) 'Critical Aspects of Parenting Plans for Young Children', *Family Court Review*, 42, 39–59.

Pryor, J. and Rodgers, B. (2001) *Children in Changing Families: Family Life after Parental Separation* (Oxford: Blackwell).

Putnam, R. (1993) *Making Democracy Work: Civic Traditions in Modern Italy* (Princeton, NJ: Princeton University Press).

Putnam, R. (1995) 'Bowling Alone: America's Declining Social Capital', *Journal of Democracy Prospect*, 6(1), 65–78.

Putnam R. (2000) *Bowling Alone: The Collapse and Revival of American Community* (New York: Simon & Schuster).

Putnam, R. (2002) *Democracies in Flux: The Evolution of Social Capital in Contemporary Society* (New York: Oxford University Press).

Pylkkänen, A. (1995) 'Substitute Children and Adoption in Finnish Legal History', *Scandinavian Journal of History*, 20(2), 129–40.

Quintaneiro, T. (2004) 'The Concept of Figuration or Configuration in Norbert Elias' Sociological Theory', *Teoria and Sociedade*, 12, 54–69.

Rands, M. (1988) 'Changes in Social Networks Following Marital Separation and Divorce' in R. Milardo (ed.) *Families and Social Networks* (London: Sage).

Reamer, F. and Siegel, D. (2007) 'Ethical Issues in Open Adoption: Implications for Practice', *Families in Society: The Journal of Contemporary Social Services*, 88(1), 11–18.

Reher, D. (1998) 'Family Ties in Western Europe: Persistent Contrasts', *Population and Development Review*, 24(2), 203–34.

Reiss, I. (1960) 'Toward a Sociology of the Heterosexual Love Relationship', *Marriage and Family Living*, 22(2), 139–45.

Rigg, A. and Pryor, J. (2007) 'Children's Perceptions of Families: What Do They Really Think?', *Children & Society*, 21, 17–30.

Riley White, M. (1983) 'The Family in an Aging Society: A Matrix of Latent Relationships', *Journal of Family Issues*, 3, 439–54.

Rochberg-Halton, E. (1986) *Meaning and Modernity: Social Theory in the Pragmatic Attitude* (Chicago and London: The University of Chicago Press).

Rosenberg, M. and Guttmann, J. (2001) 'Structural Boundaries of Single-Parent Families and Children's Adjustment', *Journal of Divorce and Remarriage*, 36(1–2), 83–98.

Rossi, G. (2003) 'Quando e come l'associazionismo familiare genera capitale? Esperienze di sussidiarietà delle politiche sociali in Lombardia' in P. Donati (ed.) *Famiglia e capitale sociale nella società italiana* (Cinisello Balsamo: Edizioni San Paolo).

Rossi, G. (2006) 'Le comunità familiari' in E. Scabini and G. Rossi (eds) *Le parole della famiglia* (Milano: Vita e Pensiero).

Rossi, G. (2007) 'Family, Social Capital and Family Associations', *International Review of Sociology*, 17(2), 279–92.

Rossi, G. (2009) 'Development and Dynamics of the Family in Southern Europe' in O. Kapella, C. Rille-Pfeiffer, M. Rupp and N. Schneider (eds) *Die Vielfalt der Familie* (Opladen & Farmington Hills: Barbara Budrich).

Rossi, G. and Bramanti, D. (2007) 'Famiglie al confine tra familiare e comunitario' in P. Donati (ed.) *Ri-conoscere la famiglia attraverso il suo valore aggiunto* (Cinisello Balsamo: Edizioni San Paolo).

Rossi, G. and Maccarini, A. (1999) 'Benessere familiare e associazionismo delle famiglie' in P. Donati (ed.) *Famiglia e società del benessere* (Cinisello Balsamo: Edizioni San Paolo).

Rustin, M. (2000) 'Reflections on the Biographical Turn in Social Science' in P. Chamberlayne, J. Bornat and T. Wengraf (eds) *The Turn to Biographical Methods in Social Science* (London: Routledge).

Rüling, A. (2007) *Jenseits der Traditionalisierungsfallen. Wie Eltern sich Familien- und Erwerbsarbeit teilen* (Frankfurt am Main u.a.: Campus).

Sabbatini, L. (2002) 'Le reti di aiuti informali' in Osservatorio Nazionale sulle famiglie (ed.) *Famiglie, mutamenti e politiche sociale* (Bologna: Il Mulino).

Safeguarding the Rights and Well-Being of Birthparents in the Adoption Process (2007). Evan B. Donaldson Adoption Institute (New York).

Sarrazin, J. and Cyr, F. (2007) 'Parental Conflicts and Their Damaging Effects on Children', *Journal of Divorce and Remarriage*, 47(1/2), 77–94.

Sayer, Andrew (2005) *The Moral Significance of Class* (Cambridge: Cambridge University Press).

Scabini, E. and Donati, P. (1988) (a cura di) *La famiglia 'lunga' del giovane adulto*, numero monografico di 'studi interdisciplinari sulla famiglia', no. 7 (Milano: Vita e Pensiero).

Scanzoni, J., Polonko, K., Teachman, J. and Thompson, L. (1989) *The Sexual Bond: Rethinking Families and Close Relationships* (London: Sage Publications).

Scheper-Hughes, N. (1992) *Death Without Weeping* (Berkeley, Los Angeles and London: University of California Press).

Schmitz, H. and Schmidt-Denter, U. (1999) 'Die Nachscheidungsfamilie sechs Jahre nach der elterlichen Trennung', *Zeitschrift für Familienforschung*, 11(3), 28–55.

Schneider, D. (1980, orig. 1968) *American Kinship: A Cultural Account* (Chicago and London: The University of Chicago Press).

Schneider, W., Hirseland, A., Ludwig-Mayerhofer, W. and Allmendinger, J. (2005) 'Macht und Ohnmacht des Geldes im Privaten. Zur Dynamik von Individualisierung in Paarbeziehungen', *Soziale Welt*, 56, 203–24.

Segalen, Martine (1980) *Mari et femme dans la société paysanne* (Paris: Flammarion).

Segalen, Martine (1981) *Amours et mariages de l'ancienne France* (Paris: Berger-Levrault).

Selman, P. (2009) 'The Rise and Fall of Intercountry Adoption in the 21st Century', *International Social Work*, 52(5), 575–94.

Sennett, R. (1998) *The Corrosion of Character: The Personal Consequences of Work in the New Capitalism* (New York: Norton).

Sgritta, G. (2002) 'La transizione all'età adulta: la sindroma del ritardo' in *Famiglie: mutamenti e politiche sociali* by Osservatorio nazionale sulle famiglie e le politiche locali di sostegna alle responsabilità familiari (Bologna: Mulino).

Shorter, Edward (1975) *The Making of the Modern Family* (New York: Basic Books).

Siikala, A-L. and Siikala, J. (2005) *Return to Culture. Oral Tradition and Society in the Southern Cook Islands* (Helsinki: Academia Scientiarum Fennica).

Simmel, G. (1908) *Soziologie: Untersuchungen Über Die Formen Der Vergesellschaftung* (Leipzig: Duncker & Humblot).

Singly (de) F. (1996) *Le soi, le couple et le mariage* (Paris: Nathan).

Singly (de) F. (1999) *Sociologie současné rodiny (Sociologie de la famille contemporaine)* (Praha: Portál).

Singly (de) F. (2000) *Libres ensemble* (Paris: Nathan).

Smart, C. (2004) 'Changing Landscapes of Family Life: Rethinking Divorce', *Social Policy & Society*, 2–4, 401–8.

Smart, C. (2007a) 'Textures of Family Life: Further Thoughts on Change and Commitment', *Journal of Social Policy*, 34(4), 541–56.

Smart, C. (2007b) *Personal Life: New Directions in Sociological Thinking* (Cambridge: Polity).

Smart, Carol (2007c) 'Same Sex Couples and Marriage: Negotiating Relational Landscapes with Families and Friends', *The Sociological Review*, 55(4), 671–86.

Smart, C. (2009) 'Family Secrets: Law and Understandings of Openness in Everyday Relationships', *Journal of Social Policy*, 38(4), 551–67.

Smart, C. and Shipman, B. (2004) 'Visions in Monochrome: Families, Marriages, and the Individualization Thesis', *British Journal of Sociology*, 55(4), 492–509.

Smart, C., Neale, B. and Wade, A. (2001) *The Changing Experience of Childhood: Families and Divorce* (Cambridge: Polity Press).

Smith, A. B., Taylor, N. J. and Tapp, P. (2003) 'Rethinking Children's Involvement in Decision-Making After Parental Separation', *Childhood*, 10(2), 201–16.

Smith, S. and Kulynych, J. (2002) 'It may be Social but Why It is Capital', *Politics and Society*, 30(1), 149–86.

Sniezek, Tamara (2005) 'Is It Our Day or the Bride's Day? The Division of Wedding Labor and Its Meaning for Couples', *Qualitative Sociology*, 28(3), 215–34.

South Africa Survey (2004/2005). South African Institute of Race Relations, Johannesburg 2006.

South African Child Gauge (2006). Children's Institute, University of Cape Town.

Sprey, J. (1969) 'The Family as a System in Conflict', *Journal of Marriage and Family*, 31(4), 699–706.

Stacey, Judith (1990) *New Brave Families: Stories of Domestic Upheaval in Late Twentieth Century America* (New York: Basic Books).

Stacey, J. (1996) *In the Name of the Family* (Boston: Beacon Press).

State of the World's Children (2007), Unicef. Available at: www.unicef.org/sowc07/. Accessed 5 May 2010.

Steedman, C. (1986) *Landscape for a Good Woman* (London: Virago).

Steedman, C. (1992) *Past Tenses: Essays on Writing, Autobiography and History* (London: Rivers Oram Press).

Steenhof, L. and Liefbroer, A. (2008) 'Intergenerational Transmission of Age at First Birth in the Netherlands for Birth Cohorts Born between 1935 and 1984: Evidence from Municipal Registers', *Population Studies*, 62(1), 69–84.

Steinfels, P. (1980) *The Neoconservatives: The Men Who are Changing America's Politics* (New York: A Touchstone Book).

Stewart, S. (2005) 'Boundary Ambiguity in Stepfamilies', *Journal of Family Issues*, 26(7), 1002–29.

Stoehr, T. (1979) *Free Love in America: A Documentary History* (New York: AMS Press).

Strathern, M. (1995) 'Displacing Knowledge: Technology and the Consequences for Kinship' in F. Ginsburg and R. Rapp (eds.) *Conceiving the New World Order* (Berkeley, Los Angeles and London: University of California Press).

Strauss, A. (1987) *Qualitative Analysis for Social Scientists* (Cambridge: Cambridge University Press).

Strauss, A. and Corbin, J. (1990) *Basics of Qualitative Research: Grounded Theory Procedures and Techniques* (Newbury Park, London and New Delhi: Sage).

Suoranta, Kirsti (2005) 'Veriside on eri side? Sukulaisuuden ja ydinperheen rakentuminen lastensa kanssa elävien naisparien sosiaalisissa verkostoissa ja puhetavoissa'. Unpublished MA thesis (Department of Sociology, Helsinki Univesity).

Swartz, L. (2003) 'Fertility Transition in South Africa and Its Impact on the Four Major Racial Groups' in *Fertility. Current South African Issues of Poverty, HIV/AIDS & Youth, Seminar Proceedings*. Human Sciences Research Council and Department of Social Development (Cape Town).

Sýkorová, D. (2006) 'Od solidarity jako základu intergeneračních vztahů v rodině k ambivalenci a vyjednávání', *Sociologický časopis*, 42(4), 683–99.

Sýkorová, D. (2007) *Autonomie ve stáří. Kapitoly z gerontosociologie* (Praha: SLON).

Théry, I. (1986) 'The Interest of the Child and the Regulation of the Post-Divorce Family', *International Journal of the Sociology of Law*, 14, 341–58.

Théry, I. (1988) 'Die Familien nach der Scheidung: Vorstellungen, Normen, Regulierungen' in K. Lüscher, F. Schultheis, and M. Wehrspaun (eds) *Die postmoderne Familie* (Konstanz: Universitätsverlag).

Thomas, A. and Mabusela, S. (1991) 'Foster Care in Soweto, South Africa: Under Assault from a Politically Hostile Environment', *Child Welfare*, 70(2).

Thomas, W. I. and Thomas, D. S. (1928) *The Child in America: Behavior Problems and Programs* (New York: Knopf).

Tronca, L. (2008) 'La consistenza del capitale sociale, le sue varie forme e la sua incidenza sull'impegno civico' in P. Donati and L. Tronca (eds) *Il capitale sociale degli italiani. Le radici familiari, comunitarie ed associative del civismo* (Milano: FrancoAngeli).

Turner, J. H. (2000) 'The Formation of Social Capital' in P. Dasgupta and I. Serageldin (eds) *Social Capital and Multiphase Perspectives* (Washington, DC: World Bank).

Valente, T., Watkins, S., Jato, M., van der Straten, A. and Tsitsol, L-P. (1997) 'Social Network Associations with Contraceptive Use among Cameroonian Women in Voluntary Associations', *Social Science and Medicine*, 45(5), 677–87.

Van Putten, A., Dykstra, P. and Schippers, J. (2008) 'Just like Mom? The Intergenerational Reproduction of Women's Paid Work', *European Sociological Review*, 24(4), 435–49.

Verhaeghe, Paul (1999) *Love in a Time of Loneliness* (New York: Other Press).

Wallerstein, J., Lewis, J. and Blakeslee, S. (2000) *The Unexpected Legacy of Divorce: A 25 year Landmark Study* (New York: Hyperion).

Wasserman, S. and Faust, K. (1994/2006) *Social Network Analysis: Methods and Applications* (Cambridge: Cambridge University Press).

Watanabe, Yasushi (2004) *The American Family Across the Class Divide* (London and Ann Arbor: Pluto Press).

Weber, F. (2005) *Le sang, le nom, le quotidien. Une sociologie de la parenté pratique* (Paris: Editions Aux lieux d'être).

Weber, F., Gojard, S. and Gramain, A. (2003) *Charges de famille. Dépendance et parenté dans la France contemporaine* (Paris: La Découverte).

Weber, M. (1985) *Wirtschaft und Gesellschaft* (Tübingen: Mohr Siebeck Verlag).

Weber-Kellermann, Ingeborg (1988) 'Immer ein Anlass zum Feiern . . . – Familienfeste gestern und heute' in Deutsches Jugendinstitut (ed.) *Wie geht's der Familie? Ein Handbuch zur Situation der Familie heute* (München: Kösel).

Wellman, B. (1979) 'The Community Question: The Intimate Networks of East Yorkers', *American Journal of Sociology*, 84(5), 1201–31.

Wertsch, J. (2007, orig. 2002) *Voices of Collective Remembering* (New York: Cambridge University Press).

Weston, K. (1991) *Families We Choose. Lesbians, Gays, Kinship* (New York: Columbia University Press).

Widmer, E. D. (1999) 'Family Contexts as Cognitive Networks: A Structural Approach of Family Relationships', *Personal Relationships*, 6(4), 487–503.

Widmer, E. D. (2006) 'Who are My Family Members? Bridging and Binding Social Capital in Family Configurations', *Journal of Social and Personal Relationships*, 23(6), 979–98.

Widmer, E. D. (2007) 'Social Capital in Wide Family Contexts: An Empirical Assessment Using Social Network Methods', *International Review of Sociology*, 17(2), 225–38.

Widmer, E. D. and Jallinoja, R. (eds) (2008) *Beyond the Nuclear Family: Families in a Configurational Perspective* (Bern: Peter Lang).

Widmer, E. D. and La Farga, L. (2000) 'Family Networks: A Sociometric Method to Study Relationships in Families', *Field Methods*, 12(2), 108–28.

Widmer, E. D., Castrén, A.-M., Jallinoja, R. and Ketokivi, K. (2008) 'Introduction', in E. D. Widmer and R. Jallinoja (eds) *Beyond the Nuclear Family: Families in a Configurational Perspective* (Bern: Peter Lang).

Widmer, E. D., Giudici, F., Le Goff, J. and Pollien, A. (2009) 'From Support to Control: A Configurational Perspective on Conjugal Quality', *Journal of Marriage and Family*, 71(3), 437–48.

Widmer, E. D., Le Goff, J., Levy, R., Hammer, R. and Kellerhals, J. (2006) 'Embedded Parenting? The Influence of Conjugal Networks on Parent–Child Relationships', *Journal of Social and Personal Relationships*, 23(3), 387–406.

Widmer, E. D. and Sapin, M. (2008) 'Families on the Move: Insights on Family Configurations of Individuals Undergoing Psychotherapy' in E. D. Widmer and R. Jallinoja (eds) *Beyond the Nuclear Family: Families in a Configurational Perspective* (Bern: Lang).

Wimbauer, C. (2003) *Geld und Liebe. Zur symbolischen Bedeutung von Geld in Paarbeziehungen* (Frankfurt a.M.: Campus Verlag).

Wolin, S. and Bennett, L. (1984) 'Family Rituals', *Family Process*, 23, 401–20.

Wolin, S., Bennett, L. and Jacobs, J. (1988) 'Assessing Family Rituals in Alcoholic Families' in E. Imber-Black, J. Roberts and R. Whiting (eds), *Rituals in Families and Family Therapy* (New York: Norton).

Wulf, Christoph (2006) 'Praxis', in J. Kreinath, J. Snoek and M. Stausberg (eds) *Theorizing Rituals: Issues, Topics, Approaches, Concepts* (Leiden: Brill).

Yngvesson, B. (2002) 'Placing the "Gift Child" in Transnational Adoption', *Law & Society Review*, 36(2), 227–55.

Yngvesson, B. (2003) 'Going "Home": Adoption, Loss of Bearings, and the Mythology of Roots', *Social Text*, 74, 21(1), 7–27.

Yngvesson, B. (2004) 'National Bodies and the Body of the Child: "Completing" Families through International Adoption' in F. Bowie (ed.) *Cross-Cultural Approaches to Adoption* (London and New York: Routledge).

Yngvesson, B. (2007) 'Refiguring Kinship in the Space of Adoption', *Anthropological Quarterly*, 80(2), 561–79.

Zartler, U., Wilk, L. and Kränzl-Nagl, R. (2004) *Wenn Eltern sich trennen. Wie Kinder, Frauen und Männer Scheidung erleben* (Frankfurt, New York: Campus).

Zelizer, V. A. (1994) *The Social Meaning of Money: Pin Money, Pay Cheques, Poor Relief, and Other Currencies* (Princeton: Princeton University Press).

Index